Maternity rights

CAMILLA PALMER is a consultant with Bindman & Partners working exclusively in the field of discrimination and maternity rights. She is also a member of the Maternity Alliance's Legal Working Group. She is the author of *Discrimination at Work* (Legal Action Group).

Maternity rights

Camilla Palmer

Legal Action Group
1996

This edition published in Great Britain 1996
by LAG Education and Service Trust Limited
242 Pentonville Road, London N1 9UN

© Camilla Palmer 1996

All rights reserved. No part of this publication may be reproduced, stored in a retrieval system or transmitted in any form or by any means, without permission from the publisher.

British Library Cataloguing in Publication Data
A CIP catalogue record for this book is available from the British Library

ISBN 0 905099 66 4

This book is published in association with the Maternity Alliance, 45 Beech Street, London EC2P 2LX (advice line 0171 588 8582). The Maternity Alliance is an independent national charity working to improve rights and services for pregnant women, new parents and their babies. It aims to improve the medical care, health education and social support given to parents before conception, during pregnancy, childbirth and the first year of life. The Maternity Alliance also encompasses the wider social context of pregancy and childbirth through research, legal action, information, campaigns and training. It provides information and legal advice on all aspects of maternity rights and benefits to employees and employers as well as to people who are not working.

Phototypeset by The Harrington Consultancy, London EC1
Printed in Great Britain by Bell & Bain Ltd, Glasgow

Foreword
by LAURA COX, QC

The concept of employment 'rights' arising out of pregnancy and childbirth is a relatively recent one. The traditional view was, and undoubtedly still is in some quarters, that a woman should work only until she became pregnant, at which point she had fulfilled her potential in life and was doing what women were designed to do, ie, have babies; and that she should thereafter concentrate exclusively on childcare and family responsibilities.

Women who wanted or needed to combine work and motherhood had no statutory rights at all until 1975, when parliament first introduced rights to maternity leave and pay and protection from unfair dismissal due to pregnancy. These rights were, however, dependent on women having been in employment for a stated minimum period (generally two years). In a society where women were systematically being dismissed or denied employment, training opportunities or promotion because they were or might become pregnant, the broader protection offered to working women by the Sex Discrimination Act 1975 was clearly of vital importance.

Ten years elapsed, however, before the Employment Appeal Tribunal first accepted that less favourable treatment on grounds of pregnancy could constitute a violation of the Sex Discrimination Act in *Hayes v Malleable Working Men's Club* (1985); and then only on the basis of a comparison with how an employer would treat a sick man. The idea that a healthy pregnant woman should be compared with a man suffering illness was viewed by many as inappropriate and demeaning to women. Further, since adverse treatment of pregnant women was much more common than that of sick men, comparisons in such cases were invariably hypothetical. In those circumstances it was very difficult to contradict an employer's assertion that he would have treated a sick male employee in the same, unfavourable way.

Europe, meanwhile, had its own agenda. The need for pregnant women and new mothers to be accorded a protected status in the workplace was seen as paramount and as fundamental to the effectiveness of that equal treatment principle. Discrimination on grounds of pregnancy was held by the ECJ, in a number of cases in the early nineties, to constitute direct sex discrimination, contrary to the Equal Treatment Directive, any comparison with how a man would be treated being unnecessary.

Thus it was that, twenty years into the life of the Sex Discrimination Act, the House of Lords held, construing our legislation in conformity with the Equal Treatment Directive, that pregnancy discrimination constitutes direct sex discrimination, contrary to the 1975 Act, in *Webb v EMO Air Cargo (No 2)* (1995).

Yet the terms of these judgments in the European Court and the House of Lords have left many questions unanswered, as has the more recent European decision on pay entitlement during maternity leave (*Gillespie*). At this moment there are four further references before the European Court in pregnancy cases. The extent of protection against discrimination for pregnant women and women on maternity leave in a variety of situations is yet to be determined.

Furthermore, 1994 saw the UK government's implementation, albeit reluctantly, of the European Pregnant Workers Directive, prohibiting dismissal on grounds of pregnancy for all women and providing minimum standards of maternity leave and pay and of health and safety protection.

All this has resulted in a confusing and complicated array of domestic and European legislative provisions, giving rights subject to different qualifying conditions and notification requirements; and, further, in a mass of discrimination case-law, answering some questions but tantalisingly posing many others. Much new law remains to be decided.

Obtaining the answers to simple and understandable enquiries from women about their rights and obligations during their pregnancies and while on maternity leave has thus become a task to be undertaken only by the brave!

How fortunate, then, for everyone who may be called upon to address these problems or answer these enquiries that this excellent and timely book has arrived on the scene. In an area of law acknowledged by many to be one of the most complex and unfathomable, its author has succeeded in producing a clear, succinct and, above all, understandable exposition of the law relating to pregnancy and maternity rights and benefits as it stands today and guidance on how it may develop in the future.

It will be of immense benefit not only to lawyers but to academics, students, advice workers, trade unionists, personnel officers and employers and employees generally.

Published by the Legal Action Group in association with the Maternity Alliance, this book has succeeded in its mission both to demystify the law and to provide answers to the problems which are most commonly encountered in practice. The different subject areas are clearly defined and easy to track down, with helpful cross-references and extremely useful appendices, including a summary of the most common questions and answers arising in this field.

Inordinate legal complexity is all the more regrettable when it occurs in laws which govern the everyday lives of working people. Explaining these laws is a challenge to which this book has risen and met with a vengeance. It should be a constant companion to all those who have to understand or apply them.

Table of cases

Hill v Supasnaps Ltd COIT 1930/200	110
Hilton International Hotels (UK) Ltd v Kaissi [1994] IRLR 273; [1994] ICR 578, EAT	57, 99, 100
Home Office v Holmes [1984] IRLR 299, EAT	82, 187
Houghton v May and Hassel Ltd COIT 837/180	77
Hughes v Gwynedd Area Health Authority [1977] IRLR 436, EAT	3, 35, 99, 100
Hurley v Mustoe [1981] IRLR 208, EAT	27, 181, 182
Huth v Davidsons COIT 1409/223	78
Igbo v Johnson Matthey Chemicals Ltd [1986] IRLR 215, CA	100
Inner London Education Authority v Nash [1979] ICR 229, EAT	36
Institute of Motor Industry v Harvey [1992] IRLR 343; [1992] ICR 470, EAT	56, 98–100
Intelligent Applications Ltd v Wilson EAT/412/92 Edinburgh	107
Iverson v P&O European Ferries (Dover) Ltd, 57265/95/C	50, 52, 57-59
James v Eastleigh Borough Council [1990] ICR 554; [1990] IRLR 288, HL	180, 181
John Menzies GB Ltd v Porter (1992) 19 February, EAT 644/91	106, 109
Johnson v Chief Adjudication Officer (No 2) [1995] IRLR 157, ECJ	206
Johnston v Fultons Fine Furnishing Ltd (1995) 30 March, Case No 02087/94; DCLD No: 25, p7	26
Johnstone v Chief Constable of Royal Ulster Constabulary [1986] IRLR 263, ECJ	205
Jones v Chief Adjudication Officer [1993] IRLR 218, CA	193
Jones v University of Manchester [1993] IRLR 218, CA	190, 195
Joyce v Northern Microwave Distributors Ltd Case No 5564/93: 22.9.93, Leeds IT	24
Kelly v Liverpool Maritime Terminals Ltd [1988] IRLR 310, CA	71, 72
Kent Management Services Ltd v Butterfield [1992] IRLR 394, EAT	63
Kidd v DRG (UK) Ltd [1995] IRLR 190, EAT	190
King v Great Britain-China Centre [1991] IRLR 513, CA	181
Kolfor Plant Ltd v Wright [1982] IRLR 311, EAT	34, 74
Küratorium für Dialyse und Nierentransplantation eV v Johanna Lewark (9.2.96)	195
Lane v Shire Roofing Company (Oxford) Ltd [1995] IRLR 495, CA	13
Larsson v Dansk Handel og Service, Case C-400/95 (96C-46/15)	101
Lavery v Plessey Telecommunications Ltd [1983] IRLR 202, CA	5, 104
Levez v T H Jennings (Harlow Pools) Ltd [1996] IRLR 499, EAT	206
Linghorn v P & O Ferries COIT 1256/60	35
London Underground Ltd v Edwards [1995] IRLR 355, EAT	190
Longmore v Lee (1989) 10 November, DCLD 4, Case No: 21745/88	229
Lucas v Norton of London Ltd [1984] IRLR 86, EAT	99
Lupeti v Wrens Old House [1984] ICR 348, EAT	212

Table of cases

MacMillan v Edinburgh Voluntary Organisations' Council
  [1995] IRLR 536, SEAT — 78
Marshall v Southampton and South-West Hampshire Area
  Health Authority [1986] IRLR 140, ECJ — 201
Marshall v Southampton and South-West Hampshire Area
  Health Authority (No 2) [1993] IRLR 445, ECJ — 202, 226, 229
Martin v McConkey Case No. 1577/89 Northern Ireland
  tribunal; DCLD — 5, 28
McCausland v Dungannon District Council [1993] IRLR 583,
  NICA — 194
McClenaghan and Rice v British Shoe Corporation Ltd (1993)
  26 July Case Nos 2688/91, 3206/91, 3207/91, Northern Ireland — 72, 228, 230
McFadden v Greater Glasgow Passenger Transport Executive
  [1977] IRLR 327, IT — 77
McLachlan v Central Scotland Health Care NHS Trust Case
  No: S/4932/94; Glasgow IT; 14.6.95 — 27
McLean v William Hill Organisation Ltd SCOIT S/3800/90 — 78
McMillan v Scottish Widows Fund and Life Assurance Society
  (1993) 6 August, Case No S/4805/92 — 40
Meade-Hill and National Union of Civil and Public Servants v
  British Council [1995] IRLR 478, CA — 78, 191, 192
Mearis v IMI Yorkshire Imperial Ltd COIT 1408/60 — 71
Mediguard Services Ltd v Thame [1994] IRLR 504, EAT — 172
Meer v Tower Hamlets LBC [1988] IRLR 399, CA — 188
Megner and Scheffel v Innungskrankenkasse Vorderpfalz [1996]
  IRLR 236 — 195
Ministry of Defence v Bristow (1995) 24 July, EAT — 226
Ministry of Defence v Cannock and Others [1994] IRLR 509,
  EAT — 224-226, 228, 229
Ministry of Defence v Hunt [1996] IRLR 140, EAT — 224-226, 229
Ministry of Defence v Meredith [1995] IRLR 539, EAT — 227, 228
Ministry of Defence v Mutton [1996] ICR 590, EAT — 24, 224-228
Mirror Group Newspapers Ltd v Gunning [1986] IRLR 27,
  CA — 166
Mitchell v Arkwood Plastics (Engineering) Ltd [1993] ICR 471
  EAT — 94
Mitchell v Royal British Legion Club [1980] IRLR 425, EAT — 61
Moxley and Cherowbrier v Governors of St Edward's School
  (1994) 18 February, Case Nos 48132/93 & 48735/93,
  Southampton IT — 63
Murray v Powertech (Scotland) Ltd [1992] IRLR 257, EAT — 227
Nagarajan v Agnew [1994] IRLR 61, EAT — 181
Nelson v Western Health & Social Services Board (1994) 10
  October, Case Ref No 887/93 SDA, Belfast IT 23 — 90
Nolte v Landesversicherungsanstalt Hannover [1996]
  IRLR 225 — 195
North Yorkshire County Council v Fay [1985]
  IRLR 247, CA — 94
Nu-Swift International Ltd v Mallinson [1978] IRLR 537, EAT — 41
O'Hare v MoD (1995) 25 September; Case No 1341/95 — 24

Preface

Maternity rights is a notoriously difficult area of employment law. This book is intended to provide a clear and concise explanation of women's statutory and contractual maternity rights and their protection from discrimination.

The changes to the law introduced to comply with the Pregnant Workers Directive only came into force in 1994. There are still relatively few cases on this 'new' law.

Maternity rights also need to be seen in the context of British and European discrimination law, and this is constantly developing. Recent European decisions (such as *Webb* and *Gillespie*) have raised as many questions as they have answered. There are inconsistencies in the complex judgments and the two decisions are not easy to reconcile. This makes it difficult to predict how the law will develop.

Thus, the law is not always clear. Where this is the case, the interpretation given in this book is mine, although it has often been developed with the Maternity Alliance and its advisers.

The chapters map women's rights during the different stages of their pregnancy, maternity leave and return to work. The concluding chapters outline the scope of relevant British and European discrimination law and how to enforce it. The appendices contain a summary of common questions and answers (which are largely based on the experience of the Maternity Alliance advice line), precedents and other reference material.

It is hoped that this book will enable lawyers, advice workers, trade unionists, personnel officers and others to advise employees and employers about maternity rights and remedies. Hopefully, it will also enable employers to formulate maternity policies. Finally, it is hoped that academics and students will find it useful for teaching and training purposes.

The law is stated for England and Wales as at 1 August 1996. Where possible, account has been taken of more recent case-law at proof stage.

The Maternity Alliance

The Maternity Alliance advice line (0171 588 8582) receives hundreds of calls each month from women either confused about their maternity rights or concerned that their employers have broken the law. The Maternity Alliance gives comprehensive legal advice to help women find a route through the labyrinth of the present law. However, in the long term there must be a change of law to achieve some much-needed clarity.

Camilla Palmer and the Maternity Alliance

Acknowledgements

I would particularly like to thank Laura Cox for writing the foreword; Joanna Wade, April Beale, Jenny McLeish (from Maternity Alliance), Jenny Earle, Isabel Manley, Pauline Matthews, Caroline Underhill and Andrew Nicol for their comments on the text. I would also like to thank the staff of the Legal Action Group for their help and support.

Camilla Palmer

Contents

Table of cases xvi
Table of statutes xxiv
Table of statutory instruments xxviii
Table of European law xxxii
Abbreviations xxxiv

1 Introduction 1
Development of the law on maternity rights 3

2 Statutory framework 6
The main statutory provisions 6
Definitions under UK and EU law 7
   UK Law 7
   EU Law 10
Summary of main UK and EU statutory provisions 11

3 Rights before the birth 17
Introduction 17
Right to paid time off for ante-natal care 17
Pregnancy-related dismissal is unlawful 20
   Automatically unfair dismissal 20
   Ordinary unfair dismissal 22
   Discriminatory dismissal 23
Other less favourable treatment of pregnant women 25
   Recruitment 25
   Other less favourable treatment 27
Sickness during pregnancy 28
Key points 30

4 General maternity leave and extended maternity absence 31
Introduction 31
Minimum 'general maternity leave' for all employees 32
   Notice provisions 32
   Medical certificate 35
   Dismissal or resignation before 11th week 35
   Commencement of leave 35
Extended maternity absence 40
   Qualifying conditions 40
   Duration of absence 43
Key points 43

5 Rights during maternity leave and absence 46
Introduction 46
No right to full pay during maternity leave/absence 47
Rights during general maternity leave 47
Rights during extended maternity absence 55
   The contract 56
   Discrimination under SDA and ETD 57
   Equal Pay Act and article 119 58
   Pregnant Workers Directive 59
   Pensions 60
   Continuity of service 60
   Dismissal 61
   Remedies 62
Key points 64

6 The right to return to work 66
Introduction 66
Returning after general maternity leave 66
   Failure to comply with notice provisions 66
   Extending maternity leave and protection from dismissal 67
   Failure to return 69
   Redundancy 69
   Return after maternity leave 69
Right to return after extended maternity absence 70
   Notice provisions 70
   Postponement by employer 70
   Postponement by employee because of sickness 70
   Industrial action 73
   Contractual rights 74

Contents xiii

    Right to return to same employer 75
    Right to return to same job 75
    Redundancy during maternity absence 79
    Exceptions to right to return 79
  Transfer of undertakings 80
  Discrimination against part-timers and job-sharers 81
  Key points 86

7 Unfair dismissal 88
  Introduction 88
  General principles relating to dismissals 88
  Protection from dismissal: statutory framework 91
    Automatically unfair dismissal 91
    Dismissal for assertion of statutory right 93
    Dismissal in health and safety cases 93
    General unfair dismissal law 93
    Deemed dismissal 95
    Sex discrimination claim 96
    Pregnant Workers Directive 96
  Dismissal during maternity leave period 97
  Dismissal at end of general maternity leave period 98
  Dismissal during extended maternity absence 98
  Dismissal while exercising right to return 103
  Dismissal on transfer of the business 104
  Redundancy 105
  Dismissal after return to work 111
  Dismissal of maternity replacement 112
  Key points 113

8 Health and safety 115
  Introduction 115
  General duties 115
  The Pregnant Workers Directive 117
  The ERA and Management of Health and Safety Regulations 118
  Discrimination 126
  Equal Treatment Directive 127
  Key points 128

9 Statutory maternity pay 130
  Introduction 130
    Pregnant Workers Directive 130
  The legislation 131

xiv *Contents*

      Eligibility for SMP   131
      The maternity pay period   144
      Calculation of maternity pay   146
   How SMP is paid   148
   Administration of SMP by employers   150
   Key points   151

10 Maternity allowance and other benefits   153
   Introduction   153
   Maternity allowance   153
      Qualifying conditions   153
      Rates of maternity allowance   155
      Payment period   155
      How to claim   157
   Effect of maternity allowance on other benefits   159
      Other benefits   160
   Disputes   162
   Key points   162

11 Discrimination and equal pay claims   164
   Introduction   164
   Sex and marital discrimination   165
   Discrimination under EU law: the Equal Treatment Directive   170
   Equal pay law: Equal Pay Act 1970   170
   Article 119 and the Equal Pay Directive   172
   Key points   173

12 Direct discrimination   175
   Less favourable treatment   175
   Key points   183

13 Indirect discrimination   185
   Introduction   185
   Definition of indirect discrimination   185
   Proving indirect discrimination (UK law)   186
      Has the employer applied any condition?   187
      The material time   189
      The 'relevant circumstances' and the pool   189
      Establishing disparate impact   192
      Can the employer justify the requirement?   194
      Can the applicant comply with the requirement?   195
      Has the applicant suffered a detriment?   196
   Key points   196

14 European Community law 198
Introduction 198
European Communities Act 1972 198
EU legislation 199
EU law in UK courts and tribunals 200
Challenging UK law through the European Commission 204
Usefulness of EU law 206
Key points 207

15 Procedure and remedies 209
Introduction 209
Framework 209
Initial steps in bringing a claim 210
How to apply 215
Stages before the hearing 216
The hearing 219
Remedies 220
Key points 231

APPENDICES

1 Tabular summary of maternity rights 234
2 Common questions 236
3 Precedents 246
4 Test period table 1996/97 (maternity allowance) 254
5 Pregnant Workers Directive 258
6 Hazards for new and expectant mothers at work 267
7 Statutory maternity pay tables 277
8 Useful addresses 279

Index 281

Table of cases

Acteson v Silent Challel Products Ltd COIT 916/36,	78
Aird v Garfunkel's Restaurant plc (1994) 20 January, Case No 26151/92	76
Alexander v Home Office [1988] IRLR 190, CA	227
Amministrazione delle Finanze dello Stato v Simmenthal SpA [1978] CMLR 263, ECJ	201
Anderson v Belcher Food Products (1995) 9 August, Case No: S/571/95: Glasgow IT	126
Arbeiterwohlfahrt der Stadt Berlin eV v Botel [1992] IRLR 423, ECJ	172, 185
BP Chemicals Ltd v Gillick and Roevin Management Services Ltd [1995] IRLR 128, EAT	170
Barber v GRE Assurance Group [1990] IRLR 240, ECJ	172, 173, 228
Barrett v Newport Borough Council Case No 34096/91, IT	81, 85
Berrisford v Woodard Schools (Midland Division) Ltd [1991] IRLR 247, EAT	24
Berry v Ravensbourne National Health Service Trust [1993] ICR 871, EAT	215
Bhatt v E D Moseley & Sons Ltd Case No 12681/94, Birmingham IT (20.3.95)	21
Bhudi and Others v IMI Refiners Ltd [1994] IRLR 204, EAT	188
Biggs v Somerset County Council [1995] IRLR 452, EAT; [1996] IRLR 203; [1996] IRLR 181, CA	200, 206
Bilka-Kaufhaus v Weber von Hartz [1986] IRLR 317, ECJ	185, 188, 194, 195
Blaik v Post Office [1994] IRLR 280, EAT	205
Bland v Laws (Confectioners) Ltd COIT 1613/4	19
Bovey v Board of Governors of Hospital for Sick Children [1978] IRLR 241, EAT	74
Brasserie du Pecheur SA v Federal Republic of Germany [1996] All ER (EC) 301; [1996] IRLR 267, ECJ	204
Briggs v North Eastern Education and Library Board [1990] IRLR 81, NICA	187, 196
British Telecommunications plc v Roberts and Another [1996] ICR 625, EAT	85, 86
Brook v London Borough of Haringey [1982] IRLR 478, EAT	188
Brown v Rentokil Ltd [1995] IRLR 211, CS	23

Table of cases xvii

Brown v Stockton-on-Tees Borough Council [1988] IRLR 263, HL	22, 88, 89, 92, 105, 107
Brown-Williams v Microgen Ltd COIT 1415/176	109
CNAVTS v Thibault (OJ no C-189/7, 22.7.95) ECJ	49
Carrington v Helix Lighting Ltd [1990] IRLR 6, EAT	211
Caruana v Manchester Airport plc [1996] IRLR 378, EAT	23, 97, 178
Cast v Croydon College, unreported EAT/161/95, June 1996	189, 212
Castles Walker v Northern Co-operative Society Ltd (1978) 11 December, Case No S/3260/78	77
Chattopadhyay v Headmaster of Holloway School [1981] IRLR 487, EAT	219
Cheshire v Intasave Travel and Shipping Ltd S/2642/89	214
Clark v Secretary of State for Employment [1996] IRLR 578, CA	58
Clarke v Eley (IMI) Kynoch Ltd [1982] IRLR 482, EAT	187, 188
Clay v Governors, English Martyrs School (1993) 8 January, Case No 52319/91, Leicester IT	83
Clayton v Vigers [1990] IRLR 177, EAT	21
Clymo v Wandsworth LBC [1989] IRLR 241, EAT	187, 188, 195, 196
Cocking v Sandhurst (Stationers) Ltd [1974] ICR 650, NIRC	216
Coleman v Skyrail Oceanic Ltd [1981] IRLR 398, CA	224
Community Task Force v Rimmer [1986] IRLR 203, EAT	108
Cowan v Western Isles Seafood Co Ltd (1994) 26 October, Case No S/3439/94 Stornoway	106
Coyne v Exports Credits Guarantee Department [1981] IRLR 51, IT	28, 58, 73
Crouch v Kidsons Impey [1996] IRLR 79, EAT	57, 98, 100, 104
Crees v Royal London Mutual Insurance Society (1996) EAT/205/96	73
Curl v Air UK Ltd (1988) 20 January, Norwich IT (COIT) 1957/26	40
Deane v London Borough of Ealing and Another [1993] IRLR 209, EAT	228
Debenham v Adams Childrenswear Ltd/Case No 49552/94; folio No 3106/127	106
Dekker v Stichting Vormingscentrum voor Jonge Volwassenen (VJV-Centrum) Plus [1991] IRLR 27, ECJ	25, 39, 176
Del Monte Foods Ltd v Mundon [1980] IRLR 224, EAT	21
Dhamrait v United Biscuits Ltd COIT 1430/192	18
DJM International Ltd v Nicholas [1996] IRLR	81
Dodd v British Telecom plc [1980] IRLR 16, EAT	215
Dowuona v John Lewis plc [1987] IRLR 310, CA	71, 72
Eagles v Cadman t/a Baby Days COIT 1334/181	35
Edgar v Giorgione Inns Ltd COIT 1803/13	18, 19
Edgell v Lloyd's Register of Shipping [1977] IRLR 463, IT	77
Edith Freers, Hannelor Speckmann v Deutsche Bundespost (7.3.96)	195
Edwards v London Underground Ltd (No 2) (1996) EAT DCLD 27 COIT Case No 04813/93	190
Emmott v Minister for Social Welfare [1991] IRLR 387, ECJ	206

Table of cases

Enderby v Frenchay Health Authority and Secretary of State for Health [1993] IRLR 591, ECJ	188
Evans v John R Clayton Ltd COIT 1514/119	35
Fallon v H C Blake & Co COIT 934/148	77
Faulkner v Fuller Foods International plc (1995) 1 March, Case No 64704/94, Leeds IT	214
Francovich v Italian Republic [1992] IRLR 84	204, 208
Garland v British Rail Engineering Ltd [1982] IRLR 111, ECJ	200
Gault v AVX Ltd (1995) 27 May, Case No 03492/94SD	76
Gay v George L Lockey & Sons Ltd COIT 1632/5	71
George v Beecham Group [1977] IRLR 43	22
Gill and Oakes v Wirral Health Authority Case No 16165-6/9O	83
Gillespie and Others v Northern Health and Social Services Board and Others (1996) *Times* 13 February; [1996] IRLR 214, ECJ	47, 49, 50, 55, 58, 59, 64, 130, 135, 148, 179
Gillespie v The Stamping Alliance Co Ltd COIT 1415/195	109
Given v Scottish Power plc (1995) 20 January, Case No S/3172/94, Glasgow IT	82, 85
Gledhill v Employment Service (1994) 24 May, Case No 2546/94, Leeds IT	213
Gold v London Borough of Tower Hamlets (1991) 9 December, Case No 05608/91/LN/C, London North IT	83
Greater Glasgow Health Board v Carey [1987] IRLR 485, SEAT	82, 192
Greater Manchester Police Authority v Lea [1990] IRLR 372, EAT	191
Greaves v Quicksave	73
Gregory v Tudsbury Ltd [1982] IRLR 267	17, 19
Griffin and Others v South West Water Services Ltd [1995] IRLR 15 ChD	201, 203
Guthrie v Royal Bank of Scotland plc (1987) 10 March, IT	82
Habermann-Beltermann v Arbeiterwohlfahrt, Bezirksverband Ndb/Opf eV (case C-421/92) [1994] IRLR 364, ECJ	22, 89, 127
Hammersmith and Queen Charlotte's Special Health Authority v Cato [1987] IRLR 483, EAT	172
Hampson v Department of Education and Science [1990] IRLR 302, HL	195
Hancock v Lloyd (1995) 10 February, Case No 56417/94, Shrewsbury IT	214
Handels-og Kontorfunktionaerernes Forbund i Danmark v Dansk Arbejdsgiverforening (acting for Danfoss) [1989] IRLR	183
Handels-og Kontorfunktionaerernes Forbund i Danmark (acting for Hertz) v Dansk Arbejdsgiverforening (acting for Aldi Marked K/S) [1991] IRLR 31, ECJ	39, 111, 112, 176, 178, 180, 183
Haughton v Olau Line (UK) Ltd [1986] IRLR 465, CA	14
Hayes v South Glamorgan County Council EAT 702/84	112
Heddles v Thorn EMI (UK) plc IT Northern Ireland 1678/92	72
Hicks v North Yorkshire County Council COIT 1643/117	81

Table of cases xxi

O'Neill v (1) Governors of St Thomas More RCVA Upper School and (2)Bedfordshire County Council [1996] IRLR 372, EAT	24, 177, 180, 181
O'Neill v Walthamstow Building Society Case No. 27886/89; DCLD 6	27
Osborne v Thomas Bolton & Sons Ltd COIT 794/248	41
Owusu v London Fire and Civil Defence Authority [1995] IRLR 574, EAT	212, 213
Ozkan-Quaynor v Optika (Ltd) Optician (1995) 11 December, Case No: 25564/95/LN/C, London (North) IT	96
P v S and Cornwall County Council [1996] IRLR 347	199
Page v Freight Hire (Tank Haulage) Ltd [1981] 1 All ER 394; [19813 IRLR 13, EAT	116, 127
Patel and Harewood v T & K Home Improvements Ltd and Johnson (1994) 24 March, Case Nos 57783/92 & 57778/92	227
Pearse v City of Bradford MC [1988] IRLR 379, EAT	190
Pearson v Swindells and British Telecommunications Ltd 14.11.94 Case No: 48222/93	27
Pepper v Hart [1993] IRLR 33, HL	48
Perera v Civil Service Commission and Department of Customs and Excise [1983] IRLR 166, CA	188
Philip Hodges & Co v Kell [1994] IRLR 568, EAT	108
Pickstone v Freemans plc [1988] IRLR 357, HL	173, 200, 205
Polkey v AE Dayton Services Ltd [1987] IRLR 503; [1988] IRLR 263, HL	106
Porter v Cannon Hygiene Ltd [1993] IRLR 329, NICA	200
Price v Civil Service Commission [1977] IRLR 291, EAT	195
Pridden v Warrington Community Health Care (NHS) Trust (1995) 6 June, Case No 66232/93, Liverpool IT	57
Quinnen v Hovells [1984] IRLR 227, EAT	166
R v Birmingham City Council ex p Equal Opportunities Commission [1989] IRLR 173	180
R v Secretary of State for Employment ex p Equal Opportunities Commission [1994] IRLR 176, HL	194, 195, 203
R v Secretary of State for Employment ex parte Seymour Smith & Perez [1995] IRLR 464, CA	14, 94, 172, 192-194, 203
R v Secretary of State for Social Services ex p CPAG [1989] 3 WLR 1116, QBD	203
R v Secretary of State for Transport ex p Factortame Ltd and Others [1996] IRLR 267, ECJ	204
Reay v Sunderland Health Authority Case No 22905/92, Newcastle IT	58
Rees v Appollo Watch Repairs plc (1996) *Times* 26 February, EAT	78, 80, 101
Rightside Properties Ltd v Gray [1974] 2 All ER 1169, ChD	34
Rinner-Kuhn v FWW Spezial-Gebaudereinigung GmbH [1989] IRLR 493 ECJ	39, 172, 185, 194
Roberts and Longstaffe v British Telecommunications plc (1995) 6 February, Southampton IT	83

Table of cases

Robinson v London Borough of Greenwich (1995) 21 November; 745/94 DCLD 27	24
Robinson v Oddbins Ltd (1996) 5 January, Case No 4224/95, CDLD No 27	84
Sajil v Carraro t/a Foubert's Bar COIT 1890/34	19
Satchwell Sunvic Ltd v Secretary of State for Employment C1979] IRLR 455, EAT	17, 41, 137
Saunders v Richmond-upon-Thames BC [1977] IRLR 362, EAT	26
Scally v Southern Health and Social Services Board [1991] IRLR 522, HL	34
Science Research Council v Nasse; Vyas v Leyland Cars [1979] IRLR 465, HL	217
Scottish Agricultural College v O'Mara (1991) 5 November, DCLD 12, Case No AT/449/91	230
Secretary of State for Employment v A Ford & Son (Sacks) Ltd [1986] ICR 882, EAT	36
Secretary of State for Employment v Doulton Sanitaryware Ltd [1981] ICR 477, EAT	137
Secretary of State for Employment v Mann and Others [1996] IRLR 4, EAT	204
Secretary of State for Scotland and Greater Glasgow Health Board v Wright and Hannah [1991] IRLR 187, SEAT	172, 200
Shirley v Anglian Windows Ltd COIT 1567/205	95
Simpson v Microponent Development Ltd COIT 1327/85	34, 42
Smith v David White and White Group Leisure Ltd (1994) 11 May, Manchester IT, Case No 01778/93	76
Smith v North Western Regional Health Authority COIT 1842/176; (1987) 15 January, Case No 29270/86	26, 182
Steenhorst-Neerings v Bestuur van de Bedrijfsvereniging voor Detailhandel [1994] IRLR 244, ECJ	206
Stewart and Gower t/a Gowers v Male (1994) 19 May, EAT 813/93	79
Street v Harry S Allen Ltd EAT 180/89	75
Stringer v Booth COIT 1533/56	61
Sworak v Pendelfin Studios Ltd COIT 1303/243	61
Taylor v Thomas Bee Ltd (1996) 4 January, DCLD No 28, Case No 63877/95	120
Tickle v Governors of Riverview CF School and Surrey County Council (1993) 24 August, COIT, Case No 32420/92, London South IT	83
Tindale v Barnsley Building Society (1992) 16 April, DCLD 15 Case No 15289/91	40
Todd v Eastern Health and Social Services Board (1989) 16 October, Case No 1149/88EP and 1150/88SD Belfast IT	28, 39, 54, 58
Trimble v Supertravel Ltd [1982] IRLR 451, EAT	220
Vyas v Leyland Cars [1979] IRLR 465, HL	217

Table of cases xxiii

Watson v Marylebone Optical Co Ltd COIT 2056/212	72
Watt v Ballantyne and Copeland (1994) 22 August, Case No S/1262/94	82
Webb v EMO Air Cargo Ltd [1994] IRLR 482, ECJ; [1993] IRLR 27, HL	24, 26, 39, 165, 198 200, 205
Webb v EMO Air Cargo (UK) Ltd (No 2) [1995] IRLR 645, HL	15, 21, 22, 39, 89, 101, 176, 177, 178, 180
West Midlands Passenger Transport Executive v Singh [1988] IRLR 186, CA	183, 217
Whiting v Harrow and Hillingdon Health Care NHS Trust (1995) 26 July, Case No 61664/93/LNIB	57
Williams v British Gas plc South Western DCLD 12; 21.4.92; Case No: 26089/91	230
Woodhead v Chief Constable of West Yorkshire Police EAT 285/89	26
Woolworth (F W) plc v Smith [1990] ICR 45, EAT	41, 61
Wright v Rugby Borough Council Case No 23528/84	83

Table of statutes

Armed Forces Act 1996	14, 171	s 56	13, 17, 20
Congenital Disabilities (Civil Liability Act 1976 s1	117	s 56 (6)	20
		s 57	20
Criminal Justice and Public Order Act 1994 s 26	14	s 57 (2) (a)	20
		s 60	125
Disabled Persons (Employment) Act 1944 s15	147	s 64 (2)	123
		s 66	13, 118, 121, 122
Employment Act 1989			
s4	126, 127	s 66 (2)	67
Sch 1	127	s 67	13, 122
Employment Protection (Consolidation) Act 1978	6, 12, 104, 198	s 68	13, 118, 123
		s 70	7, 13, 31, 125
s60	89		
Employment Rights Act 1996	4-6, 10, 12-15, 17, 20, 32, 46, 50, 53, 54, 74, 96, 97, 112, 114, 116, 118, 140, 147, 164, 166, 175, 198, 200, 202, 207, 209–211, 214, 215, 220, 230, 231	s 71	32, 41, 48, 50, 54, 89, 97
		s 72	7, 39
		s 72 (1)	36
		s 72 (2)	39
		s 73 (2)	67
		s 73 (3)	96
		s 73 (4)	67
		s 74	7
		s 74 (1)	33, 34
		s 74 (2)	7, 35
		s 74 (4)	32
		s 74 (4) (b)	37
		s 74 (5)	33
s 13 (3)	63	s 74 (5) (b)	37
s 23 (3)	213	s 74 (6)	33, 37
s 27	63	s 75	33
s 55	13, 17	s 75 (1)	34
s 55(2)	18	s 75 (2)	35
s 55 (3)	18	s 76	38, 66
s 55 (4)	20	s 76 (1)	67

Table of statutes xxv

s 76 (2)	67		105, 118, 140, 141
s 76 (3)	67		
s 76 (4)	67	s 99 (1) (a)	91, 92, 111
s 77	69, 107, 109	s 99 (1) (b)	91
s 78	8, 32	s 99 (1) (c)	91, 92, 111
s 79	7, 13, 40, 97	s 99 (1) (d)	22, 91, 92, 126
s 79 (2)	60, 75		
s 80	41	s 99 (1) (e)	92
s 80 (2)	42	s 99 (2) (b)	98
s 80 (3)	42	s 99 (3)	68, 92
s 81	107, 109	s 99 (3) (b)	68
s 82 (1)	42	s 99 (3) (c)	68
s 82 (2)	70	s 99 (4)	92
s 82 (3) (a)	70	s 100	93
s 82 (4)	70	s 104	20
s 82 (5)	71	s 104 (1)	93
s 82 (6)	73	s 105 (1)	105
s 82 (7)	73	s 105 (2)	105
s 82 (8)	74	s 106	112
s 82 (9)	74	s 108 (3) (a)	105
s 83	8	s 108 (3) (b)	105
s 83 (2)	8	s 111 (2)	214
s 84	90, 97, 104	s 114	221
s 85	32, 74	s 114 (2)	221
s 86	90	s 114 (5)	221
s 87	90	s 115	221
s 88	90	s 115 (2)	221
s 88 (2)	90	s 115 (4)	221
s 88 (3)	90	s 117	223
s 89	90	s 118 (1) (a)	222
s 89 (4)	90	s 118 (1) (b)	222
s 92 (4)	92	s 119-122	222
s 92 (5)	92	s 123	222
s 93	92	s 123(4)	223
s 95 (1) (a)	89	s 124	222
s 95 (1) (b)	90	s 126	230
s 95 (1) (c)	90	s 127	222
s 96	90, 95	s 137 (2)	111
s 96 (1)	76, 95	s 139	106
s 96 (2)	79, 80	s 141 (2)	110
s 96 (3)	79, 110	s 192	14
s 96 (4)	79	s 196	14
s 96 (5)	79	s 196 (4)	190
s 97 (6)	212	s 196 (5)	14
s 98	94	s 197	90
s 98 (4)	95	s 199	14
s 98 (5)	95	s 199 (3)	190
s 99	10, 13, 21, 22, 66, 89, 91, 103,	s 200	14
		s 203	100, 220
		s 210ff	40

Table of statutes

s 212ff	137	Sex Discrimination Act 1975	4-6, 15, 20
s 212(2)	60, 61		22, 25, 26
s 212(3)	61		28, 39, 46
s 218	81		51, 55-58,
s 220ff	10, 20, 48, 123		62, 63, 96, 97, 115,
s 223 (5)	166		126-128,
s 225 (5) (b)	123		164-168,
s 226	111		170-172,
s 226 (3) (a)	223		174, 175,
s 230	13, 62		183, 186
s 235	7, 8, 39		189, 192
s 235 (1)	8, 76		196, 198,
Pt II	46, 62		200, 202,
Pt XI	14		207, 209-
Pt XIII	62		215, 220,
Equal Pay Act 1970	4-6, 15, 25, 28, 30, 39,		223, 229-232
	46, 50, 51,	s 1(1) (a)	165, 175
	55, 56, 63,	s 1(1) (b)	186, 188
	65, 130,	s 2(2)	167
	164, 165,	s 3	164
	170-172,	s 4	166
	174, 179,	s 5 (2)	166
	200, 206,	s 5(3)	175
	207, 210,	s 6	57, 166, 167
	215, 220,	s 6 (1) (a)	167
	231, 232	s 6 (1) (b)	167
s 1 (2)	171	s 6 (1) (c)	167
s 1 (6) (a)	171	s 6 (2)	27
s 1 (9)	171	s 6 (2) (a)	167
s 2 (4)	213	s 6 (2) (b)	167
s 6 (1) (b)	171	s 7	168
s 6 (1A) (b)	171	s 9	169
European Communities Act 1972	198, 209	s 10	167, 171
		s 11	166
s 2 (1)	198	s 12	166
s 2 (4)	198	s 13	166
Factories Act 1961	116, 127	s 14	166
Health and Safety at Work Act 1974	115, 116, 127, 128	s 15	166, 169, 170
		s 35A	166
s 2	116	s 35B	166
s 2 (1)	116	s 41	168
s 18	116	s 45	52
Pt I	127	s 51	126
Offices, Shops and Railway Premises Act 1963	127	s 56A (10)	164
		s 65 (1) (a)	223
Public Health Act 1936		s 65 (1) (b)	223
s 205	68, 124	s 65 (1) (c)	223

s 65 (2)	224	s 164 (3)	135
s 66 (3)	27, 229	s 164(4) (b)	142
s 74	211	s 164 (6)	38
s 74 (2) (a)	211	s 165 (1)	9
s 74 (2) (b)	211	s 165 (4)	146
s 75	210	s 165 (6)	146
s 76	212	s 166 (2)	160
s 76 (5)	214	s 166 (4)	160
s 76 (6) (a)	213	s 169	132
s 76 (6) (b)	212	s 170	136
s 82 (1)	166	s 171	9
s 82 (1A)	167	s 171 (1)	132
s 85	168	Sch 3	154
Social Security Act 1989	5, 6, 46, 53, 54	Sch 3 para 1	149
		Sch 3 para 2	149
Sch 5	53, 62, 75	Sch 3 para 3	154
Sch 5 para 3	54	Sch 3 para 3 (2)	154
Sch 5 para 9	54	Sch 11	159
Sch 6 para 25	132	Sch 11 para 2 (h)	54
Social Security Act 1990		Trade Union Reform and Employment	
Sch 6 para 25	132	Rights Act 1993	102, 123
Social Security Contributions		s 23	48
and Benefits Act 1992	5, 6, 15, 131, 153	Trade Union and Labour Relations (Consolidation) Act 1992	
s 13	149	s 188	106
s 35	153	Trade Union Reform and Employment	
s 35 (2)	155	Rights Act 1993	121
s 153	54	Wages Act 1986	4, 5, 46, 62, 63, 213
s 153 (2) (d)	159		
s 153 (12)	159		

Table of statutory instruments

County Court Rules 1981	
Order 14 r 8(1)	217
Education (Modification of Enactments Relating to Employment) Order 1989 SI No 901	
Art 4	210
Art 6 (3)	210
Employment Protection (Part-Time Employees) Regulations 1995 SI No 31	31
Employment Protection (Recoupment etc) Regulations 1977 SI No 664	223
Industrial Tribunals (Constitution and Rules of Procedure) Regulations 1993 SI No 2687 Sch 1	209
r 4 (1) (a)	216
r 4 (1) (b)	217
r 4 (3)	216
r 11	220
r 12 (5)	220
r 13 (1)	209
Industrial Tribunals (Constitution and Rules of Procedure) (Amendment) Regulations 1996 SI No 1757	216
Industrial Tribunals (Extension of Jurisdiction) (England and Wales) Order 1994 SI No 1623	
reg 7	213
Judgments Debts (Rate of Interest) Order 1993 SI No 564	229
Management of Health and Safety at Work Regulations 1992 SI No 2051	11, 115, 117-119, 125
reg 2	118
reg 3	119
reg 3 (1)	118
reg 3 (3)	120
ref 3 (4)	121
reg 13A	118, 119
reg 13A (2)	122
reg 13A (4)	119
reg 13C	118
reg 13C (2)	118
reg 15 (2)	125

Table of statutory instruments

Management of Health and Safety at Work (Amendment) Regulations 1994 SI No 2865	115, 117, 122
Maternity Allowance and Statutory Maternity Pay Regulations 1994 SI No 1320	16
Maternity (Compulsory Leave) Regulations 1994 SI No 2479	
reg 2	67
reg 3	68
Police Regulations 1995 SI No 215	14
Sex Discrimination Act (Application to Armed Forces etc) Regulations 1994 SI No 3276	168
Sex Discrimination and Equal Pay (Miscellaneous Amendments) Regulations 1996 SI No 438	230
Sex Discrimination and Equal Pay (Remedies) Regulations 1993 SI No 2798	224
reg 3	228
reg 6	229
Sex Discrimination (Questions and Replies) Order 1975 SI No 2048	211
Social Security (Claims and Payments) Regulations 1987 SI No 1968	
reg 14	157
Social Security (Contributions) Regulations 1979 SI No 591	
reg 11	135
reg 119 (1) (b)	16, 136
reg 19B	147
Social Security Contributions, SMP and SSP (Miscellaneous Amendments) Regulations 1996 SI No 777	136
Social Security (Maternity Allowance) Regulations 1987 SI No 416 (as amended)	16, 153
reg 2	155
reg 3	156, 157
reg 3 (2)	156
reg 3 (2A)	157
Social Security (Maternity Allowance) (Work Abroad) Regulations 1987 SI No 417	154
Social Security (Maternity Benefits and Statutory Sick Pay) (Amendment) Regulations 1994 SI No 1367	16, 153, 159
Social Security (Medical Evidence) Regulations 1976 SI No 615	
reg 2 (3)	158
Sch 2 Pt I	158
Statutory Maternity Pay (Compensation of Employers) and Miscellaneous Amendment Regulations 1994 SI No 1882	151
Statutory Maternity Pay (General) Regulations 1986 SI No 1960 (as amended)	15, 131
reg 2 (1)	144
reg 2 (2)	144
reg 2 (3) (a)	144
reg 2 (3) (b)	144

reg 2 (4)	38, 145
reg 2 (5)	144
reg 3	140
reg 4 (2)	139
reg 4 (3)	134
reg 5	135
reg 7	141, 149
reg 8	146
reg 11 (1)	138
reg 11 (1) (a)	137
reg 11 (1) (b)	137
reg 11 (1) (c)	138
reg 11 (3)	138
reg 11 (3A)	139
reg 11 (4)	137
reg 12	141
reg 13 (1)	140
reg 13 (2)	140
reg 13 (3)	140
reg 15	140
reg 16A	137
reg 17	132
reg 17 (3)	16, 136
reg 19	147
reg 19 (b)	147
reg 20 (2)	147
reg 20 (2) (a)	147
reg 20 (2) (b)	147
reg 20 (2) (d)	147
reg 20 (2) (f)	147
reg 20 (2) (g)	147
reg 20 (2) (h)	147
reg 20 (2) (i)	147
reg 20 (3)	147
reg 20 (4) (a)	147
reg 20 (4) (d)	147
reg 20 (6) (a)	148
reg 20 (6) (b)	148
reg 21 (2) (3)	133
reg 22 (1)	142
reg 23 (1)	143
reg 23 (3)	143
reg 23 (4)	141, 143
reg 24	146
reg 26 (1)	150
reg 26 (3)	150
reg 27	148
reg 28	148
Statutory Maternity Pay (General) Amendment Regulations 1996 SI No 1335	148

Statutory Maternity Pay (Medical Evidence) Regulations 1987 SI No 235	
reg 2	35
Statutory Maternity Pay (National Health Service Employees) Regulations 1991 SI No 590	135
Statutory Maternity Pay (Persons Abroad and Mariners) Regulations 1987 SI No 418	136
Statutory Sick Pay (General) Regulations 1982 SI No 894	
reg 3 (4)	159
reg 3 (5)	159
Transfer of Undertakings (Protection of Employment) Regulations 1981 SI No 1794	81, 141
reg 5	80
reg 7	80
reg 8	81, 104
reg 14	141, 142

Table of European law

Equal Pay Directive (75/117/EEC)	5, 6, 46, 165, 172, 173, 199, 207
Equal Treatment Directive (76/207/EEC)	4-6, 15, 21, 22, 25, 39, 46, 49, 55, 57, 63, 90, 91, 96, 111, 112, 115, 127, 164, 170, 174-176, 185, 188, 194, 196, 199, 202-204, 207, 215, 220
Art 2 (3)	170
Art 2(4)	170
Art 5	39
Art 6	202
Equal Treatment (Social Security) Directive (79/7/EEC)	5
Pregnant Workers Directive (92/85/EEC)	3-6, 10, 14, 17, 38, 46, 47, 55, 59, 65, 71, 90, 91, 96, 97, 112, 113, 115, 117, 119, 120, 124, 130, 135, 136, 198, 199, 202-204, 207, 215
Annex I	117, 119
Annex II	117, 119
Art 1	12
Art 2	12
Art 2 (a)	10
Art 2 (b)	11
Art 2 (c)	11
Art 5	122, 124
Art 5 (1)	122
Art 6	121, 122
Art 8	11, 59
Art 8(2)	67
Art 9	12, 17
Art 10	12
Art 10 (2)	92
Art 11	12

Art 11 (2)	59
Art 11 (2) (b)	130
Art 11 (3)	130
Art 11 (4)	12, 135
Art 12	12, 126, 202
Treaty of Rome	
Art 117	205
Art 119	4-6, 15, 28, 30, 39, 46, 51, 55, 58, 63-65, 136, 165, 172-174, 179, 199, 200, 202, 206, 207, 215, 220, 231

Abbreviations

ACAS	Advisory, Conciliation and Arbitration Service
AWC	actual week of childbirth (or confinement)
EAT	Employment Appeal Tribunal
ECJ	European Court of Justice
EEC	European Economic Community; EEC Treaty
EOC	Equal Opportunities Commission
EOR	Equal Opportunities Review
EPCA	Employment Protection (Consolidation) Act 1978
EPD	Equal Pay Directive (75/117/EEC)
EqPA	Equal Pay Act 1970
ERA	Employment Rights Act 1996
ETD	Equal Treatment Directive (76/207/EEC)
EU	European Union
EWC	expected week of childbirth (or confinement)
HSE	Health and Safety Executive
IT	industrial tribunal
MA	maternity allowance
MAP	maternity allowance period
MA Regs	Social Security (Maternity Allowance) Regulations 1987 SI No 416 (as amended)
MHSWR	Management of Health and Safety at Work Regulations 1992 SI No 2051 (as amended)
MLP	maternity leave period
MPP	maternity pay period
NDR	notified day of return

NI	national insurance
PWD	Pregnant Workers Directive (92/85/EEC)
QW	qualifying week
SDA	Sex Discrimination Act 1975
SMP	statutory maternity pay
SMP Regs	Statutory Maternity Pay (General) Regulations 1986 SI No 1960 (as amended)
SSCBA	Social Security Contributions and Benefits Act 1992
SSP	statutory sick pay
TUPE	Transfer of Undertakings (Protection of Employment) Regulations 1981 SI No 1974 (as amended)

CHAPTER 1
Introduction

The House of Commons Employment Committee report on mothers in employment[1] points out that one of the most profound social changes in recent years has been the increase across the industrialised world of the number of women who combine a job with family life. Increasingly, women with young children are returning to work within a year of giving birth.

Between 1984 and 1994 the proportion of women of working age who were economically active rose from 66 to 71 per cent. Among mothers the growth was even more noticeable.[2] During the same period the percentage of men who were economically active dropped from 88 to 85 per cent. However, most of the growth in women's labour has been in part-time work, where pay is lower and terms and conditions worse.[3] 44 per cent of women of working age in 1994 worked part-time and the trend is more pronounced among women with dependent children. Women returning from maternity leave tend to return to a part-time job, often requiring fewer skills and less responsibility than their previous job.

Despite the increasing number of women in the labour market, a study conducted by NACAB[4] found that employers were gener-

1 House of Commons Employment Committee, *First Report on Mothers in Employment* HC 227–I Session 1994–95; price £12.15.
2 In 1984, 55 per cent of mothers with children under 16 were economically active; in 1994, 64 per cent were active.
3 'Mothers in the Labour market', *Employment Gazette*, November 1994, pp403–407. In 1994 the female part-time hourly wage was on average 79.5 per cent of the male full-time hourly wage. Terms and conditions of part-time workers are usually much worse (see 'Flexible Working: the impact on women's pay and conditions' *EOR* No 65 January/February 1996, p19 and Employment Committee report above).
4 'Not in Labour: CAB evidence on pregnancy, dismissal and employment', available from NACAB, Myddelton House, 115–123 Pentonville Road, London N1 9LX. This was carried out before the changes introduced as a result of the Pregnant Workers' Directive.

ally hostile to pregnant women. Some employers used maternity leave as an opportunity to dismiss pregnant employees and women were reluctant to take action because of lack of awareness about their rights, the stress involved in taking action and their desire to look forward to the birth rather than face an industrial tribunal.

Yet, there is evidence that the provision of more generous maternity rights (than the statutory minimum) is in the interests of both employees and employers. For example, the Chairman of Sainsbury's estimated that it cost £5,000 to find and train a new recruit to the same standard as an experienced employee and for store managers and their deputies the figure was nearer £10,000. As he said, 'No business can afford this level of waste'.[5]

An *Equal Opportunities Review* survey of maternity arrangements[6] showed that most employers in the survey offered maternity provisions in excess of the statutory minimum:[7]

- 85 per cent of respondents have improved on the current statutory minimum maternity provision;
- the average return-to-work rate of women employed by organisations offering improved maternity provision was 15 per cent higher than that of women employed by organisations which offer only the basic statutory provision;
- about 80 per cent of respondents gave more than the statutory minimum period of maternity leave;
- 78 per cent of respondents gave maternity pay in excess of the statutory minimum;
- on average, 84 per cent of leavers returned to employment; the majority of women, around two-thirds, returned to full-time employment. Women employed in organisations with more than the statutory minimum maternity provision are more likely to return to work.[8]

---

5 House of Commons Employment Committee, (n1 above), p.xxxvi.
6 The survey was based on 243 organisations, where on average 1.8 per cent of the workforce was on maternity leave each year. The average number of female staff on maternity leave as a proportion of female staff was 3.3 per cent.
7 'Maternity Arrangements '95', *EOR* No 63, September/October 1995 and *EOR* No 64, November/December 1995.
8 It should be noted, however, that the majority of the respondents were *EOR* subscribers and therefore more likely to offer more generous provisions.

One company found that improving maternity benefits and 'phasing in' women on return through part-time working reduced the loss of over 80 per cent of skilled and experienced women to less than 20 per cent. Over five years, after allowing for the additional cost of the programme, this had brought a 'return' of some £1 million through savings in recruitment, retraining and lost productivity.[9] Another company found that the provision of flexitime, part-time, job-sharing, maternity and other family leave provisions, together with a childcare support scheme, benefited the company by a significant improvement in retention rates, from 50 per cent in 1990 to 90 per cent in 1994. The provisions provided an environment where women and men wanted to work and give their continued commitment.

Development of the law on maternity rights

Before 1994, only women working for at least 16 hours per week, with two years' service, or working between 8 and 16 hours per week for at least five years (as at the beginning of the 11th week before the week the baby was due) were entitled to maternity absence. Many women with less than two years' continuous employment were dismissed when pregnant.[10]

In October 1994 the government was forced to implement the EU Pregnant Workers Directive (PWD). The directive sets minimum standards of health and safety protection, maternity leave and pay and prohibits dismissal on grounds of pregnancy. Employees whose babies were due on or after 16 October 1994 are now entitled to 14 weeks' maternity leave irrespective of length of service or hours of work. The directive also provides that member states cannot reduce existing protection.

The British government was the only one of the member states of the European Union opposed to the directive. Thus, only the minimum requirements of the directive were implemented. The UK statutory maternity provisions are, in many respects, worse than in most other EU countries, with the shortest period of maternity leave and lowest amount of maternity pay.[11]

9 'Making the Most of Women in Science, Engineering and Technology: Building a workforce for sustained competitiveness', October 1995; Rank Xerox experience.
10 NACAB, 'Not in Labour' (n4 above).
11 Conditions of Work Digest 'Maternity and work', Volume 13, International Labour Office, 1994 and H Foster ed, *Employee Benefits in Europe and the USA*, Longman, 1994.

Fourteen weeks' maternity leave is far too short, particularly without any provision for parental leave as in other EU countries. The UK has refused to adopt the parental leave directive, which is to be implemented by 1998 in other European contries. If a woman is forced, because of pregnancy-related sickness or absence, to start her leave six weeks before the expected week of the birth, and then the baby is late, she could be left with as little as four weeks' leave after the birth.

For those employees entitled to longer maternity absence (of up to 29 weeks after the beginning of the week of the birth), maternity pay runs out after 18 weeks. Many women are forced to choose between returning to work sooner than may be good for them and their children and staying off work without any independent means of support.

The present scheme comprises the European minimum rights superimposed on the pre-existing UK scheme. In addition, the UK and EU discrimination legislation provides some protection.[12] The statutory framework is therefore a hotchpotch of European and UK employment, discrimination and social security legislation providing a patchwork of rights which are subject to different qualifying conditions and notification requirements.

A woman who is dismissed while pregnant or on maternity leave (or absence) will have to consider a claim for automatically unfair dismissal (on pregnancy-related grounds), ordinary unfair dismissal (both under the Employment Rights Act 1996 (ERA)), sex discrimination (under the SDA and ETD) and protection from dismissal under the PWD. If the dismissal occurs when she is on maternity leave and she has also been denied a contractual benefit to which she is entitled, she may have additional claims under her contract, under the EqPA or article 119, under the provisions of the ERA which prohibit deductions from wages[13] and/or the SDA. That makes eight potential causes of action. There are also confusing inconsistencies in the scheme. For example, all women have a right to a minimum of 14 weeks' maternity leave, but maternity pay is payable for 18 weeks.

The House of Commons Employment Committee[14] recom-

---

12 Under the Sex Discrimination Act 1975 (SDA), Equal Pay Act 1970 (EqPA), article 119 EEC, Equal Treatment Directive (ETD) and Equal Pay Directive (EPD).
13 Formerly contained in the Wages Act 1986.
14 See n1 above.

mended that the system of maternity pay and leave should be simplified and be the responsibility of one, not three, government departments to make it accessible and comprehensible to employers and employees.[15] None of the recommendations were accepted by the government.

The increasing number of women entering and remaining in the labour market makes the provision of clear, comprehensive maternity rights all the more important. Yet the legal provisions are, as pointed out by a current Law Lord, Lord Browne-Wilkinson,[16] in a dismissal case, of 'inordinate complexity exceeding the worst excesses of a taxing statute', which 'is especially regrettable bearing in mind that they regulate the everyday rights of ordinary employers and employees'. Lord Browne-Wilkinson, in the same case, said that 'even with the skilled assistance of experienced advocates, he had no confidence that he correctly understood them'.[17]

How then can pregnant women and women on maternity leave be expected to find their way through the maze of legislation? No less than five pieces of European legislation,[18] five UK statutes[19] and ten statutory instruments are relevant. There are few specialist advisers and fewer solicitors who understand the provisions.

The complexity of the provisions means that they will be misunderstood by employers and employees alike. The Pregnant Workers Directive requires member states to introduce measures 'as are necessary to enable all workers who [consider] themselves wronged by failure to comply with the obligations arising from this Directive to pursue their claims by judicial process ...' Effective implementation of the directive is dependent on national provisions being comprehensible and readily enforceable. It is arguable that the complexity and multiplicity of potential claims relating to maternity rights makes it neither. It is in the interests of employers and employees alike for the law to be simplified.

---

15 Employment Committee Report (n1), para 43.
16 When he was sitting in the Court of Appeal.
17 *Lavery v Plessey Telecommunications Ltd* [1983] IRLR 202, CA.
18 Article 119 EEC, Equal Pay Directive (75/117/EEC), Equal Treatment Directive (76/207/EEC), Equal Treatment (Social Security) Directive (79/7/EEC) and Pregnant Workers Directive (92/391/EEC).
19 Employment Rights Act 1996, Sex Discrimination Act 1975, Equal Pay Act 1970, Social Security Contributions and Benefits Act 1992, Social Security Act 1989.

CHAPTER 2

Statutory framework

The main statutory provisions

The lack of any coherent legislative framework for maternity rights means that it is necessary to piece together the following UK and EU legislation:

a) the maternity provisions of both UK and EU law, ie:
   - the Employment Rights Act 1996 (ERA);[1] and
   - the Pregnant Workers Directive (PWD) (92/85/EEC);

b) the ordinary unfair dismissal provisions of the ERA;

c) the UK and EU sex discrimination and equal pay provisions in:
   - the Sex Discrimination Act 1975 (SDA);
   - the Equal Pay Act 1970 (EqPA);
   - article 119 EEC;
   - the Equal Pay Directive (EPD) (75/117/EEC); and
   - the Equal Treatment Directive (ETD) (76/207/EEC).

d) the social security provisions which provide for pension rights during paid leave or absence, for statutory maternity pay (SMP) and for maternity allowance (MA), namely:
   - the Social Security Contributions and Benefits Act 1992 (SSCBA);
   - the Social Security Act 1989; and
   - the Pregnant Workers Directive (PWD) (92/85/EEC).

EU legislation is relevant where it provides more favourable rights than the UK law (see chapter 14).

---

1 The ERA consolidated various employment law statutes including the Employment Protection (Consolidation) Act 1978 (EPCA).

It is also important to consider whether a woman has more favourable rights under her contract of employment (see pp 8 and 74).

Definitions under UK and EU law

Definitions under UK law: maternity leave

General maternity leave and maternity leave period (MLP)

All employees are entitled to 14 weeks *general maternity leave*.[2] The leave can start at any time from the beginning of the 11th week before the expected week of childbirth (EWC) and lasts for a continuous period of 14 weeks. This is known as the *maternity leave period*.[3]

Extended maternity absence

Women who have been continuously employed for at least two years at the beginning of the 11th week before the expected week of childbirth are entitled to return to work within 29 weeks of the beginning of the week in which birth occurs. This period is known as *extended maternity absence*. It is in addition to the 11 weeks a woman is entitled to take before the EWC.[4] Women were entitled to maternity absence before the changes introduced in 1994 and this term covers this absence.

11th week before the EWC

A week runs from Sunday to Saturday.[5] The 11th week is the earliest date on which general maternity leave, SMP and maternity allowance can commence (unless the baby is born before this date).[6]

Notified leave date

This is the day the woman notifies her employer she intends to start her general maternity leave.[7] This cannot be before the beginning of the 11th week before the expected week of childbirth.

---

2 ERA ss71–73, 235.
3 ERA ss72, 73, 235.
4 ERA s79.
5 ERA s235.
6 ERA s74(2).
7 ERA s74.

Childbirth

This means the birth of a living child (however premature) or of a child, living or dead, after 24 weeks of pregnancy.[8]

Expected week of childbirth (EWC)

This is the week the baby is due. It begins at midnight on the Saturday, so the first day is Sunday.[9]

Actual week of childbirth (AWC)

This is the week in which the baby is born. The 29 weeks of extended maternity absence are calculated from the beginning of the *actual* week of childbirth.[10] A week for these purposes ends on a Saturday, unless the employee's pay is calculated weekly by a week ending with a day other than Saturday, in which case it is that other day.[11]

Maternity certificate (MAT B1)

This is the certificate issued by the woman's doctor or midwife showing the date on which the baby is due.

Right to return

Women entitled to extended maternity absence have a 'right to return' to work up to 29 weeks from the beginning of the week of childbirth.[12]

Notified day of return (NDR)

This is the day the woman notifies her employer she intends to return to work after extended maternity absence.[13] It may be postponed in certain circumstances, in which case the NDR is the postponed date.[14]

Composite right

Employees who have a statutory right to maternity leave and absence and a contractual right have a 'composite' right.[15] This means an employee can take advantage of whichever right is, in any particular respect, the more favourable.

8 ERA s235.
9 ERA s235.
10 ERA s79.
11 ERA s235(1).
12 ERA s79.
13 ERA ss83, 235.
14 ERA s83(2).
15 ERA ss78, 85.

Maternity pay and allowance

Statutory maternity pay (SMP)
This is paid by the employer to employees who satisfy the qualifying conditions, for up to 18 weeks while they are on maternity leave. 90 per cent of earnings is paid for the first six weeks and £54.55 (1996/97 rates) for up to 12 weeks thereafter.

Maternity pay period (MPP)
This is the period during which SMP is payable. It always starts on a Sunday – usually the Sunday after the woman stops working.[16]

Maternity allowance (MA)
Women not entitled to SMP may be entitled to maternity allowance if they have paid sufficient national insurance contributions. It is paid by the Benefits Agency.

Maternity allowance period (MAP)
This is the period during which maternity allowance is payable. Like SMP, it is payable for up to 18 weeks. A week runs from Sunday to Saturday.

Maternity allowance test period
This is the period of 66 weeks immediately before the week in which the baby is due.

Expected°week of confinement (EWC)
This has the same meaning as the expected week of childbirth and is still used in the statutory maternity pay and maternity allowance legislation.

Actual week of confinement (AWC)
This is still used in the statutory maternity pay and maternity allowance legislation. It has the same meaning as the actual week of childbirth.

Qualifying week (QW)
This is the 15th week before the EWC and runs from Sunday to Saturday. It is used to calculate entitlement to SMP and higher rate maternity allowance.

16 SSCBA s165(1), 171.

Maternity rights/Chapter 2

Normal weekly earnings (for SMP)
These are the woman's actual earnings during the relevant calculation period for SMP (ie, the eight weeks or two months before the end of the qualifying week). They are calculated differently depending on whether she is paid weekly, monthly or at other intervals.

Dismissal

Week's pay for employment rights under the ERA
Compensation for breach of an employee's employment rights (eg, unfair dismissal, redundancy) is based on a week's pay. If there are fixed hours, a week's pay is the amount payable under the contract. Otherwise it may be averaged over a 12 week period. There is a maximum limit (at present £210) on the amount of a week's pay taken into account and it is subject to annual review. The calculation of a week's pay is set out in ERA ss220ff. It is beyond the scope of this book.

Automatically unfair dismissal
It is automatically unfair to dismiss a woman because she is pregnant, has had a baby or taken maternity leave. All employees are protected irrespective of length of service or hours they work.[17]

Ordinary unfair dismissal
Employees with two years' qualifying service with the same employer are protected from ordinary unfair dismissal.[18]

Definitions under the Pregnant Workers Directive

These are only relevant where the directive provides additional rights to those under the ERA. Where there is reference to the worker having informed her employer of her condition, she must have complied with the notice provisions in the ERA.

A pregnant worker means a pregnant worker who informs her employer of her condition, in accordance with national legislation or practice.[19]

A worker who has recently given birth means a worker who has recently given birth within the meaning of national legislation

17 ERA s99.
18 This qualifying period may be indirectly discriminatory (see p203).
19 PWD article 2(a).

Statutory framework 11

or practice and who informs her employer of her condition.[20] In the UK this means a woman who has given birth or had a stillbirth (after 24 weeks' pregnancy) in the previous six months (Management of Health and Safety at Work Regulations).

A *worker who is breastfeeding* means a worker who is breastfeeding within the meaning of national legislation or practice and who informs her employer of her condition.[21] There is no limit under UK law on the length of time a woman may continue breastfeeding.

Summary of main UK and EU statutory provisions

The following is a summary of the main UK and EU statutory provisions on maternity rights. The EU law is set out first, as rights under the ERA are based on the Pregnant Workers Directive. Where EU law provides greater rights than the national legislation, the latter should be interpreted in line with EU law, where possible (see chapter 14).

Maternity rights under EU law: the Pregnant Workers Directive[22]

This European directive was adopted in October 1992 and member states were given until October 1994 to implement its provisions (see p3). The PWD's stated aim is 'to encourage improvements in the safety and health at work of pregnant workers and workers who have recently given birth or are breastfeeding'. The main provisions are:

a) employers must carry out a health and safety assessment where there is a risk to pregnant or breastfeeding women and take such steps as are necessary to minimise the risks; this may include adjusting working conditions, moving the woman to another job or giving her paid leave;
b) all pregnant workers are entitled to a minimum of 14 weeks general maternity leave;[23]

---

20 Article 2(b).
21 Article 2(c).
22 92/85/EEC.
23 Article 8.

c) all pregnant workers are entitled to paid time off for ante-natal examinations;[24]
d) it is prohibited to dismiss a worker during the period from the beginning of her pregnancy to the end of the maternity leave (and probably absence) save in exceptional cases not connected with pregnancy or childbirth;[25]
e) employment rights, apart from pay, must be maintained during general maternity leave;[26] (it is not clear whether they must also be maintained during extended maternity absence; see p59);
f) an adequate allowance must be paid during maternity leave which must be no less than the woman would receive if she were absent sick.[27]

The directive protects all 'workers' (see pp10–11).

There are no exceptions to protection under the PWD, though entitlement to maternity pay is dependent on the worker satisfying eligibility conditions laid down under national law.[28]

The directive does not allow any reduction in pre-existing levels of protection provided under national law. Article 1 provides that the 'Directive may not have the effect of reducing the level of protection afforded to pregnant workers, workers who have recently given birth or who are breastfeeding as compared with the situation which exists in each Member State on the date on which this Directive is adopted'.

Where there is no protection under UK law, reference should always be made to EU law, as it may provide greater protection than UK law. Possible areas of conflict are highlighted in the relevant sections of this book.

Maternity rights under UK law: Employment Rights Act 1996

The provisions of the Employment Protection (Consolidation) Act 1978 and other employment statutes have now been consolidated by the Employment Rights Act 1996 (ERA). It came into force on 22 August 1996. There have been changes in the wording of many

24 Article 9.
25 Article 10.
26 Article 11.
27 Article 11.
28 Article 11(4).

Statutory framework

of the sections, but as it is a consolidation Act, these changes are not intended to be substantive.

The rights under the ERA are subject to qualifying conditions, including notice provisions, which are set out later. The main provisions are:

a) where working conditions cannot be adjusted to avoid a health and safety risk, a right to be given alternative work on health and safety grounds, or suspended on full pay in the absence of suitable alternative work (ss66–68); this was implemented in 1994;

b) a right to 14 weeks' general maternity leave irrespective of length of service or hours of work; this was also implemented in 1994 (s71). The right to extended maternity absence (of up to 29 weeks after the beginning of the actual week of childbirth) for women with two years service (as at the 11th week before the expected week of childbirth) is maintained (this now includes part-timers);

c) a right to time off for ante-natal care without loss of pay, irrespective of length of service (ss55 and 56); this provision has not changed since the implementation of the directive;

d) a right to protection from dismissal for specified grounds related to the woman's pregnancy, childbirth or maternity leave (s99). Before implementation of the directive, a woman could be fairly dismissed if she was incapable of adequately doing the work;

e) employment rights (apart from remuneration) continue without reduction during general maternity leave (s71); this was implemented in 1994;

f) a right to return to work up to 29 weeks after the beginning of the week the baby was born (where there is a right to extended maternity absence) (s79).

Employees only protected

The ERA only applies to an 'employee', ie, 'an individual who has entered into or works under (or, where the employment has ceased, worked under) a contract of employment'. A contract of employment means a contract of service or apprenticeship, whether express or implied, and (if it is express) whether it is oral or in writing.[29]

---

29 ERA s230. See *Lane v Shire Roofing Company (Oxford) Ltd* [1995] IRLR 495, CA.

General exclusions from ERA

Not all employees are protected by ERA. The following are outside its scope:[30]

a) *Women who ordinarily work outside Great Britain.* Where, under her contract of employment, a woman ordinarily works outside Great Britain she is not protected unless she is covered by the offshore employment provisions.[31] If the woman works in the EU, she should be protected by the law of the member state in which she works. A woman who works on board a ship will be protected by the ERA if the ship is registered in the UK unless the employment is wholly outside Great Britain or she is not ordinarily resident in Great Britain.[32]

b) *Share fisherwomen.* Women who are either the master or crew of a fishing vessel and are paid by a share in the profits or gross earnings of the vessel are not protected.[33]

c) *Police officers.* Women employed in the police service are excluded, though they have similar protection under the Police Regulations 1995.[34] This no longer includes prison officers, who are now protected.[35]

d) *Armed forces.* When ERA s192 is brought into force armed forces employees will be within the protection of the ERA in relation to the maternity provisions.[36] The Armed Forces Act 1996, when implemented, will oblige a complainant to go through an internal complaints procedure before bringing proceedings in an industrial tribunal. In order to allow time for the internal procedure, the time limit for bringing IT proceedings will be extended to six months.

Ordinary unfair dismissal provisions of ERA

In addition to the automatically unfair dismissal provisions of ERA, women who have two years' service[37] are protected from

30 They are excluded from the right to paid time off for ante-natal care, maternity leave (general and extended), continued contractual rights during general maternity leave, the right to return to work, the right not to be dismissed and the right to suspension on health and safety grounds.
31 ERA s196 (but see p90 for protection from unfair dismissal).
32 ERA s196(5); see *Haughton v Olau Line (UK) Ltd* [1986] IRLR 465, CA.
33 ERA s199 (but see p90 for protection from unfair dismissal).
34 ERA s200.
35 Criminal Justice and Public Order Act 1994 s26. The exclusion of share fisherwomen and police officers may be in breach of the PWD.
36 The only relevant exception is in Part XI, which deals with redundancy.
37 This service qualification may itself be discriminatory; see *R v Secretary of State for Employment ex p Seymour Smith & Perez* [1995] IRLR 464.

ordinary unfair dismissal (see pp93ff). The definition of employee and the exceptions are the same as above.

Protection from discrimination

Less favourable treatment of a woman on grounds related to her pregnancy or childbirth will usually be direct discrimination on grounds of sex and a breach of both the SDA and Equal Treatment Directive.[38] The advantage of making a discrimination claim is that the questionnaire procedure can be used (see p211) and, unlike unfair dismissal, compensation is not subject to any limit and can be awarded for injury to feelings.

The Equal Pay Act 1970 covers pay and other contractual terms where there is a comparable man as a fellow employee (see p170). Article 119 provides for equal pay for work of equal value. Maternity pay is pay under article 119 (see p47).

Statutory maternity pay

Statutory maternity pay is payable under the Social Security Contributions and Benefits Act 1992 (SSCBA) and the Statutory Maternity Pay (General) Regulations 1986 SI No 1960 (as amended) to women who have been continuously employed by the same employer for 26 weeks to the end of the 15th week before the expected week of childbirth. It is paid by the employer for up to 18 weeks, at 90 per cent of full pay for the first six weeks and £54.55 (1996/97 rates) per week for up to 12 weeks.

Employee

The definition of employee is different under the ERA and the SSCBA. For the purposes of maternity pay an employee is a woman over the age of 16 who is employed in Great Britain under a contract of service or who holds an office (including elective office), and whose employer pays income tax (PAYE) for her. The self-employed are not entitled to statutory maternity pay, but may be entitled to maternity allowance (see below).

Exclusions

Where the woman's employer is not resident or present in Great

---

38 *Webb v EMO Air Cargo (UK) Ltd (No 2)* [1995] IRLR 645, HL.

Britain or does not have a place of business in Great Britain where NI contributions are payable, the employee will not be entitled to SMP.[39] The only other employees excluded from entitlement to SMP are those in custody and foreign-going mariners (see p136).

Maternity allowance

Maternity allowance is paid under the Maternity Allowance Regulations 1987 SI No 416 (as amended)[40] to women who have been in employment and have paid 26 weeks' national insurance contributions in the 66 weeks immediately before the EWC. The allowance is paid for 18 weeks at a higher rate of £54.55 (1996/97 rates) to women employed in the qualifying week (the 15th week before the EWC) and at a lower rate of £47.35 per week (1996/97 rates) to women who are self-employed or who are not employed in the qualifying week.

---

39 Statutory Maternity Pay (General) Regulations 1986 SI No 1960 reg 17(3) and Social Security (Contributions) Regulations 1979 SI No 591 reg 119(1)(b).
40 The main amending regulations are the Maternity Allowance and Statutory Maternity Pay Regulations 1994 SI No 1320 and the Social Security Maternity Benefits and Statutory Sick Pay (Amendment) Regulations 1994 SI No 1367.

CHAPTER 3
Rights before the birth

Introduction

This chapter looks at the rights and protection given to pregnant women up to the time they go on general maternity leave. It covers the right to paid time off for ante-natal care and pregnancy-related sickness. It also covers other less favourable treatment (such as in recruitment, training, promotion, access to benefits and dismissal).

Right to paid time off for ante-natal care

All pregnant employees, irrespective of length of service or hours of work, whether permanent or temporary, are entitled to paid time off during working hours for ante-natal care.[1] The employer cannot unreasonably refuse time off (see below). The Pregnant Workers Directive contains a similar right to time off, without loss of pay, in order to attend ante-natal examinations.[2]

What is ante-natal care?

Ante-natal care is not defined by the ERA. In *Satchwell Sunvic Ltd v Secretary of State for Employment*,[3] the EAT held that ante-natal care covered non-medical care such as relaxation classes.[4] The Under-Secretary of State for Employment said in

---

1 ERA ss55 and 56. The limited exclusions are set out on p14.
2 Article 9. This does not provide any greater protection than exists under the ERA.
3 [1979] IRLR 455, EAT.
4 See also *Gregory v Tudsbury Ltd* [1982] IRLR 267, IT.

parliamentary debates that ante-natal care would include relaxation classes.[5] As the government pointed out, there is no need to show the specific reason for an ante-natal appointment. The DTI guide[6] also states that ante-natal care may include relaxation and parentcraft classes.

Requirement for appointment for ante-natal care and certificate

The woman must have an appointment given on the advice of a registered doctor, midwife or health visitor. There is no obligation to provide proof of the appointment in relation to the first visit, though she should obtain the employer's permission to attend. For subsequent appointments, however, if the employer so requires, the woman must provide written proof of the appointment (such as an appointment card) and a certificate or note from a doctor, midwife or health visitor stating that she is pregnant.[7]

Can the employer refuse time off for ante-natal care?

Time off cannot be unreasonably refused. The amount of time off needed for ante-natal care is fairly standard for most women who have uncomplicated pregnancies. There are unlikely, therefore, to be many situations when an employer could justify refusing time off. Clearly, it would not be reasonable for a woman to take part of every day off in order to attend relaxation classes, nor to take off more than a few hours at a time. Time should be allowed for waiting and travelling to and from the appointment. For example, in *Dhamrait v United Biscuits Ltd*[8] the appointment lasted longer than expected and as a result the woman missed the works bus (her only means of transport). The IT held she was entitled to be paid for the whole shift.

It would not generally be reasonable to expect a woman to attend work for as little as half an hour before or after the appointment. Thus, in *Edgar v Giorgione Inns Ltd*[9] the woman worked from 9 am to 3 pm. The tribunal expected her to work before an appointment fixed at 3 pm (she had to leave at 2 pm)

---

5 Hansard (HC) Standing Committee F, 12.1.93, cols 291–292; Hansard (HL) 25.3.93, cols 531–532 (Trades Union Reform and Employment Rights Bill 1993).
6 DTI, *Maternity Rights: a guide for employers and employees*; August 1995.
7 ERA s55(2) and (3).
8 COIT 1430/192. There have been a number of tribunal decisions on time off for ante-natal care but these are not binding.
9 COIT 1803/13.

and after an appointment at 9.05 am, but said it was not reasonable for her to attend work before or after appointments fixed between 10.30 am and 11.15 am. It will be a question of fact in each case and the type of work may be a relevant factor.

There is no obligation on the woman to arrange ante-natal care outside working hours or to make up the time.[10] Although in *Gregory v Tudsbury Ltd* (above) the tribunal suggested that an employer could reasonably refuse time off if a woman worked part-time and could arrange ante-natal care outside work, this is not binding and is arguably wrong. The woman may not be able to choose the time of her appointment. The statute states that there is entitlement to time off during working hours and there is no proviso that this is subject to the woman not being able to attend outside working hours. In *Sajil v Carraro t/a Foubert's Bar*[11] the IT said it was important not to allow employers scope for requiring women to change their working hours or make up for lost time.

An employer can refuse paid time off if the woman fails to comply with the requirement to produce proof of the appointment (for the second and subsequent visits) and a certificate stating she is pregnant, after being requested to do so by the employer (see above and *Edgar v Giorgione Inns Ltd*).

The right to be paid for time off

A woman who takes time off for ante-natal care is entitled to be paid as though she was still at work. Once the employer has allowed time off, s/he must pay for it.[12]

Pay is calculated as follows:

a) If a week's pay is always the same, the hourly rate is calculated by dividing the week's pay by the hours worked; or
b) If the pay varies, it should be averaged over a 12-week period, ending with the last complete week before the day on which the time off is taken; or
c) If the pay varies and the woman has not been employed for 12 weeks, the pay should be calculated by taking into account:

---

10 *Edgar v Giorgione Inns Ltd* COIT 1803/13, *Bland v Laws (Confectioners) Ltd* COIT 1613/4 and *Sajil v Carraro t/a Foubert's Bar* (below).
11 COIT 1890/34.
12 *Gregory v Tudsbury Ltd* (n4 above).

- the average number of normal working hours a week which the employee could expect; and
- the average number of such hours of other employees engaged in relevant comparable employment with the same employer.[13]

'Normal working hours' and 'a week's pay' are defined by the ERA.[14] Pay includes overtime where it is compulsory under the contract. There is no maximum limit on a week's pay.

Payment made by the employer under the contract of employment discharges liability under statute and vice-versa.[15]

Remedies

If an employer refuses to give time off for ante-natal care or refuses to pay (in full or in part), the woman can complain to a tribunal within three months from the date of the appointment or such further period as is reasonable where it was not reasonably practicable for the complaint to be presented within three months (see p214).[15A]

If the tribunal upholds the woman's complaint, it must make a declaration to that effect and award compensation equal to the amount the woman should have received had she been given the time off.[16]

Dismissal of a woman who enforces her right to time off

Dismissal of a woman who takes time off or alleges that the employer has failed to give paid time off or who complains to a tribunal is automatically unfair.[17]

Pregnancy-related dismissal is unlawful

Automatically unfair dismissal under ERA

It is automatically unfair to dismiss a woman for any reason connected with her pregnancy. There are no minimum service

13 ERA s56.
14 ERA ss55(4) and 220ff.
15 ERA s56(6).
15A ERA s57(2)(a).
16 ERA s57.
17 Under ERA s99, as it would be a reason 'connected with' her pregnancy (see below) and ERA s104 (see p93).

qualifying conditions nor is there any exemption for small businesses. It is irrelevant how a man would be treated. The limited exceptions are set out on p14.

A dismissal which is automatically unfair (under ERA s99) will generally also be discriminatory (ie, a breach of the SDA and ETD).[18] The dismissal may also be an ordinary unfair dismissal (see pp93ff).

It is automatically unfair to dismiss a woman because she is pregnant or for 'any other reason connected with her pregnancy'. In *Clayton v Vigers*[19] the EAT held that 'connected with' means 'associated with' and the words should be given a wide meaning. A woman found guilty of dishonesty would clearly not be protected from dismissal, unless a man guilty of similar conduct was not dismissed (in which case she might be able to claim sex discrimination). However, if the reason for dismissal has anything to do with pregnancy, such as taking time off for ante-natal care, a miscarriage, pregnancy-related sickness, lateness due to morning sickness, inability to do the work because of pregnancy-related tiredness or health and safety reasons, the dismissal will be automatically unfair.

Employer must know of pregnancy

In order to claim that the dismissal was for a pregnancy-related reason, the employer must be aware that the woman is pregnant. In *Del Monte Foods Ltd v Mundon*[20] the woman was dismissed because of continued absence caused by gastroenteritis. The day after the dismissal the company discovered she was pregnant. The EAT held that the dismissal was not automatically unfair because the employers were unaware that the absence was connected to her pregnancy.[21]

What is pregnancy-related sickness?

It includes morning sickness, fatigue, threatened or actual miscarriage or any other illness connected with the pregnancy (see p37).

Is there a limit to the amount of pregnancy-related absence?

If a woman is absent because of pregnancy-related sickness for the

---

18 *Webb v EMO Air Cargo Ltd (No 2)* [1994] IRLR 482, ECJ; [1995] IRLR 645, HL.
19 [1990] IRLR 177, EAT.
20 [1980] IRLR 224, EAT.
21 See also *Bhatt v E D Moseley & Sons Ltd* Case No 12681/94, Birmingham IT (20.3.95).

whole of her pregnancy (until she goes on maternity leave), she should still be protected. The sickness must be genuine and caused by the pregnancy.

'Ordinary' sickness followed by 'pregnancy' sickness
If pregnancy has exacerbated an existing condition, this should be sufficient to establish that it is 'related to pregnancy'. If the employee would not have been dismissed 'but for' the pregnancy-related sickness absence, the dismissal will be unfair. In *George v Beecham Group*[22] the applicant received two written warnings about her sickness absences followed by a final warning after she went into hospital for a gynaecological operation. She then told her manager she was pregnant. Soon after, she was admitted to hospital after a miscarriage and was dismissed on her return to work. The tribunal held that her dismissal was automatically unfair because the main reason for the dismissal was her absence caused by the miscarriage.

Dismissal for health and safety reasons
If a pregnant woman is unable to continue working for health and safety reasons, the employer must either alter her working conditions or offer her suitable alternative work, or suspend her on full pay. It is automatically unfair to dismiss a woman to avoid having to comply with these duties or suspend her[23] (see chapter 8). It is also a breach of the Equal Treatment Directive[24] (see p127).

Selection for redundancy because of pregnancy
It is automatically unfair under ERA s99 to make a woman redundant because she is pregnant (see pp105ff and *Brown v Stockton-on-Tees Borough Council*).[25]

Ordinary unfair dismissal

Dismissal of a pregnant woman may also be an ordinary unfair dismissal (see p93). This would include dismissal for sickness not related to pregnancy.

---

22 [1977] IRLR 43, IT.
23 ERA s99(1).
24 *Habermann-Beltermann v Arbeiterwohlfahrt, Bezirksverband Ndb/Opf eV* [1994] IRLR 364, ECJ.
25 [1988] IRLR 263, HL.

Rights before the birth

Discriminatory dismissals under SDA and ETD

The HL and ECJ held in *Webb v EMO Air Cargo Ltd* (n18 above) that it is a breach of the SDA and the Equal Treatment Directive to dismiss a woman (at least with a permanent contract) because she is pregnant (see p176). The position in relation to fixed-term contracts is set out on pp177–178. The House of Lords expressed some doubt whether the same principles would apply to fixed-term contracts where a woman would, because of her pregnancy, be unavailable for the whole of the period.

In *Brown v Rentokil Ltd*,[26] which is being appealed, and is arguably wrong in the light of *Webb*, the Court of Session held that a pregnant woman dismissed as a result of absence due to a pregnancy-related illness, had not been discriminated against on grounds of sex. She had been treated like a male employee absent through long-term illness.[27]

Similar principles apply to fixed term contracts. In *Caruana v Manchester Airport plc*[28] the applicant had been employed (as an independent sub-contractor) on a series of fixed-term contracts. Soon after she told her employers that she was pregnant, she was informed that her current 12-month contract would not be renewed. The tribunal found that the reason was because she would not be available for work (because of her maternity leave) at the beginning of the renewed contract. Following *Webb*, the EAT held that the failure to renew the fixed-term contract was because of the applicant's pregnancy and was therefore discriminatory.

The EAT did not consider that the ECJ and HL judgments in *Webb* necessarily meant that a woman with (or about to be offered) a fixed-term contract should be treated any differently from a woman with a permanent contract. Thus, too much weight should not be given to the comments (which were obiter) made in the House of Lords in *Webb* about fixed-term contracts, particularly where a woman is available for part of the contract (see p178).

---

26 [1995] IRLR 211, CS. This has been referred to the ECJ.
27 Note that at the time of the decision it was not automatically unfair to dismiss a woman for a pregnancy-related reason.
28 [1996] IRLR 378, EAT. See also *Nelson v Western Health & Social Services Board* Case No 887/93SDA: 10.10.94, Belfast IT where the applicant's fixed term contract was not renewed after she was off sick having had an ectopic pregnancy. The tribunal, following the ECJ decision in *Webb*, held that her operation was pregnancy-related and the failure to renew her contract was a discriminatory dismissal.

Fertility treatment

In *Joyce v Northern Microwave Distributors Ltd*[29] the IT held that a woman who was dismissed because she was on a course of fertility treatment had suffered discrimination. The IT said that the assumptions which were made about the fertility treatment and the possible pregnancy were totally stereotyped. They were evidence of a discriminatory attitude and a man would not have been treated in the same way. The employer admitted that the applicant had been dismissed because she would be away having fertility treatment *and* she might get pregnant.[30]

Dismissal on 'moral' grounds

In *O'Neill v (1) The Governors of St Thomas More RCVA Upper School and (2) Bedfordshire County Council*[31] the applicant was an unmarried pregnant teacher, working in a Catholic school, who was dismissed when the school discovered that the father was a Catholic priest. The EAT held, overruling the IT, that the critical question is whether, on an objective consideration of all the circumstances, the dismissal was on the ground of pregnancy, motive being irrelevant. The EAT acknowledged that there may have been other grounds for the dismissal (such as the paternity of the child) – but as these were pregnancy-related and it was the applicant's pregnancy which precipitated the decision to dismiss her, the dismissal was unlawful. As it was not possible on the facts to find that the dismissal was caused by anything other than the pregnancy, this was, following *Webb,* sex discrimination.

Abortion to avoid dismissal

A woman who had an abortion to avoid being dismissed by the army was awarded £10,000 for discrimination.[32] The tribunal

---

29 Case No 5564/93: 22.9.93, Leeds IT.
30 In *Robinson v London Borough of Greenwich* [1995] 21 November, 745/94 DCLD 27 the EAT held that an employer could take account of absence due to infertility treatment when comparing the woman's absence levels to those of other employees in deciding whom to select for redundancy.
31 [1996] IRLR 372, EAT. The EAT decision in *Berrisford v Woodard Schools (Midland Division) Ltd* [1991] IRLR 247, EAT was distinguished on the basis that in *Berrisford* the applicant was dismissed not because of her pregnancy but because she did not intend to marry and this 'manifested extra-marital sex', which was unacceptable in a religious school.
32 *O'Hare v MOD* (1995) 25 September; Case No 1341/95. See also *Ministry of Defence v Mutton* [1996] ICR 590, EAT.

held that 'the policy of dismissal for pregnancy must be taken to include as reasonably foreseeable ... that some servicewomen who wish to continue their service would, on finding that they were pregnant, not only seek a termination but would be reasonably able to obtain one.'

Other less favourable treatment of pregnant women

Other less favourable treatment of women because of their pregnancy may be unlawful under the SDA (see p166–167) or the ETD (see p170). Where there is discrimination in pay or contractual terms, there may be a breach of the EqPA (see p170).

Recruitment

Refusal to recruit

In *Dekker v Stichting Vormingscentrum voor Jonge Volwassenen (VJV-Centrum) Plus*[33] the ECJ held that it was a breach of the Equal Treatment Directive for an employer to refuse to employ a suitable female applicant on the ground of 'possible adverse consequences for him arising from employing a woman who is pregnant at the time of the application'. The employers had refused to employ Mrs Dekker as a training instructor because they would not be reimbursed the sickness benefits which the employer would have to pay her during her maternity leave. As a result they would lose some of their training places. The ECJ held that a refusal to employ because of the financial consequences of absence connected with pregnancy must be deemed to be based principally on the fact of the pregnancy and was as such discriminatory. It was irrelevant that there was no male candidate. The ECJ stressed that no account could be taken of justification provided under national law.

Whether the applicant intends to return after maternity leave (or absence) should not make any difference (except to the level of compensation). There is no obligation for an employee who is entitled to only 14 weeks' maternity leave to state whether she intends to return to work. Women often do not, at this stage, know whether they will return, as their circumstances may

---

33 [1991] IRLR 27.

change. In addition, no other employee would be asked how long s/he intended to stay; it is surely discriminatory to ask this of a pregnant woman (see also chapter 12).

Discriminatory questions at interview
The EOC Code of Practice (see p164) recommends that interview questions should relate to the requirements of the job.

> Where it is necessary to assess whether personal circumstances will affect performance of the job (for example, where it involves unsocial hours or extensive travel) this should be discussed objectively without detailed questions based on assumptions about marital status, children and domestic obligations. Questions about marriage plans or family intentions should not be asked, as they could be construed as showing bias against women. Information necessary for personal records can be collected after a job offer has been made.

For example, in *Johnston v Fultons Fine Furnishing Ltd*[34] an IT held that a woman who was asked at her job interview questions aimed at filtering out female candidates of childbearing age (such as whether she intended to have any more children) suffered unlawful discrimination. The tribunal found she was better qualified than two candidates invited to a second interview who were aged 38 and 43, at which age the tribunal considered it was uncommon for women to have children.[35]

Arguably, any questions about childbearing are themselves discriminatory after *Webb*. The only question which needs to be asked is whether the applicant can do the hours.[36] Even if the questions are not in themselves discriminatory,[37] they will be strong evidence of discrimination if a male applicant is not asked similar questions and the woman fails to get the job – particularly if the woman is better qualified.[38]

---

34 (1995) 30 March, Case No 02087/94; DCLD No 25, p7.
35 The applicant was awarded £3,000 compensation for injury to feelings on the basis that she suffered considerable upset and embarrassment.
36 Though in *Woodhead v Chief Constable of West Yorkshire Police* EAT 285/89 the EAT held that it may be legitimate for an employer to ask questions about whether the applicant's circumstances would affect her performance in the job.
37 See *Saunders v Richmond upon-Thames BC* [1977] IRLR 362, EAT.
38 See *Smith v North Western Regional Health Authority* COIT 1842/176.

Rights before the birth

A refusal to recruit a woman because she has children (and so is assumed to be unreliable) was held to be discriminatory in *Hurley v Mustoe*.[39] The EAT said there were other ways of establishing whether the applicant was reliable such as by taking up references.

Other less favourable treatment

The SDA[40] makes it unlawful for an employer to discriminate against a woman in relation to promotion, transfer, training or other benefits or to subject her to any other detriment.

Transfer

In *McLachlan v Central Scotland Health Care NHS Trust*,[41] for example, the tribunal held that a decision to transfer the applicant was made because she was female, part-time and due to go on maternity leave. This was direct discrimination, because it was related to the applicant's maternity leave, and indirect discrimination in that she was selected because she worked part-time.[42]

Promotion

In *Pearson v Swindells and British Telecommunications Ltd*[43] the IT held that the applicant failed to obtain promotion because of her absence on maternity leave. She had attended an interview while eight months pregnant and no account had been taken of the possibility that her poor performance at interview might have been affected by being eight months pregnant and on leave. Similar principles apply to promotion as to recruitment.

Appearances

It is likely to be unlawful to move a woman to a different job because she is pregnant and 'would not look good' dealing with customers. For example, in *O'Neill v Walthamstow Building Society*[44] Ms O'Neill was told that her attempt to conceal her stomach by wearing her shirt outside her skirt made her look a

---

39 [1981] IRLR 208, EAT. It was held to be direct sex discrimination and indirect marital discrimination (see chapters 11 and 12).
40 s6(2).
41 Case No S/4932/94; Glasgow IT; 14.6.95.
42 Although the move was cancelled, and the applicant incurred no financial loss, she was awarded £500 for injury to feelings.
43 Case No 48222/93 14.11.94.
44 Case No 27886/89; DCLD 6.

mess and if she did not wear her uniform properly she would be transferred out of sight of the public. Feeling humiliated the applicant resigned and the tribunal upheld her complaint of discrimination.

In *Martin v McConkey*[45] the applicant was told she would have to leave when her pregnancy showed 'because he did not want people talking in the shop'. She won her sex discrimination claim.

Note that the SDA protects not only employees but also contract workers, partners, trainees, and those working for employment agencies.

Sickness during pregnancy

Sickness during pregnancy may lead to an employer taking disciplinary action and dismissing her. This may be unfair and discriminatory (see pp93 and 96). There are also the following issues to consider.

Exclusion of pregnancy-related sickness from contractual sick pay

If a contractual sick pay scheme excludes pregnancy-related sickness, this may be a breach of the EqPA or article 119. In *Coyne v Exports Credits Guarantee Department*[46] a tribunal held that the exclusion of pregnancy-related sickness from a contractual sick pay scheme was a breach of the EqPA. A man covered by a medical certificate showing he was unfit for work was automatically entitled to his full pay for six months, with no restrictions, whereas a woman's right to sick pay following maternity absence was restricted to an absence which arose from some illness or condition unconnected with confinement.[47]

Effect on entitlement to statutory maternity pay (SMP)

If a woman is sick during the eight weeks or two months before the qualifying week (and is on unpaid leave or only getting statutory sick pay), she may not be entitled to SMP because she has not complied with one of the qualifying conditions, ie, to have earned

45 Case No 1577/89, Northern Ireland tribunal; DCLD 5.
46 [1981] IRLR 51, IT.
47 See also *Todd v Eastern Health and Social Services Board* Case Ref 1149/88EP and 1150/88SD.

on average the amount of the lower earnings limit (ie, £61) during the eight-week or two-month period (see pp132ff), because statutory sick pay is below the lower earnings limit.

Triggering provisions

A woman who is absent because of her pregnancy during the six weeks before the EWC may be forced to start her maternity leave immediately (see p35). Her SMP period will always start immediately (see pp36, 38 and 144ff).

RIGHTS BEFORE THE BIRTH: KEY POINTS

- All pregnant women are entitled to paid time off for antenatal care; this includes relaxation classes. It is automatically unfair to dismiss a woman for enforcing this right.
- Pregnancy-related dismissal is automatically unfair and discriminatory; this includes dismissal because of pregnancy-related sickness provided the employer is aware of the pregnancy.
- Dismissal during pregnancy may also be an ordinary unfair dismissal.
- Selection of a woman for redundancy because she is pregnant is automatically unfair.
- Employers have a duty to carry out an assessment of the health and safety risks to women of childbearing age and pregnant women. Where there is a risk, the employer must alter the woman's working conditions, or offer suitable alternative work and if this is not possible, suspend her on full pay.
- Dismissal of a woman in order to avoid health and safety duties is automatically unfair.
- Other less favourable treatment which is a breach of the SDA includes:
  - failure to recruit a woman because she is pregnant,
  - transferring a woman because she is due to go on maternity leave,
  - failure to promote a woman because she is pregnant or about to go on maternity leave,
  - different treatment because of the woman's appearance during pregnancy.
- Sickness during pregnancy can also lead to the following problems:
  - reduction in the woman's earnings which may disentitle her to SMP if they fall below the lower earnings limit in the eight weeks or two months before the qualifying week,
  - pregnancy-related sickness may be excluded from contractual sick pay schemes; this will probably be a breach of article 119 and the EqPA,
  - a woman who has a pregnancy-related absence in the six weeks before the expected week of childbirth may be forced to start her maternity leave immediately.

CHAPTER 4

General maternity leave and extended maternity absence

Introduction

This chapter is about women's entitlement to 'general maternity leave' (of 14 weeks), to which all women are entitled, and 'extended maternity absence' (of up to 29 weeks after the beginning of the week the baby was born), for which there is a two-year qualifying period.

It is important to distinguish between 'leave' and 'absence'; not all women are entitled to maternity absence and women's rights during the two periods are different. The term 'general maternity leave' refers to the 14-week 'maternity leave period'. The term 'extended maternity absence' is the period which commences at the end of the 14-week 'maternity leave period' and lasts up to 29 weeks after the beginning of the week of the birth. The term 'absence' is also used to refer to the maternity absence to which women were entitled before 1994, when there was no right to maternity leave for all employees.

There is no longer any requirement (for either leave or absence) for the employee to have worked a minimum number of hours per week.[1] The limited exclusions are set out on p14.

Women may be entitled, under their contract of employment or by agreement, to more favourable terms than the statutory minimum, such as a longer period off work. It is always important to establish whether there is any such agreement (written or oral) between employer and employee and the terms of any agreement. Where there is a statutory and a contractual right to maternity leave or absence, the woman may take advantage of whichever

1 Employment Protection (Part-Time Employees) Regulations 1995 SI No 31.

right is, in any particular respect, the more favourable[2] (see p74). This is called a *composite right*.

The rights to maternity leave and absence are dependent on strict compliance with notice provisions. These are set out in this chapter, together with the consequences of failure to comply with them. Women entitled to extended maternity absence must first comply with the notice provisions for maternity leave. The date for commencement of maternity leave is discussed together with the effect of premature births and pregnancy-related absence in the six weeks before the expected week of childbirth (EWC). Rights during maternity leave and absence are discussed in chapter 5. The right to return to work is covered in chapter 6.

There are no provisions in the ERA for adoption leave. Failure to allow a woman to take time off to care for an adopted child may be directly discriminatory, particularly if employees are allowed time off for other reasons (see p40). It may also be indirectly discriminatory, the requirement being that the woman must not take any unpaid leave in order to care for the child. The key question will then be whether this is justifiable (see chapter 13).

Minimum 'general maternity leave' for all employees

This section looks at the provisions relating to general maternity leave of 14 weeks to which all employees, irrespective of the hours they work and length of service, and whether permanent or temporary, are entitled. During this period the contract continues.[3] Usually, the woman can choose when her leave starts, though it cannot begin earlier than the 11th week before the EWC (see pp35ff).

Notice provisions

There are two separate requirements:

a) The woman must notify her employer *in writing* at least 21

---

2 ERA s78 and s85.
3 ERA 71. The legislation does not provide that there is a right to 'maternity leave' but that during the maternity leave period (the 14 weeks) the woman is entitled to the benefit of her terms and conditions of employment (except remuneration).

General maternity leave and extended maternity absence

days before her maternity leave starts[4] or, if that is not reasonably practicable, as soon as reasonably practicable, of:
- the fact that she is pregnant; and
- the expected week of childbirth; or
- the date of the birth (if it has occurred);[5]
- the fact that she wishes to be paid SMP (see p142).

A woman entitled to 'extended maternity absence' must at the same time give written notice that she intends to return to work (see p41). If the baby is born before the woman has had a chance to give notice, she should give written notice of the birth as soon as possible.

b) The woman must inform her employer at least 21 days before her general maternity leave starts, or, if that is not reasonably practicable, as soon as is reasonably practicable of the date she intends to start her leave.[6]

The 21-day time limit (under (b)) does not apply if:
- a woman is absent because of her pregnancy in the six weeks before the EWC and the employer requires her to start her leave; or
- she gives birth before she has notified the employer; or
- she gives birth before the notice expires.

In these circumstances (when the woman's maternity leave will automatically start), notice must be given to the employer (either of the birth or that the absence is due to pregnancy), as soon as practically possible.[7] The leave will start immediately (see p36), so there is no longer any need to give notice of the start of leave.

Notice under (b) need only be in writing if requested by the employer.[8] However, in order to avoid any argument about whether notice has been given, it is preferable to put it in writing (at the same time as notice under (a) above is given) and keep a copy.

Notice required for contractual rights to return

Where the woman claims the benefit of more favourable contractual terms but there is no provision in the contract (or by agree-

---

4 Which must not be earlier than the beginning of the 11th week before the expected week of childbirth.
5 ERA s75.
6 ERA s74(1).
7 ERA s74(4) and (5).
8 ERA s74(6).

ment with the employer) for notice, then the statutory provisions regarding notice will apply.⁹

21 clear days' notice

21 clear days' notice should be given, excluding the day of notification and the day when maternity leave begins.¹⁰ The 21 days include bank holidays and weekends.

Not reasonably practicable

Failure to comply with the notification provisions may deprive the woman of her *statutory* right to maternity leave (and absence).¹¹ It will be a question of fact whether it was reasonably practicable to give the 21 days' notice. In the unfair dismissal context the question is whether it is 'feasible'; whether the woman was at fault will be relevant. Absence from work because of pregnancy complications may constitute a good reason, particularly if the woman was unaware of her rights.¹² The cases about failure to give notice of intention to return from maternity absence may be relevant in this context (see pp41-42). Having said that, notice should *always* be given on time; it is never safe to assume it can be given late.

Employer's obligation to advise about rights

Employers have an obligation to advise employees of their contractual rights where these are not agreed with the employee but incorporated into the contract through a collective agreement. In *Scally v Southern Health and Social Services Board*¹³ the House of Lords held that there was a contractual obligation on employers to take reasonable steps to bring the existence of a right to enhanced pension entitlement to the attention of employees. The same principle should apply to contractual maternity rights. It would be good practice for employers to advise employees about their statutory maternity rights.

---

9 *Kolfor Plant Ltd v Wright* [1982] IRLR 311, EAT.
10 *Rightside Properties Ltd v Gray* [1974] 2 All ER 1169, ChD (a case involving the sale of property), where the court held that a condition requiring a period of 'at least 21 days' was not satisfied by giving notice that something was to be done 'within 21 days'; the words 'at least' indicated that the period allowed was to be exclusive of the day of service and the day of expiry of the notice.
11 ERA s74(1) and s75(1).
12 *Simpson v Microponent Development Ltd* COIT 1327/85.
13 [1991] IRLR 522, HL.

Provision of certificate giving EWC

If the employer asks the woman to provide a doctor's or midwife's certificate giving the EWC, she must do so.[14] Failure to provide a certificate will deprive the woman of her right to *statutory* maternity leave (and absence).[15] The employer's request must clearly require a certificate, which will generally be a MAT B1.[16] There is no time limit laid down for producing a certificate, though it should be produced within a reasonable timescale. There is no obligation to provide a certificate if it is not requested.[17]

Dismissal or resignation before 11th week

A woman who is dismissed or resigns before she reaches the 11th week will not be employed and will not have the automatic right to maternity leave (or absence).[18] However, if she is dismissed for a reason related to her pregnancy, it will automatically be unfair and discriminatory (see p20). She will be entitled to compensation (and possibly reinstatement or re-engagement) for unfair dismissal, which should include an amount for loss of maternity rights[19] (see pp224ff).

Commencement of leave

Maternity leave cannot start earlier than the 11th week before the expected week of childbirth (unless the baby is born before the 11th week).[20] Nor can the leave start later than the birth.

---

14 ERA s75(2). For the purposes of SMP the certificate must not be signed by the doctor or midwife before the beginning of the 14th week before the EWC: Statutory Maternity Pay (Medical Evidence) Regulations 1987 SI No 235 reg 2.
15 ERA s75(2).
16 *Eagles v Cadman t/a Baby Days* COIT 1334/181.
17 However, if the woman wants to claim SMP, she must provide medical evidence within the time limits (see p142).
18 However, if she merely says that she does not intend to return, this should not count as a resignation. If she then complies with all the notice provisions, she should be entitled to return (see *Hughes v Gwynedd Area Health Authority* p99).
19 See *Linghorn v P & O Ferries* COIT 1256/60, where there was a declaration that all rights in connection with maternity leave were to be restored, and *Evans v John R Clayton Ltd* COIT 1514/119, where the compensatory award included an amount for maternity pay.
20 ERA s74(2).

Otherwise it is generally up to the woman to decide when her maternity leave starts. It will be the date she notifies to her employer (as above), unless she is forced to commence her leave because of pregnancy-related absence during the six weeks before the EWC (see below).

A week begins on a Sunday. To calculate the earliest that maternity leave can start:

a) start with the Sunday at the beginning of the EWC;
b) count back 11 weeks (to the 11th Sunday); a week ends on a Saturday;[21]
c) the earliest leave can start is the 11th Sunday.

For example, if the baby was due on Thursday 27 June 1996, the EWC began on Sunday 23 June, and 11 Sundays before this date will be 7 April 1996. Maternity leave could commence on any day from 7 April.

Even where there is a provision in the contract stating that the woman must start her maternity leave at a specified time, this is overridden by the statute which allows women to choose the start date.[22] Many women will want to start their maternity leave as close as possible to the EWC in order to maximise the number of weeks off after the birth. There is no obligation on the woman to provide a medical certificate to show she is fit. The 14 weeks run continuously from the actual day it starts.[23]

Absence due to pregnancy during six weeks before EWC

A woman who, in the six weeks before the expected week of childbirth, is absent wholly or partly because of her pregnancy (because, for example, she is sick) will have to commence her maternity leave from this date, unless her employer agrees otherwise (see below).[24] If she has given birth, her leave will start immediately.

This means that a woman who is off work for as little as half a day because of her pregnancy may, in theory, have to start her

---

21 See *Secretary of State for Employment v A Ford & Son (Sacks) Ltd* [1986] ICR 882, EAT.
22 *Inner London Education Authority v Nash* [1979] ICR 229, EAT.
23 ERA s73.
24 ERA s72(1). See pp144 and 156 for the effect of pregnancy-related absence on entitlement to statutory maternity pay and maternity allowance.

General maternity leave and extended maternity absence 37

leave and cannot take sick leave or pay (but see below). If the woman is not aware of these provisions, she may return to work for a few days only to discover that, when she tells her employer she was off for a pregnancy-related reason, she is informed that her maternity leave started from the time she was off. If this happens she will have lost some of her leave.

If the absence is not related to the woman's pregnancy, it does not trigger maternity leave and she can take sick leave (and receive statutory or contractual sick pay) in the normal way.

What is pregnancy-related absence?

General guidance on pregnancy-related illness is provided by the Benefits Agency Medical Service.[25] Absence at an ante-natal class should not count; the DTI and DSS guide confirms this.[26]

It is not clear whether a woman who has been suspended for health and safety reasons will be treated as absent because of her pregnancy and therefore forced on to maternity leave from the sixth week (see p124).

Duty to notify employer of pregnancy-related absence

A woman who is absent because of her pregnancy (or where the baby is born early) in the six weeks before the EWC must inform her employer of this as soon as is reasonably practicable or she will lose her statutory right to maternity leave (and absence).[27] This need not be in writing unless the employer so requests.[28]

Right of woman to work following pregnancy-related absence

An employer need not force the woman to start her maternity leave if she has a pregnancy-related absence. The contract of employment may give the woman the right to choose when her leave starts, in which case this overrides the statutory provisions. Alternatively, the employer may agree to the woman starting it later. It is advisable, if possible, to get such agreement in writing. The DTI booklet says that employers may ignore 'odd days'.

If the employer allows a woman to return to work after pregnancy-related absence and nothing is specifically agreed, there

---

25 *Pregnancy-Related Illness*, ref NI200, available free from Benefits Agency offices.
26 See *Maternity Rights*, ref PL958 (Rev 1).
27 ERA s74(4)(b) and (5)(b).
28 ERA s74(6).

may be a waiver of these triggering provisions. In such a case maternity leave should start at the date given in the notice.

A woman may want to return to work after a short absence in order to receive her full pay for the maximum period of time. If the employer requires the maternity leave to start at the time of the pregnancy-related absence but the woman wants to return to work, then arguably she should be allowed to do so.[29] However, she will lose a day of maternity leave for each day she works.[30]

In addition, a woman wanting to return to work before the end of her maternity leave must give her employer at least seven days' notice[31] (unless this is waived by the employer). This provision is aimed at women who wish to return to work after the birth but before the expiry of the 14 weeks. It is not clear if a woman must give seven days' notice if she wants to return to work (and be paid) after pregnancy-related absence but before the birth. It would be safer to assume that notice must be given.

Commencement of statutory maternity pay period

The statutory maternity pay period is automatically triggered if there is pregnancy-related absence in the six weeks before the EWC and this cannot be overridden[32] (see chapter 9).

Are the trigger provisions a breach of EU law?

There is no parallel provision in the PWD which triggers a woman onto maternity leave if she has a pregnancy-related absence during the six weeks before the EWC; this may be a breach of EU law because:

a) the trigger provisions are new for women entitled to extended maternity absence (which existed before the implementation of the Directive); this may be in breach of the provision in the Pregnant Workers Directive which states that there must be no derogation of existing rights (see p12);

b) failure to allow a woman to take sick leave or pay because her sickness is pregnancy-related is itself discrimination, on the basis that any less favourable treatment of a pregnant woman

---

29 Refusal to allow her to return may be constructive dismissal if she resigns.
30 She will lose her SMP for each week or part she works (at the lower rate first (see p146).
31 ERA s76.
32 Statutory Maternity Pay (General) Regulations 1986 reg 2(4) and SSCBA 1992 s164(6).

General maternity leave and extended maternity absence 39

is unlawful under EU law (see *Webb, Dekker,* and *Hertz,* pp176ff); or

c) even if it is not discriminatory in itself to deny a woman sick leave or pay because the illness is pregnancy-related, it is arguable that if a man who is on long-term sick pay would not be disqualified from sick pay or leave for any period of his sickness, then nor should a woman.[33]

Under (b) or (c) above there may be a breach of either article 119 and the Equal Pay Act or the Sex Discrimination Act and the Equal Treatment Directive. Sick pay is 'pay' under article 119.[34] Failure to pay sick pay to a woman because her illness is related to her pregnancy is probably a breach of article 119 and the EqPA (see p28). The Equal Treatment Directive provides that there shall be equal treatment with regard to working conditions. This means that men and women shall be guaranteed the same conditions without discrimination on grounds of sex.[35] Thus, a woman who is absent from work because of sickness should not be deprived of sick leave only because the sickness is pregnancy-related.

Premature births

The maternity leave period will automatically start with the day on which the baby is born.[36] There is no right to postpone all or part of maternity leave unless this is negotiated with the employer.

Stillbirths

Childbirth is defined as the birth of a living child (however premature) or of a child (whether living or dead) after 24 weeks of pregnancy.[37] A woman who has a stillbirth after 24 weeks will be entitled to 14 weeks' maternity leave. If the stillbirth occurs before the 11th week before the EWC, the maternity leave period will start from that date.

---

33 See *Todd v Eastern Health and Social Services Board* (1989) 16 October, Case No 1149/88EP, 1150/88SD, Belfast IT (see p54).
34 *Rinner-Kuhn v FWW Spezial-Gebäudereinigung GmbH* [1989] IRLR 493 ECJ.
35 ETD article 5.
36 ERA s72(2).
37 ERA s235.

Extended maternity absence

A woman who has been employed continuously, by the same employer, for two years at the beginning of the 11th week before the expected week of childbirth is entitled to return to work up to 29 weeks after the beginning of the week in which the baby was born.[38] This means that the woman must usually return by the Friday of the 29th week; she cannot leave it until the Monday unless agreed with the employer.

A woman who does not have the relevant qualifying service may be able to argue for a longer period if employees are allowed longer periods of absence for other reasons, such as sickness, or a sabbatical. For example, in *McMillan v Scottish Widows Fund and Life Assurance Society*[39] the tribunal held that an employer discriminated by not holding open a woman's job because she did not have two years' service. Men were allowed time off for sporting activities or to accommodate short-term illnesses without their job being threatened.[40]

Qualifying conditions for extended maternity absence

Continuous employment

The woman must still be employed at the beginning (ie, on the Sunday) of the 11th week before the expected week of childbirth (or have already given birth). Basically one must work out the Sunday at the beginning of the EWC and count back 11 Sundays.

Continuous employment includes any week in which the employee has a contract of employment (written or oral) with her employer. Thus an employee may be on sick leave, on holiday, or on unpaid leave and still have a contract of employment.

There are also special rules as to when an absence from work, when there is no contract, may still be treated as continuous employment. These absences between contracts include up to 26 weeks sickness absence, and leave of absence by arrangement or custom.[41] This may apply, for example, to seasonal workers who may have successive short-term contracts with gaps in between.

---

38 ERA s79. For definition of 'week' see p8.
39 (1993) 6 August, Case No S/4805/92.
40 See also *Curl v Air UK Ltd* (1988) 20 January, Norwich IT (COIT) 1957/26 and *Tindale v Barnsley Building Society* (1992) 16 April, DCLD 15 Case No 15289/91.
41 ERA ss210ff. See p137 for comparable provisions for statutory maternity pay.

General maternity leave and extended maternity absence

Even if the woman stopped working for her employer before the 11th week, she may still have a contract of employment (to which she can return) if this was the intention of the parties. For example, in *Satchwell Sunvic Ltd v Secretary of State for Employment*[42] the woman stopped work 12 weeks before the EWC but, as the employers expected her to return (and kept her on the payroll, retaining her P45), her contract was held to continue.

Notice provisions for 'extended maternity absence'

The woman must first qualify for maternity leave, in other words she must have complied with all the relevant notice provisions.[43] There are also the following additional requirements:

a) The employee must inform her employer, *in writing*, at least 21 days before her maternity leave begins, or, if that is not reasonably practicable (see p33 above), as soon as reasonably practicable, that she intends to return to work.[44] This must be included with the information about her pregnancy and EWC (see p33). The provision of a certificate of expected confinement is not sufficient if the woman fails to state that she intends to return.[45] A conditional notice to return is not sufficient.[46]

In *Nu-Swift International Ltd v Mallinson*[47] the woman failed to give the required written confirmation about whether she intended to return. She said she was worried that the child might have some deformity and she was waiting for assurance that this was not the case and she did not know if she could make suitable childcare arrangements. The EAT held that she was aware of her rights and it was reasonably practicable for her to notify the employer before she left. The Act did not

---

42 [1979] IRLR 455, EAT.
43 ERA s79 provides that women entitled to rights conferred under s71 (the general right to maternity leave) have a right to return after 'extended maternity absence'.
44 ERA s80.
45 *F W Woolworth plc v Smith* [1990] ICR 45, EAT.
46 In *Osborne v Thomas Bolton & Sons Ltd* COIT 794/248 the tribunal held that it was not enough for the applicant to say that she wanted to return if the circumstances were right.
47 [1978] IRLR 537, EAT.

cover the situation where an employee had not made up her mind so she lost her statutory right to return.

If notice has not been given a woman can argue it was not reasonably practicable to give notice. For example, in *Simpson v Microponent Development Ltd* COIT 1327/85, the tribunal held that, because of the applicant's difficult pregnancy and her ignorance of her statutory rights, it was not reasonably practicable for her to inform her employers of her intention to return within the prescribed period.

An employee is well advised to give notice of intention to return, even if she does not plan to or is unsure of her future plans. This will protect her position if she subsequently decides that she does wish to return. Uncertainty about whether or not to return is no excuse, and the right to return is lost. An employee who gives notice to return but who is unable or unwilling to return can change her mind at a later stage at no loss to herself.

b) The woman must give written notice to the employer, at least 21 days before the day on which she proposes to return, of her proposal to return on that day.[48] She must therefore give the notice not later than 26 weeks after the actual week of childbirth. Note that there is no provision for this notice to be waived on the grounds that it was not reasonably practicable to give it.

c) Where, not earlier than 21 days before the end of her maternity leave period (ie, after 11 weeks of maternity leave) the employer makes a written request for *written* confirmation that she intends to return, the employee must provide such written confirmation within 14 days of receiving the request (or, if that is not reasonably practicable, as soon as is reasonably practicable). Thus, the employer can write 11 weeks into the woman's maternity leave, at a time when she may still not have had the baby.[49]

The employer's request must be in writing and must explain the effect of this provision (ie, that the woman will lose her right to return if she does not reply in writing within 14 days).[50] Failure to provide the explanation probably means that the employer will not be able to deprive the woman of her right to return if she fails to reply. The woman is not obliged to give an

---

48 ERA s82(1).
49 ERA s80(2).
50 ERA s80(3).

General maternity leave and extended maternity absence

actual date for her return until 21 days before she is due to return; she need only say that she intends to return.

As with general maternity leave, it is crucially important that the notice requirements are followed; failure to do so may result in the *statutory* right to return being lost.

Even if the woman wants to return the day after the expiry of her maternity leave period, she must comply with these notice provisions relating to maternity absence. There is no reason, however, why she should not return at the end of the 14 weeks if she has failed to comply with these notice provisions, or if she simply changes her mind about taking the longer period.

Provision of certificate giving EWC

As with general maternity leave there is a requirement to provide a doctor's or midwife's certificate giving the EWC, if requested by the employer (see p35).

Duration of absence

Maternity absence begins at the end of maternity leave. The woman has a right to return to work up to 29 weeks after the beginning of the week of the birth (see pp70ff for right to return).

MATERNITY LEAVE: KEY POINTS
- All women employees are entitled to 14 weeks' general maternity leave irrespective of length of service, the hours they work, and whether they have permanent or temporary contracts.
- A woman must be employed at the 11th week before the EWC or she will not be entitled to maternity leave or absence. If she has been dismissed because of her pregnancy this will be automatically unfair. If she has resigned she will have no right to leave or absence.
- Entitlement to maternity leave and absence depends on giving notice, ie
  - *written notice* at least 21 days before maternity leave starts (or as soon as reasonably practicable) that she is pregnant; she must give the expected week of childbirth; a woman entitled to extended maternity absence must, at the same time, give written notice that she intends to return.

- *notice*, at least 21 days before maternity leave starts (or as soon as reasonably practicable), of the date she intends to start maternity leave. This notice need not be in writing unless requested by the employer.
- *a medical certificate,* giving the EWC, must be provided if the employer asks for it or if the employee wants SMP.
• The earliest maternity leave can start is the 11th week before the EWC (unless the baby is born earlier).
• After the 11th week the woman can choose when to start her maternity leave unless:
  - she is absent because of her pregnancy in the six weeks before the EWC – in which case her leave will start then. If she is absent because of her pregnancy in these six weeks, she must inform her employer of this. These provisions may be in breach of EU law;
  - the baby is premature; in which case the leave will start immediately.
• Women continuously employed by the same employer for two years (at the beginning of the 11th week before the EWC) are entitled to maternity absence and the right to return up to 29 weeks after the beginning of the week the baby is born.
• There are additional notice requirements for maternity absence:
  - the woman must have complied with the notice requirements for maternity leave;
  - she must inform her employer, *in writing,* at least 21 days before her leave begins (or as soon as reasonably practicable) that she intends to return to work;
  - she must give written notice, at least 21 days before the day of her return, of her proposal to return; and
  - where, not earlier than 21 days before the end of her MLP, the employer makes a written request for confirmation that she intends to return, the employee must provide written confirmation within 14 days of receiving the request.
• General maternity leave lasts for 14 weeks and the woman can simply turn up to work at the end of the period; she must give seven days' notice if she wants to return earlier.
• Maternity absence begins at the end of the MLP and lasts up to 29 weeks after the beginning of week of the birth.

General maternity leave and extended maternity absence 45

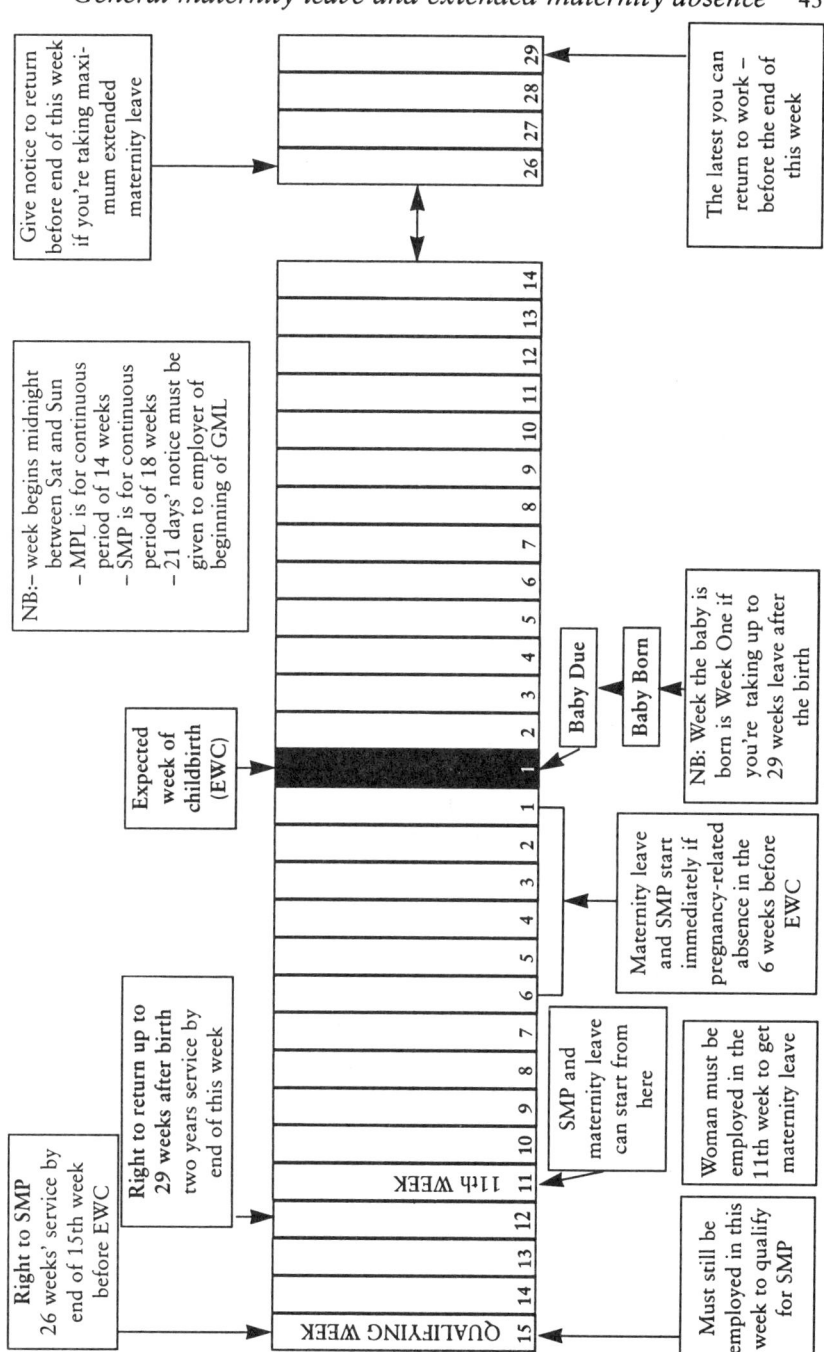

CHAPTER 5
Rights during maternity leave and absence

Introduction

There is no right to receive full pay during maternity leave or absence unless the contract of employment makes provision for it. Women may, however, be entitled to other benefits which they receive from their employer, such as holidays, sick pay, bonuses, commission and fringe benefits (such as a company car, health insurance, mortgage subsidy). Different principles apply to the maternity leave period (the 14 weeks) and extended maternity absence (the period which starts at the end of the leave and lasts up to 29 weeks after the beginning of the week of the birth).

The position is complicated because maternity rights under the ERA need to be considered along with other provisions, ie
- contractual terms (whether written or oral, express or implied);
- the discrimination provisions of the SDA and Equal Treatment Directive;
- the equal pay provisions of the Equal Pay Act, as well as article 119 EEC and the Equal Pay Directive;
- the Pregnant Workers Directive, which may, in some situations, provide more protection than the ERA;
- Part II of ERA (formerly in the Wages Act 1986), under which a claim may be made on the basis that there has been an unlawful deduction of pay;
- the Social Security Act 1989, which prohibits unfair maternity provisions in pension schemes.

No right to full pay during maternity leave/absence

In *Gillespie and Others v Northern Health and Social Services Board and Others*[1] the ECJ held that although maternity pay was 'pay' within article 119, there was no right to full pay during maternity leave or absence. The ECJ made a distinction between:
- pay (which is not payable) and,
- a pay rise relating to the period before the end of paid maternity leave or absence but after the beginning of the period when maternity pay was calculated (see p148).

In *Gillespie* the calculation of contractual maternity pay (under the collective agreement) was based on the average weekly pay received by employees for the two months preceding the reference week (which was the 15th week before the expected week of childbirth). No provision was made for an increase in maternity pay if there was a subsequent pay rise. A pay increase was agreed in November 1988 and backdated to the eight-week calculation period. The ECJ held that they were entitled to the benefit of the pay rise awarded any time after the beginning of the calculation period where it relates to the paid part of their maternity leave or absence (see p148). In *Gillespie* the increase was payable on the earnings-related part of contractual maternity pay.

Any pay increase should also be payable in full immediately on the woman's return to work. This would include any incremental rise up a pay scale, a pay review relating to an individual and any inflationary award, which is often backdated.

For the effect on the calculation of statutory maternity pay see p148.

Rights during general maternity leave

Although the main provisions are to be found in the ERA, these need to be considered in the context of the Pregnant Workers Directive on which they are based. In addition, where there is no entitlement to a benefit under the ERA, there may be a claim under the discrimination or equal pay legislation.

The Pregnant Workers Directive provides that 'the rights connected with the employment contract of workers ... must be ensured' during maternity leave 'other than those referred to in point (b)'. Point (b) provides for the maintenance of an adequate

1 [1996] IRLR 214, ECJ.

allowance during maternity leave. Thus all rights apart from 'the adequate allowance' should continue during maternity leave (and possibly maternity absence; see p59). The ERA should be interpreted so as to accord with the Directive (to the extent that it provides more favourable rights), particularly as the provisions (introduced via the Trade Union Reform and Employment Rights Act 1993) were intended to implement the directive.

Remuneration

During the maternity leave period women are entitled, under ERA s71, to the same terms and conditions, *other than remuneration*, as they would have received if they had been at work.[2] The definition of remuneration is therefore crucial. The Hansard debates are useful as an aid to interpretation.[3]

There is no statutory definition of remuneration, but it is clearly narrower than pay as defined by article 119. In the debates on Trade Union Reform and Employment Rights Act 1993 s23 (where, in the predecessor of ERA s71, the word 'remuneration' was substituted for 'pay'), Patrick McLoughlin, for the government, said that the use of the word 'pay' would risk too wide an interpretation and could mean that benefits in kind might be withheld during maternity leave. He went on to say, 'This is clearly not the intention of the directive and it is not our intention in implementing it. Only monetary payment is not required to be continued, to be replaced by maternity pay. The employee will continue to enjoy all other benefits under her contract.'[4]

The government said that guidance could be drawn from the definition of remuneration used to calculate a week's pay.[5] In this context remuneration would include wages, salaries, contractual bonuses and other 'profits' but not benefits in kind (such as a company car or free insurance) or holiday pay.

Arguably, remuneration should only include money, such as

---

2 Provided they have complied with the notice requirements for maternity leave. See p32 above.
3 In *Pepper v Hart* [1993] IRLR 33 the House of Lords allowed reference to parliamentary material as an aid to construction.
4 Hansard, Standing Committee F 12.1.93, cols 310, 316, 317. See also col 396 14.1.93, where he said that all the terms and conditions of the contract, with the sole exception of those relating to wages and salary, will continue.
5 ERA ss220 ff. This is used for calculating entitlement to redundancy payments, guarantee payments etc.

the salary or wages which would have been earned by the woman during the 14-week period if she had been at work. It is, in other words, what she would expect to receive in her basic pay at the end of the week or month (excluding 'perks'). This is the amount which is replaced by maternity pay.[6] Thus, a bonus payable to all employees at Christmas should also be paid to a woman on maternity leave as it is not part of her basic pay.

The following is a summary of how different payments are likely to be treated under the ERA and, where relevant, article 119.

Wages, salary and overtime pay

Wages and salary are clearly 'remuneration' (under the ERA) and not payable during general maternity leave, unless there is a more favourable contractual maternity scheme. Overtime will also come within the definition of remuneration. Following *Gillespie* (above), failure to pay wages or salary during maternity leave would not be a breach of article 119.

Pay reviews or increase

Where a woman's pay review is due to be carried out during her maternity leave, failure to carry it out may be a breach of contract or discrimination. Either a review should be brought forward to before the woman goes on leave or should take place immediately on her return. If it is based on productivity, this should be assessed on the basis of an average over a period which does not include the maternity leave period or a period where the woman's earnings are unusually low because of her pregnancy. The Advocate General pointed out in *Gillespie* that 'the fact that a woman is pregnant cannot be relied on in order to reduce her pay on the grounds that she has become less productive or that her pregnancy entails special arrangements justifying a pay cut'.

Where a pay review is due during maternity absence, similar principles apply. The ERA also provides that a woman is entitled to the same terms and conditions, except as to remuneration, as those which would have applied had she not been absent (see p48). A French case has been referred to the ECJ to decide whether failure to assess a woman's performance because she was on maternity leave is a breach of the ETD.[7]

---

6 As pointed out by Patrick McLoughlin in the debates (see above).
7 *CNAVTS v Thibault* (OJ no C-189/7, 22.7.95) ECJ.

Bonuses and commission

The position in relation to bonuses and commission is unclear. A woman denied such a payment would be well advised to make a claim under the ERA, article 119 or the Equal Pay Act.

(a) *Under ERA.* Whether bonuses and commission count as 'remuneration' will depend on the type of bonus and the terms of the particular bonus scheme. A contractual bonus or commission payable in respect of work which would have been done by the woman if she had not been on maternity leave may count as remuneration and therefore not be payable during the 14 weeks. This would apply to productivity pay based on the individual's performance.

A bonus or commission which is payable in respect of work done by the whole workforce should arguably be paid to a woman on general maternity leave; it is not dependant on her being at work.

If the bonus or commission is not paid in full but relates to work done by the woman in a period outside the maternity leave, arguably it should be paid on a proportionate basis.[8] ERA s71 is only concerned with the period the woman is absent from work on maternity leave, so any payment relating to a period either before or after this 14 weeks should be paid as normal (see below for position in relation to maternity absence).

(b) *Article 119 and Equal Pay Act.* Under article 119 bonuses and commission are 'pay' and, unlike the EqPA, it is not relevant whether they are contractual or not. In *Gillespie* the ECJ held that 'a woman who is still linked to her employer by a contract of employment or by an employment relationship during maternity leave must, like any other worker, benefit from any pay rise ... To deny such an increase to a woman on maternity leave would discriminate against her purely in her capacity as a worker since, had she not been pregnant, she would have received the pay rise'. Thus, where the bonus or commission is paid irrespective of the work actually done by the individual, such as a Christmas or other one-off bonus paid to all workers, it should be paid. This approach was taken by the IT in *Iverson v P&O European Ferries (Dover) Ltd* (57265/95/C) in relation to profit-related pay, paid irrespective of whether an

---

8 A woman should still not be penalised, however, if, while at work, she has earned less because of pregnancy-related absence (see p49).

employee had earned profit. However, it may be argued that no comparison can be made between a woman on maternity leave and an employee at work, thus there can be no discrimination (see p58). There is no clear answer.

There may also be a claim under article 119 or the Equal Pay Act on the basis that where a man or woman who had been away from work for a similar period would receive a bonus, so too should a woman absent on maternity leave. Where the bonus is discretionary (ie, non-contractual), the claim would be under the SDA (see chapter 11).

Company cars, mobile phones and other perks
Where a company car or mobile phone (or other perk) is restricted to business use only, there is no entitlement to continued use of it during the general maternity leave period.

Where the car and/or phone are for personal and business use, the woman should be entitled to use it during maternity leave. It was implicitly accepted by the government in the debates referred to above that entitlement to use of a company car continued during the MLP as it was not 'remuneration'.[9]

If the employer pays a car allowance or a contribution towards a car or phone (such as rental, insurance, repairs), these payments should not be classified as 'remuneration' where they are for both personal *and* business use.

Other benefits in kind and 'perks'
Benefits in kind include subsidised loans and mortgages, participation in share schemes, private health insurance, professional subscriptions, free or subsidised travel, subsidised child care or child care vouchers, club membership and any other 'perks'. The employer must continue to provide these benefits during maternity leave; they should not be treated as remuneration.[10] This probably applies even where cash is paid to an employee who can then chose which benefit to take.

---

9 Standing Committee F; 12.1.93, col 314
10 During the debates the reason why the government substituted the word 'remuneration' for 'pay' was to avoid the wider definition of pay under article 119. The purpose was to ensure that benefits whether in cash or in kind continued to be paid. See p48 above.

Private health insurance

Where a private health insurance scheme excludes pregnancy-related illness, the insurance company may refuse to insure the woman, relying on the exception which allows differential treatment for actuarial reasons.[11] There is no equivalent exception for an employer. If an employer fails to provide an equivalent benefit, the woman may arguably have an equal pay claim against him/her.

Luncheon vouchers

These are a benefit in kind and arguably should continue to be paid during maternity leave. This was the view of the government spokesman Viscount Ullswater.[12]

Holidays

Holiday entitlement is not remuneration so continues to accrue during general maternity leave and it will count towards the woman's normal leave entitlement.[13] For bank holidays see p55. If it has not been possible to take accrued holiday leave before going on maternity leave, the woman should ask for the holiday leave to be carried over into the following year or to be paid in cash instead. The right to carry over leave or to receive pay in lieu will depend on the terms of the contract and the employer's normal practice. If there is no entitlement to carry holiday leave over or to be paid in lieu, then it is advisable to take the leave before going on maternity leave. A claim for holiday *pay* (as opposed to *leave*) may succeed if a man on sick leave would be entitled to it (see *Iverson*).

Annual shut-down

If the workplace closes for a period, and this coincides with the woman's maternity leave, she may be able to claim this period as accrued holiday if an employee who was sick during this period is entitled to take the time off (though this is unlikely). It will be necessary to look carefully at the contract and custom and practice.

---

11 SDA s45.
12 Hansard (HL) 25.3.93, col 548.
13 Before October 1994 there was no automatic right to accrue holiday entitlement during maternity absence.

School holidays

If maternity leave (or absence) falls during school holidays there is no entitlement to take leave to make up for missing the holidays. If, however, a woman returns to work before the beginning of the holidays, she will get paid for them in the normal way.

Occupational pensions

During the 14 weeks maternity leave the employer must continue to pay pension contributions as though the woman was working normally and irrespective of whether she returns to work at the end of the leave (or absence).[14] This applies irrespective of whether the woman is entitled to maternity pay. In the debates (above) Patrick McLoughlin said that using the word 'pay' might throw doubt on whether pension contributions were payable during maternity leave. That, he said, was clearly not the intention of the directive nor was it the government's intention (see p48).[15]

In addition, under the Social Security Act 1989 Sch 5, a woman on paid maternity leave or absence must be treated for all purposes (except her liability to pay contributions) as though she was at work and receiving full pay. The provisions apply whether or not the woman returns to work at the end of her leave or absence. The woman will continue to accrue rights and benefits during her paid leave (and absence) but is only required to pay contributions on the maternity pay she actually receives. These provisions do not apply to women who are not entitled to maternity pay (contractual or statutory), who will have to rely on their rights under the ERA during the maternity leave period. Rights at the end of the paid period will depend on the contract and the pension scheme (see p60 for provisions on continuity of service).

Where the pension is a money purchase scheme (ie, based on actual contributions made as opposed to the final salary), a woman who has been on maternity leave and thus paid fewer contributions will receive less than an employee who has not. It is not clear what, if any, remedy she would have.

These provisions are enforced in the civil courts (usually the county court). The Social Security Act 1989 provides that where

---

14 Occupational pension rights are not 'remuneration' and should therefore be maintained during the maternity leave period.
15 Hansard 13.1.93 Standing Committee F col 310.

54 Maternity rights/Chapter 5

any provision is in breach of the principle of the Act it may be overridden.[16] Thus, for example, if the employer fails to maintain the pension contributions during paid maternity leave (or absence), an application can be made (by an 'interested person') to the county court for payment to be made.[17]

Continuity of service is preserved during maternity leave

During the 14-week maternity leave period the contract of employment continues, irrespective of pay, length of service or hours of work.[18] This applies in relation to contractual and statutory benefits.

Statutory sick pay

There is no entitlement to statutory sick pay during the 18-week maternity pay period.[19] This is the case even if the woman returns to work before the end of the period and then falls sick. She would then have to re-claim statutory maternity pay (or maternity allowance) for any week in which she was not working (see p159).[20]

Contractual sick pay

This covers sick pay schemes which are part of the contract and provide more favourable terms than the statutory scheme. Under the ERA a woman would not be entitled to contractual sick pay as she is to be treated as though she were not absent. In any event, such pay is likely to be treated as 'remuneration'. However, she may have an equal pay claim. In *Todd v Eastern Health and Social Services Board*[21] the applicant argued that she was entitled, while absent from work during pregnancy, to the benefit of her contractual sick pay scheme which was more favourable than the maternity pay she would receive. A Northern Ireland tribunal held that the applicant, by being denied access to the sickness provisions when disabled through pregnancy, was treated less favourably than a man doing like work. The tribunal said that it did not make its decision on the basis of a comparison between a

---

16 Social Security Act 1989 Sch 5 para 3.
17 Sch 5 para 9.
18 ERA s71.
19 SSCBA s153 and Sch 11 para 2(h).
20 If she does any work in the week, she cannot claim SMP (see p146).
21 (1989) 16 October, Case Nos 1149/88EP, 1150/88SD, Belfast IT. This may be referred to the ECJ.

pregnant female employee and a sick male employee, as they felt that no such comparison could be made. The difference in treatment was because there was no limit on that man's entitlement related to the nature of his disability. The applicant was awarded the difference between what she would have received if she had been off sick and what she actually received in maternity pay (see also p28).

Although it is not possible to compare a woman on maternity leave with a man at work (at least for the purposes of 'pay', following *Gillespie*), a comparison can arguably be made between a woman on maternity leave with an employee on sick leave or other leave. However, it is unlikely that a woman can take advantage of both maternity pay and sick pay during the same period. The uncertainty of the comparative approach following the decision in *Gillespie* (see p179) makes the abandonment of any claim to statutory maternity rights inadvisable.

Time off in lieu for missed bank holidays
Apart from maternity pay, there are other benefits which may be given to employees absent from work (because of sickness or other reasons) but not to women on maternity leave. For example, if there is a bank holiday during the woman's maternity leave, there is normally no entitlement to take a day off at a later stage. If, however, employees who are sick on a bank holiday are entitled to take a day off in lieu then it may well be discriminatory to refuse to allow a woman on maternity leave to do the same (see p58).

Rights during extended maternity absence

Extended maternity absence commences from the end of the 14-week general maternity leave period and lasts for up to 29 weeks after the beginning of the week in which the baby is born. Entitlement to preserved contractual terms and conditions (ie, those set out on pp48–55) during extended maternity absence is unclear. There are a number of possible claims based on:

a) the contract;
b) the SDA and Equal Treatment Directive;
c) the EqPA and article 119;
d) the Pregnant Workers Directive;
e) the statutory provisions for pensions and continuity of service.

The contract

The status of a woman's contract during maternity absence is very unclear and it is important to consider the terms of the contract and any agreement (written or verbal) between employer and employee. The options are:

a) there is no continuing contract, in which case there will be no entitlement to the benefits of the contract; or

b) the contract, or part of it, is suspended until the woman returns to work; any part of the contract which is 'suspended', such as the obligation on the employee to work and the obligation on the employer to pay the employee, is not enforceable during the period. However, it is arguable that the suspension should be restricted to these two obligations; or

c) the contract continues as normal so that all obligations (apart from the duty to work and obligation to pay wages) continue. If this is correct, then the position during maternity absence would be the same as it is during maternity leave.

Where the contract has been terminated, by dismissal or resignation, there will clearly be no continuing entitlement to benefits during maternity absence.[22] This will also be the case where the employer provides in the contract that all the terms of the contract are suspended during maternity absence. Arguably, however, such a provision may itself be discriminatory (and a breach of the EqPA or SDA), particularly if it only applies to women on maternity absence.

Even where the contract of employment does subsist during maternity absence (see p98), it is not clear to what extent, if at all, a woman is entitled to benefits under the contract. In *Institute of the Motor Industry v Harvey*[23] the EAT said the basic obligations of a contract of employment, for the employer to provide reasonable work and to make payment, and for the employee to carry out that work, were suspended 'as indeed *may* be other terms which do not depend upon continuity for their effectiveness'. Does this mean that a woman will be deemed to be continuously employed (during her absence) for the purpose of calculating service-related benefits, such as sick pay or holiday, but otherwise the benefits of her contract are suspended?

---

22 Except to pension rights during the SMP period (see p53).
23 [1992] IRLR 343, EAT.

In *Hilton International Hotels (UK) Ltd v Kaissi*[24] the EAT reiterated that the contract may continue even though the requirement to perform the basic obligations may be suspended. In *Kaissi*, however, there was no reference to 'other terms'. The idea of a suspended contract is a novel one which has only been applied to maternity absence. It should be noted that the comments were obiter (not binding) as both cases were concerned only with unfair dismissal (see also *Crouch v Impey* (p99)).

Where, as is common, there are no provisions about what happens to the contract during maternity absence and there is no agreement between the parties, it is arguable that it should be treated as continuing along with the terms and conditions (apart from remuneration) (see *Iverson* (p50)). However, it will depend on all the circumstances of the case (see also pp98–100).

Discrimination under SDA and Equal Treatment Directive

A woman denied a benefit during maternity absence may be able to claim discrimination if an employee on other leave would be entitled to the benefit. This would be a detriment under SDA s6 (see chapter 11). There are as yet no binding decisions on the point. In an IT case, *Whiting v Harrow and Hillingdon Health Care NHS Trust*,[25] the applicant argued that she was entitled to accrue holiday leave during the unpaid part of her maternity absence. She claimed that a man on paid sick leave would be entitled to accrue holiday leave, so failure to allow her to accrue leave was discriminatory. The IT held that no comparison could be made between the applicant and a man on *paid* sick leave as the relevant circumstances were not the same (see p175). Any comparison had to be with a man on *unpaid* sick leave – who in this case would not have been entitled to accrue holiday leave. Thus, held the IT, there was no discrimination.[26]

In *Pridden v Warrington Community Health Care (NHS) Trust*[27] the IT held that the denial of days in lieu of bank holidays was sex discrimination as only in maternity absence was the benefit of days in lieu of bank holidays denied; an employee on sick leave was given credit for bank holidays.

24 [1994] IRLR 273, EAT.
25 (1995) 26 July, Case No 61664/93/LNIB.
26 The IT only considered the claim under the SDA, the EqPA claim having been withdrawn.
27 (1995) 6 June, Case No 66232/93, Liverpool IT.

Equal Pay Act and article 119

EqPA covers discriminatory contractual terms, whether or not they relate to pay. Article 119, however, covers 'pay' (defined very widely (see p172)), but does not distinguish between contractual and non-contractual benefits. Although in *Gillespie* (see p179) the ECJ held that no comparison could be made between a woman on maternity absence and an employee at work (at least for the purposes of pay), it is not clear if the same approach will be adopted under the EqPA. In *Iverson* a woman successfully claimed profit-related pay and holiday entitlement on the basis that a man would have received them had he been off sick.

Equal Pay Act

In *Reay v Sunderland Health Authority*[28] the contract allowed employees to accrue bank holidays that fell during a period of sick leave but not maternity absence. This was held by the IT to be a breach of the EqPA. The contractual term was less favourable, as it did not give the applicant the same rights to accrue holidays as her comparators who did not lose the right in any circumstances. The tribunal also considered this to be a detriment under the SDA.[29] See also the decisions in *Coyne* (p28) and *Todd* (p54).

Article 119

Gillespie (see p47) was only concerned with maternity pay, not other contractual benefits, but the ruling is likely to have implications for the treatment of such benefits. The main question is whether, and to what extent, a woman on maternity absence can compare herself with an employee who is similarly absent. In *Clark* [1996] IRLR 578, the CA held that in relation to 'notice pay', no comparison could be made.

In *Gillespie* the ECJ said, in relation to the pay rise (see p47), that 'to deny such [a pay increase] to a woman on maternity leave would discriminate against her purely in her capacity as a worker since, had she not been pregnant, she would have received the pay rise'. It is arguable that all the ECJ was saying in *Gillespie* was that for the purposes of maternity pay (and other payments received for work actually done) a woman cannot be compared to an employee at work. However, to deny her any other benefit

---

28 Case No 22905/92, Newcastle IT.
29 Though note that the SDA and EqPA are meant to be mutually exclusive (see p171).

which does not depend on her being 'at work' would discriminate against her because of her pregnancy.

Thus any payment or benefit which is only payable when the employee is actually at work comes within *Gillespie* (and so is not payable because no comparison with an employee at work is possible). Other benefits or perks (such as subsidised loans or private insurance), are paid as a result of the employment relationship and are not dependent on a woman being at work. In order to prove this, you would look at the position of another employee who is absent from work. Thus, if an employee on sick leave would continue to retain the benefit of the subsidised loan, private insurance etc, it should be provided to a woman on maternity absence. This was the approach in *Iverson* (see p50).

There is also the comparative approach, ie, a woman on maternity absence should not be treated any worse than any other employee on leave for another reason. Following *Gillespie,* a woman on maternity absence may not be able to compare herself with an employee at work, but she can arguably compare herself with an employee *not* at work.

Thus if an employee who is absent for another reason (such as sickness, study leave or sabbatical) would continue to receive benefits which are not payable to a woman on maternity absence, this is less favourable treatment. For example, if an occupational sick pay scheme allows an employee on long-term sick leave the benefit of her/his contractual terms, a woman on maternity absence should be treated in the same way.

Pregnant Workers Directive

The PWD article 11(2) states that in relation to article 8 (which provides that workers are entitled to a continuous period of maternity leave of at least 14 weeks), rights connected with the employment contract must be ensured. This does not apply to maternity pay. What is not clear is whether, under the PWD, the contractual rights must be maintained only during the minimum 14-week period or during extended maternity absence as well. Arguably they must, because all that article 8 does is to set a *minimum* period for the length of maternity leave. If the leave or absence is longer than the minimum, contractual rights should be maintained throughout. Note, however, that only public sector employees can rely on the directive. Private sector employees may have a remedy against the government (see p203).

Pensions

The position during paid leave and absence is set out on p53 above.

There is no statutory entitlement to maintained pension rights at the end of the 18-week period of SMP entitlement or the end of the period of entitlement to contractual maternity pay, whichever is the later. However, if the contract of employment continues during this period, entitlement will depend on the contractual terms. Usually, however, employers' contributions are based on earnings. So, if the woman is on unpaid leave, the employer will not be obliged to pay contributions.

Continuity of service during extended maternity absence

During extended maternity absence, whether the contract subsists will be a question of fact (see p98). If it does, continuity for the purposes of calculating service-related contractual benefits (such as holiday leave entitlement) is preserved.

Continuity for contractual rights

If there is no continuing contract during maternity absence, then for the purposes of the woman's seniority and similar contractual rights (including pensions) the period of employment after extended maternity absence is to be treated as continuous with the period of employment before the end of the maternity leave period.[30] The period of absence (ie, from the end of maternity leave until the date the woman returns) does not itself count (except for pensions during paid leave, see p53). Thus, if sick pay entitlement increases with length of service, the period before her absence will be added to the period after the absence. The period of the absence will not count. However, it may well be the case that the contract continues, so it will not be necessary to rely on this provision (see p98).

Continuity for statutory rights

Where the contract continues, any period of maternity absence also counts in working out the employee's continuous employment for the purposes of statutory rights (such as redundancy).[31]

30 ERA s79(2); though see p53 for special provisions relating to pensions.
31 ERA s212(2).

Rights during maternity leave and absence

Even where there is no continuing contract during the absence, continuity is maintained if the woman returns to her original job or accepts suitable alternative employment in accordance with the right to return.[32] In *Woolworths plc v Smith*[33] the applicant failed to give the appropriate statutory notice but the tribunal held that even so the employer had offered her a different but suitable job and this was suitable alternative employment. Her continuity was therefore preserved during her absence.

Continuity of service with break for up to 26 weeks

Where a woman is absent from work because of pregnancy for up to 26 weeks (with no statutory right to return, because, for example, she failed to give appropriate notice) and is then allowed to return by the employer, she will be treated as continuously employed for that period.[34] The 26 weeks applies to periods where there is no contract of employment.[35]

In *Mitchell v Royal British Legion Club*[36] the applicant wrote stating that she would be leaving her employment due to personal reasons. She returned to work 16 weeks later but was dismissed two days later. The EAT held that if, during a period when there is no contract of employment, a woman is absent from work wholly or partly because of pregnancy, then those weeks count in computing her period of employment and there is no break in continuity. It does not matter if the reason there is no contract is because the employee has resigned or been dismissed; the employers knew the applicant intended to return.

There may be other situations in which continuity is preserved, such as 26 weeks' sickness absence. These may be added together.[37] Absences, where there is no contract, for more than 26 weeks will break continuity.

Dismissal

If the employer dismisses a woman in order to avoid the contract

---

32 ERA s212(2).
33 (1989) 3 October (337/88), EAT.
34 See *Stringer v Booth* COIT 1533/56.
35 ERA s212(3). This is in addition to any period when the contract continues, so may in fact allow a longer absence to be counted.
36 [1980] IRLR 425, EAT.
37 See *Sworak v Pendelfin Studios Ltd* COIT 1303/243, where a woman was absent for over nine months because of sickness after the birth. She was able to add the period of absence due to the birth to the sickness absence.

continuing during extended maternity absence, this will be automatically unfair, as the reason for the dismissal will be a reason connected with pregnancy or maternity leave (or absence) (see p91).

Remedies

If the employer refuses to provide a benefit to which the woman is entitled, she may have the following claims.

Action in the county court

An action can be brought in the county court for:

a) breach of contract, where the woman has not received the benefit of her contractual terms during her leave (and, where she is entitled to them, during her absence; or
b) breach of Social Security Act 1989, Sch 5 (see p53). Legal aid may be available (see p210).

Contract claim in industrial tribunal

A breach of contract claim may be brought in an industrial tribunal but only where the woman's employment has ended (see p213).

Deduction of wages

A claim under ERA Part II (formerly the Wages Act 1986) may be made where, for example, an employer does not pay a bonus to which an employee is entitled.

The Act prevents an employer making any deductions from a worker's wages unless:

- it is allowed under statute (for example, tax and national insurance), or
- authorised under the contract, or
- agreed by the worker.

'Worker' includes employees, apprentices and the self-employed.[38] It is similar to the definition under the SDA. Some workers, such as mariners, the armed forces or those working outside Great Britain are excluded from the Act.[39]

---

38 ERA s230.
39 ERA Part XIII. The detailed provisions are outside the scope of this book.

Rights during maternity leave and absence

Wages are defined widely as 'any sums payable to the worker by his employer in connection with his employment, including any fee, bonus, commission, holiday pay or other emolument referrable to his employment'. They include statutory sick pay and maternity pay but not pensions.[40] Wages also include discretionary and ex gratia payments, such as a bonus or commission, if it is reasonably expected that the worker will receive them.[41]

In *Moxley and Cherowbrier v The Governors of St Edward's School*[42] the IT held that failure to give the applicants a single lump sum (awarded to all teachers as part of a pay review) because they were on maternity absence was an unlawful deduction under the Wages Act 1986. Where the total wages paid are less than those due, the amount of shortfall be will treated as an deduction.[43] Thus, failure to pay statutory maternity pay, sick pay or holiday pay, where payments are due, will be an unauthorised deduction.

Equal Pay Act, article 119 and Equal Pay Directive

A claim may be made under the EqPA where the woman is employed on like work, equivalent work or work of equal value and there is no 'material factor' defence (see p171). The EqPA only applies to contractual terms, though it is not restricted to pay. Article 119 only covers 'pay' (widely defined) but no distinction is made between contractual and non-contractual terms.

Sex Discrimination Act and Equal Treatment Directive

A claim may also be made under the SDA in relation to non-contractual benefits (see p172). The ETD does not distinguish between contractual and non-contractual terms.

If there is any doubt about which claim to bring, it is advisable to make alternative claims.

There may be circumstances where the employee is entitled to resign and claim constructive dismissal. There is always a risk, however, that the tribunal will hold that the employee resigned voluntarily (see p85).

---

40 ERA s27.
41 *Kent Management Services Ltd v Butterfield* [1992] IRLR 394, EAT.
42 (1994) 18 February, Case Nos 48132/93 and 48735/93, Southampton IT.
43 ERA s13(3).

KEY POINTS

- Maternity pay is pay for the purposes of article 119.
- There is no entitlement to full pay during maternity leave (or absence) unless the contract provides for it (*Gillespie*).
- A woman on maternity leave or absence is arguably entitled to receive the benefit of any pay rise awarded after the period when her earnings-related maternity pay is calculated and before the end of the earnings-related part of leave or absence.
- **Rights during general maternity leave**
  - The contract continues during the MLP.
  - There is no right to receive remuneration – ie, salary, wages, overtime pay.
  - All other contractual benefits must be maintained during the MLP; this includes
    - certain bonuses and commission (where they are not 'remuneration')
    - company car and mobile phone (where not exclusively for business use),
    - other benefits or perks, such as subsidised loans, insurance, professional subscriptions, subsidised travel, club membership etc,
    - luncheon vouchers (probably),
    - holiday entitlement (but not pay),
    - occupational pensions.
  - There is no entitlement to SSP during the maternity pay period. The exclusion of pregnancy from occupational sick pay schemes may be discriminatory.
  - Pensions must be maintained during *paid* maternity leave and absence; the woman must be treated as though at work though her contributions will be based on her maternity pay.
  - Continuity of service is preserved during the MLP.
  - Where a woman on maternity leave or absence is treated less favourably than an employee on other leave, this may be discriminatory.
  - Claims for continued benefits may be made in the county court (for breach of contract) or in the tribunal if there has been an unlawful deduction of wages or for breach of contract if the employee has left.

Rights during maternity leave and absence

- **Rights during maternity absence depend on:**
  - Whether *the contract continues during the absence and, if so, whether and which terms and conditions are 'suspended';*
  - whether, under the SDA or Equal Treatment Directive, there is discrimination because a woman on maternity absence is treated less favourably than an employee on comparable 'leave';
  - whether, under the EqPA, there are less favourable terms and conditions of the contract;
  - whether, under article 119, benefits, which do not depend on the woman being at work, should continue to be paid or whether an employee who is absent for a different reason would be treated more favourably;
  - whether the provisions in the PWD, which provide for the continuation of employment rights during maternity leave, apply also to maternity absence; if they do the woman is entitled to the benefit of terms and conditions (apart from pay).
- Continuity of service is maintained during maternity absence for the purpose of calculating statutory rights, provided the woman returns to work.
- Where the contract does not continue during the absence, the period of employment after maternity absence is treated as continuous with the period before the leave for the purpose of calculating contractual rights; the period of absence does not count.

CHAPTER 6

The right to return to work

Introduction

This chapter covers the right to return to work after the maternity leave period and after extended maternity absence, the possibility of extending the leave or absence, exceptions to the right to return, the job on return and the right to return part-time.

Women who return to work at the end of general maternity leave can simply turn up for work at the end of the 14 weeks (provided they complied with the notice provisions before going on maternity leave). They are in the same position as an employee returning from any other type of leave. Women exercising their right to return after extended maternity absence must comply with additional notice provisions before returning (see below).

Returning after general maternity leave

A woman returning after maternity leave has a right to return to the same job with the same terms and conditions. Where the employer refuses to take a woman back after maternity leave, this will be a dismissal (see p98).

Failure to comply with notice provisions

A woman who fails to give the appropriate notice does not have a statutory right to general maternity leave (or absence) or the benefit of her terms and conditions during leave (see pp47ff). However, her contract should not come to an end unless and until terminated by the employer or employee (see p100). If the employer terminates a woman's contract for a reason related to her pregnancy, childbirth or maternity leave, this will be automatically unfair under ERA s99 (see p91). It may also be an ordinary unfair dismissal (see p93) and discriminatory (see p96).

Return before expiry of 14 weeks

A woman who wants to return to work before the expiry of the 14 weeks must give her employer seven days' notice of the date she intends to return.[1] The notice need not be in writing. Failure to give notice means that the employer is entitled to postpone the woman's return to work until she has given seven days' notice, or to accept her back but not pay her;[2] the employer is entitled to refuse to pay the woman until she has given the required notice.[3] The employer is not, however, entitled to postpone the woman's return beyond the end of her maternity leave period.[4]

Extending general maternity leave and protection from dismissal

Maternity leave may be extended where there is a statutory prohibition on working. There is also protection from dismissal for four weeks for women who cannot return to work because they are ill and provision on health and safety risks.

Statutory prohibitions

Where a statutory requirement prohibits a woman from working for any period after the end of her maternity leave because she has recently given birth, the maternity leave period continues for as long as there is a statutory prohibition.[5]

Working within two weeks of childbirth

A woman is not allowed to work for two weeks after the birth. This period begins with the day the baby was born.[6] This applies even if the woman has used up her 14 weeks maternity leave (for example, because she started her leave at the 11th week before the expected week of childbirth and the baby was two or more weeks late). Her maternity leave period will be extended until two weeks after the birth.

---

1 ERA s76(1).
2 ERA s76(2).
3 ERA s76(4).
4 ERA s76(3).
5 ERA s73(2) and (4). ERA s73(4) specifically excludes health and safety requirements or recommendations made under s66(2). These are the subject of separate provisions (see p68).
6 Pregnant Workers Directive article 8(2) implemented by the Maternity (Compulsory Leave) Regulations 1994 SI No 2479 reg 2.

It is an offence for an employer to allow an employee to return to work within these two weeks, punishable by a fine not exceeding level 2 on the standard scale (currently £500).[7] The Health and Safety Executive has the responsibility for enforcing these provisions.

Women working in a factory or workshop
Health and safety legislation provides that a woman working in a factory or workshop must not return to work within four weeks of childbirth.[8] This covers people doing manual work involving the making, repairing or cleaning of any goods. Breach of the prohibition by the employer is a criminal offence punishable by a fine on level 1 (presently £200).

Protection from dismissal for further four weeks in case of illness
There is protection against dismissal for women unable to return to work because of sickness in the four weeks after the end of maternity leave, provided a medical certificate is given to the employer before the end of the maternity leave period[9] (see p92). The illness does not have to be related to the pregnancy or childbirth, though the dismissal must be for a reason connected with the woman having given birth.[10] The protection from dismissal only lasts as long as the woman continues to be incapable of work and has a current medical certificate.[11]

The woman is not treated as on maternity leave during this four-week period, so she is not entitled to the benefit of her contractual terms (see chapter 5).[12] Arguably, however, she should be treated like any other employee who is off sick, and she should receive contractual sick pay where this is payable (see p72).

Health and safety reasons
Where there would be a health and safety risk, either to the woman (as a new or breastfeeding mother) or to the baby, if the woman returned to work, the employer's health and safety duties apply (see

7 Ibid reg 3.
8 Public Health Act 1936 s205 (as amended).
9 ERA s99(3).
10 ERA s99(3)(c).
11 ERA s99(3)(b).
12 Though she is entitled to SMP, as this is paid for 18 weeks. She will not be entitled to SSP (see p159).

p122). This will only apply in limited circumstances, for example, where the woman is dealing with potentially dangerous substances. If the working conditions cannot be satisfactorily adjusted to remove the risk and there is no alternative suitable available work, the woman must be suspended on full pay.

Failure to return at the end of MLP

A woman who does not return after her leave should be treated like any other employee who does not return after authorised leave. The employer should not assume that, because the woman has not returned, she is not intending to return. The employer should investigate. If the reason is because she is ill, she should be able to go on sick leave and claim occupational sick pay (where it exists) or SMP if within the 18-week period (see p145).[13] If she cannot return because, for example, the baby is sick, she should negotiate a longer period of leave with her employer (see p102). If the employer dismisses her because she does not return or because she is sick, this may be automatically unfair or discriminatory, if the reason is related to her pregnancy, childbirth or maternity leave. These issues are dealt with in chapter 7.

Redundancy during general maternity leave

Where it is not practicable, because of redundancy, for the woman to return to the same job, she must be offered a suitable available vacancy.[14] The new contract must take effect at the end of the previous one (see p109).

Return after general maternity leave

A woman is entitled to return to exactly the same job on the same terms and conditions. She has the same contract as before she went on leave. If she is only allowed to return on less favourable terms and conditions, she may be entitled to resign and claim constructive dismissal. She will be in a similar position to any other employee whose job has been changed. If the change is due to the woman having been on maternity leave, it is likely to be automatically unfair and discriminatory (see pp91 and 96).

13 Note that this SMP is not payable during any week in which the woman works.
14 ERA s77.

Right to return after extended maternity absence

Notice provisions

In order to exercise the right to return (up to 29 weeks after the beginning of the week of the birth), a woman must have complied with the notice provisions set out on p32 for maternity leave and the additional requirements for extended maternity absence set out on p41).

Unfair dismissal

Even where the woman has failed to comply with the notice provisions and has therefore lost the *statutory* right to return, she may have a claim for unfair dismissal if her contract subsists and the employer refuses to have her back (see p102).

Postponement of return by employer

The employer may postpone the woman's date of return by up to four weeks after the notified date of return if s/he notifies the woman, before the notified date of return, that for specified reasons s/he is postponing her return. The postponement by the employer may be for any reason and need not be connected to the maternity leave or absence. The woman must then return on this later date.[15] She is not entitled to be paid during this period.

Postponement of return by employee because of sickness

A woman may postpone her return for up to four weeks if she is sick either at the time she is due to return or at the end of the 29-week period.

She must give her employer a doctor's certificate stating that (by reason of disease or bodily or mental disablement) she will be incapable of work on the date she was due to return or, where no date has been given, within the 29-week period.[16] This certificate must be given to the employer before the notified date of return (NDR) or before the 29-week period expires. Her return may then be delayed for up to four weeks from the NDR or, where no NDR

---

15 ERA s82(2).
16 ERA s82(3)(a) and (4).

has been given, up to four weeks from the end of the 29-week period. In the latter case, the 21 days' notice must still be given.

A woman who has failed to give the required 21 days' notice of her intention to return (before the expiry of the 29 weeks) will seemingly not lose her right to return if the reason for postponing her return is sickness. She only has to give the employer a doctor's certificate before the expiry of the 29 weeks and can then give the required 21 days' notice of her intention to return. The notice must therefore be given no later than a week after the end of the 29-week period.

The requirement to provide a doctor's certificate at the appropriate time is a strict one and failure to do so will mean the woman loses her statutory right to return.[17] If, however, the employer waives the requirement, the employee may have a contractual right to return (see p74).

Sickness postponement only allowed once
A woman can only postpone her return to work because of sickness on one occasion.[18] If she has had one postponement, even if it is only for a week, she has no *statutory* right to a further postponement. Similarly, if she is still ill at the end of the four week period, she will lose her statutory right to return.

In *Dowuona v John Lewis plc*[19] the applicant postponed her return for four weeks on medical grounds and then added one week's holiday leave. She was still unfit to return and the Court of Appeal held that she lost her right to return when she tried to return at a later date.[20] It is arguable that the dismissal in Dowuona was connected to the woman's pregnancy or maternity absence, in that the dismissal would not have taken place at all if the woman had not been on maternity absence. If this can be proved, the dismissal will be automatically unfair (see p91).[21]

If there is a more favourable contractual right to return, this

---

17 See *Mearis v IMI Yorkshire Imperial Ltd* COIT 1408/60, where the doctor's certificate was dated one day after the end of the 29-week period. See also *Gay v George L Lockey & Sons Ltd* COIT 1632/5, where the applicant failed to send the doctor's certificate.
18 ERA s82(5).
19 [1987] IRLR 310, CA.
20 See also *Kelly v Liverpool Maritime Terminals Ltd* [1988] IRLR 310, CA (see p72).
21 Note that *Dowuona* was decided before the Pregnant Workers Directive was implemented.

will override the statutory right. Thus, in *Watson v Marylebone Optical Co Ltd*[22] the employee twice postponed her return on medical grounds. The contract did not limit the number of postponements on medical grounds. The IT held she was entitled to rely on the contractual provision which allowed her to return up to the end of the 33rd week and that her dismissal was unfair.

Exercising right to return while sick

A woman who is sick during her maternity absence may be able to exercise her right to return (by giving 21 days' notice) and then claim contractual sick pay, if it exists, or SSP if she qualifies (see p159). She will then have to return to work after her sickness; she cannot go back on maternity absence.

In *Kelly v Liverpool Maritime Terminals Ltd*[23] the Court of Appeal held that an employee who sent a letter to her employers saying that she could not return to work after her absence (together with a doctor's certificate) could not be said to be exercising her right to return and then claiming sick leave. Thus, it appears that a woman must physically return to work (for however short a time) in order to go on sick leave. Although this is probably discriminatory (as an employee returning from any other leave will usually be able to telephone in sick), it is safer for the woman to return to work for a short time, if possible. If it is not possible, the woman should notify the employer that she wishes to go on sick leave and claim sick pay (see also *Dowuona*).

Two Northern Ireland tribunal decisions adopted a different approach to that taken in *Kelly* and *Dowuona* (though they are not binding). In *Heddles v Thorn EMI (UK) plc*[24] a woman was unable to return to work after maternity absence because of postnatal depression. Her employer said she lost her right to return. The applicant successfully complained that failure to give her sick leave was discriminatory. The IT held that after the period of statutory maternity absence, during which she was entitled to special protection, she should be treated in the same way as other sick employees, with the period of maternity absence being ignored. Similarly, in *McClenaghan and Rice v British Shoe Corporation Ltd*[25] the IT held that employees unable, because of

22 COIT 2056/212.
23 [1988] IRLR 310, CA.
24 IT Northern Ireland 1678/92.
25 (1993) 26 July Case Nos 2688/91, 3206/91, 3207/91, IT Northern Ireland.

illness, to return to work after maternity absence were entitled to be treated like any other sick employee (with a similar employment history) as regards sickness pay or leave. The period of maternity leave (or absence) should be disregarded (see p101).[26]

In *Crees* (EAT/205/96), the EAT, following *Kelly*, held that there must be a physical return to work. However, discrimination was not argued and a further EAT decision is expected in *Greaves v Quicksave*.

The disadvantage of exercising a right to return and going on sick leave (as opposed to postponing the return for four weeks) is that the absence is likely to be added to the woman's sickness record. If the sickness is related to pregnancy or childbirth and is a relevant factor in a subsequent dismissal or redundancy, it may be automatically unfair or discriminatory. Many women are not entitled to contractual sick pay (and are unlikely to get SSP); so there is no advantage in them returning to work as opposed to taking advantage of the four-week postponement.

Industrial action preventing a return to work

Where the employee has given an NDR

Where an employee has notified a day of return but there is an interruption of work (eg, industrial action) and it is unreasonable to expect the woman to return to work on that day, she may return when work resumes or as soon as reasonably practicable afterwards.[27]

Where the woman has not notified a day of return

Where there is an an interruption of work which makes it unreasonable for her to return to work before the end of the 29-week period (or which appears likely to have that effect), she may give an NDR which is not more than 28 days from the end of the interruption. Twenty-one days' notice of the NDR must still be given.[28]

Sickness followed by interruption of work or vice-versa

If the woman has already extended her maternity absence because of sickness (see above) and then there is an interruption of work,

26 See also *Coyne v Exports Credits Guarantee Department* [1981] IRLR 51, IT, where a restriction in the woman's contract on entitlement to sick pay after childbirth was removed.
27 ERA s82(6).
28 ERA s82(7).

the 28-day extension (because of the interruption of work) may be in addition to the four-week sickness period. The interruption of work must commence before the expiry of the four-week period, ie, before the woman would have been due to return. Similar principles apply where an interruption of work is followed by sickness.[29] The employer can also postpone the woman's return after she has already postponed her return on medical grounds.

Contractual rights – 'composite rights'

An employee may have both a statutory right to return and a contractual right; this is known as a composite right. The ERA provides that an employee who has both the right to return to work under the ERA and another right to return to work after absence because of pregnancy or childbirth (under a contract of employment or otherwise) may not exercise the two rights separately. She may, however, in returning to work, take advantage of whichever right is, in any particular respect, the more favourable.[30] It is not clear what the words 'or otherwise' mean but presumably they would cover, for example, an oral agreement between employer and employee.

In *Bovey v Board of Governors of the Hospital for Sick Children*,[31] Ms Bovey wanted to return to work part-time but her employers gave her the option of returning to her original job full-time or to a lower grade job part-time. She argued she was entitled to return to her original job. The EAT held that there was a limit to the extent to which the right (in this case to return to work) could be subdivided so as to identify the particular respects in which it was more favourable. The EAT upheld the tribunal finding that the contractual right to work part-time on the lower grade was indivisible.[32]

If the contractual right is less favourable than the statutory right, the statutory right will apply.

In *Kolfor Plant Ltd v Wright*[33] the EAT held that if an employee's contract is silent on the notice to be given on return to

29 ERA s82(8), (9).
30 ERA s85.
31 [1978] IRLR 241, EAT.
32 The applicant could have argued she had a right to return to her original job and refusal to allow her to return part-time was indirectly discriminatory (see p81).
33 [1982] IRLR 311, EAT.

work, then the statutory requirements apply.[34] Thus, if a woman is entitled to 18 weeks leave, and the contract says nothing about notice, she should give 21 days notice of her return date.

Right to return to same employer

The right to return is the right to return to the same employer or (where appropriate) his/her successor.[35] If there has been a transfer of the business, the woman has a right to return with the new employer (see p80).

Right to return to same job

A woman who returns to work after extended maternity absence has a right to return to work in the job in which she was previously employed:
a) on no less favourable terms and conditions as to remuneration than she would have received if she had not been absent since the beginning of her maternity leave period; this means that if there have been changes affecting the workforce while the woman was away, she will be subject to these changes, whether good or bad;
b) with preserved seniority, pension rights and other rights; periods of continuous employment prior to the end of maternity leave must be treated as continuous with the woman's employment following her return;[36] the period of maternity absence will not count unless there the contract continues during the absence; and
c) otherwise on terms and conditions no less favourable than she would have received if she had not been absent after the end of her maternity leave period.[37]

For the two exceptions to the right to return, see p79.

If the woman is not allowed to return or if she is only offered a less favourable job, she will be deemed to have been dismissed

---

34 See also *Street v Harry S Allen Ltd* EAT 180/89, where there was an agreement for the woman to return to work but in a different location. The applicant refused to say when she would return until she was given the exact terms of employment. The EAT held that the employers had given sufficient details of the terms and she should have given her proposed date of return.
35 ERA s79(2).
36 Subject to Social Security Act 1989 Sch 5 (see p53).
37 ERA s79(2).

unless one of the two exceptions apply (see p79). She is treated as having been continuously employed until her NDR (see p103).

A woman may find, on return to work, that her work has been reallocated to another employee or she is expected to do a job with less responsibility and/or lower status. If a woman is not offered the same job, she will be treated as having been denied her statutory right to return to work. It will be deemed to be a dismissal for the reason that she was not allowed to return and may be an automatically unfair dismissal, an ordinary unfair dismissal or discriminatory (see chapter 7).

For example, in *Smith v David White and White Group Leisure Ltd*[38] Ms Smith was demoted from manageress to general assistant after she became pregnant. A new manageress was appointed. The IT found that the reason for the demotion was Ms Smith's pregnancy. She should have been allowed to return to work as a manageress and was therefore entitled to resign and claim constructive dismissal.[39] As the employer had failed to discharge the burden of establishing a reason for the dismissal, it was unfair and it was discriminatory.[40]

In *Aird v Garfunkel's Restaurant plc*[41] the applicant returned to a less favourable job and complained she had been dismissed because she had not been allowed to return to her original job. The IT held that, as she had been redeployed into work which was not the 'same job', she had been dismissed even though she continued in the respondent's employment.

What is the 'same job'?

'Job' means the nature of the work which the employee is employed to do under her contract and the capacity and place in which she is employed.[42] It is important to consider both the contract and what the employee does in practice. For example, in

---

38 (1994) 11 May, Manchester IT, Case No 01778/93.
39 This was a deemed dismissal under what is now ERA s96(1).
40 However, the tribunal also decided that the applicant failed to mitigate her loss by refusing the offer of reinstatement as general assistant. The reason they gave was because she had worked, without protest, as general assistant before her maternity leave. In *Gault v AVX Ltd* (1995) 27 May, Case No 03492/94SD, a Belfast tribunal held that a woman who was demoted immediately on her return from maternity leave had been discriminated against. She was awarded £4,000 for injury to feelings (see DCLD No 25).
41 (1994) 20 January, Case No 26151/92.
42 ERA s235(1).

Edgell v Lloyd's Register of Shipping[43] there was a reorganisation while the applicant was on maternity absence. As a result her duties no longer included signing cheques and she had to report to a supervisor as opposed to a manager. The tribunal held that her right to return had not been breached as she had been offered a job in the same grade.

An employee may be asked to do the same work in a different department. Provided there is no loss of responsibility or status, this may be treated as the same job.[44]

Loss of status and job security

Loss of status and job security led to a finding of unfair dismissal in *McFadden v Greater Glasgow Passenger Transport Executive.*[45] The applicant had a permanent position as a clerk in the Engineering Department. While she was on maternity absence, another clerk was promoted to fill her job on a permanent basis. When the applicant returned to work she was told there were no permanent jobs available and she was placed in another section as a supernumerary (unestablished) clerk. Despite the fact that the hours of work, pay, holiday entitlement etc were the same, the tribunal held that the new terms and conditions were less favourable. She no longer had her own desk and she was no longer sure of getting a full day's work. The tribunal held that there were new and less favourable conditions of work and she had therefore been unfairly dismissed.[46]

Different location

A requirement that the woman must move to a different location may also constitute less favourable terms.

Where there is no mobility clause in the contract of employment, the employee should not have to work from a different location. If the job has been made redundant, she must be offered alternative available work (see pp108ff). However,

---

43 [1977] IRLR 463, IT.
44 See *Houghton v May and Hassell Ltd* COIT 837/180 and *Fallon v H C Blake & Co* COIT 934/148.
45 [1977] IRLR 327, IT.
46 See also *Castles Walker v Northern Co-operative Society Ltd* (1978) 11 December, Case No S/3260/78, where a tribunal held that a job of confidential secretary to the chief accountant was not of the same status as the applicant's original post of confidential secretary to the chief executive.

The right to return to work

where there is no redundancy situation and no 'other substantial reason' (such as a reorganisation) a requirement that she must move may be a breach of contract entitling her to resign. It is no excuse for her employer to say that her old job has been filled by another employee. In these circumstances she should be able to show that 'but for' the fact that she had been pregnant and on maternity leave, she would not have been forced to move; this will make the dismissal automatically unfair and discriminatory.[47]

Where there is a mobility clause, this must be construed strictly. A clause which requires an employee to be temporarily placed in another location does not mean that she can be permanently moved.[48]

The requirement to be mobile may be indirectly discriminatory. In *Meade-Hill v British Council*[49] the Court of Appeal held that a mobility clause requiring that an employee must work in whatever location in the UK her employers may direct had a disproportionate impact on women. Whether such a requirement is justifiable will depend on the facts in each case (see p194).

Different hours

The imposition of different hours is likely to mean 'less favourable terms'. In *Acteson v Silent Challel Products Ltd*[50] the woman's set hours were changed to shifts. The tribunal held that the employer had unfairly dismissed the applicant, as she was not allowed to return to the same job.

If the reason for the change in hours is due to the woman's maternity absence, this will be automatically unfair. 'But for' her pregnancy or maternity absence her hours would not have changed. It may also be unintentional indirect discrimination, as it was in *MacMillan v Edinburgh Voluntary Organisations' Council*[51] where the applicant was dismissed from her part-time job because her employer wanted to appoint a full-time manager.

---

47 See *Rees v Appollo* (p101) and *Huth v Davidsons* COIT 1409/223, where the tribunal held that the employer's refusal to allow the applicant to return to her job (in the same office) was unfair dismissal. The fact that the job was being done by somebody else meant that there was no redundancy situation so no question of alternative work arose.
48 See *McLean v William Hill Organisation Ltd* SCOIT S/3800/90.
49 [1995] IRLR 478, CA.
50 COIT 916/36.
51 [1995] IRLR 536, SEAT.

Maternity rights/Chapter 6

Options if job not same or suitable

The woman can resign and claim constructive dismissal (see p85). If she does not want to risk this – it is difficult to predict whether the tribunal will hold that the employer's breach entitled her to resign – she can continue working under protest and make a claim for any loss as well as reinstatement into the job she had before she went on leave (see p85).

Redundancy during maternity absence

Where a woman is made redundant during her maternity absence, she is entitled to suitable available work (see p108).

Exceptions to right to return

There are two exceptions to the right to return after maternity absence. If either apply, there is no deemed dismissal if the employer does not allow the woman to return to work.[52] In either case, the failure to allow her to return may still be unfair or discriminatory (see chapter 7). In both cases the burden of proof lies with the employer.[53]

Small employers

The employer must show that:
- immediately before the end of the woman's maternity leave period, the total number of employees did not exceed five; and
- it is not reasonably practicable for the employer or any successor to allow the woman to return to her original job; and
- it is not reasonably practicable for the employer, or any successor or associated employer, to offer suitable alternative work. The work must be suitable for the woman and appropriate for her in the circumstances and the terms and conditions must not be substantially less favourable. The test is similar to that for suitable alternative work on redundancy (see p109).

In *Stewart and Gower t/a Gowers v Male*[54] the EAT stressed that the employer had to show it was not reasonably practicable for the woman to return. The employer had restructured to cover for the applicant's absence but had not considered whether other

---

52 ERA s96(2)–(5).
53 ERA s96(5).
54 (1994) 19 May, EAT 813/93.

employees could cover for her, as they had done when she had been off sick. The dismissal was therefore unfair.

Offer of suitable alternative work
Where:
- it is not reasonably practicable for a reason *other than redundancy* for the employer or any successor to permit the woman to return to her old job; and
- the employer, or a successor or associated employer, has offered her suitable alternative work which she has either accepted or unreasonably refused,[55]

the right to return to her old job is lost.

This might arise where there has been a business reorganisation.[56] The alternative work must be suitable for the employee and appropriate in the circumstances. Other terms and conditions of the contract must not be substantially less favourable. Thus, a move to a different location which would involve more travelling is unlikely to be suitable (see above).

Although an employer might rely on this exception if the s/he has employed a permanent replacement, there will be a heavy burden on the employer to show that it was not 'reasonably practicable' for the employer to allow the woman to return. This might apply where the replacement was about to complete a complex piece of work and it would not be practical for the returning employee to take it over. A dismissal in these circumstances is also likely to be discriminatory (see *Rees v Appollo Watch Repairs plc*, p101).

Transfer of undertakings

The transfer does not terminate the contract but transfers it to the transferee organisation, including all the rights and obligations under or in connection with the contract.[57] This means that if there is a transfer during the time when a woman is exercising her maternity rights, she has the same rights against the new employer. If there is a transfer to a new employer while the

---

55 ERA s96(2).
56 Which falls within 'some other substantial reason' for dismissal.
57 Transfer of Undertakings (Protection of Employment) Regulations 1981 SI No 1794 (TUPE) reg 5. The only exception is rights and obligations under or in connection with an occupational pension scheme (reg 7).

woman is on maternity leave or absence, her right to return is with the new employer. She is entitled to the benefit of her terms and conditions during maternity leave and her service will be treated as continuous.[58]

It is unlawful to dismiss an employee as a result of the transfer unless there is an 'economic, technical or organisational reason entailing changes in the workforce of either the transferor or the transferee before or after a relevant transfer'.[59]

The woman must enforce her rights against the new employer, even if the breach was by the old employer.[60]

Discrimination against part-timers and job sharers

Is there a right to work part-time or job share?

A woman may want to reduce her hours when she returns from maternity leave or absence. This may be done by returning to the same job on a part-time basis, or sharing the same full-time job with another person (ie, a job-share). Or she may wish to work flexible hours, work from home, or vary her hours in other ways. Where the refusal to allow a woman to change her hours (in one of these ways) is indirectly discriminatory she should return to the same job with the same terms and conditions – except hours of work.

The complex legal principles relating to indirect discrimination are set out in chapter 13. The main issue relates to justifiability. This will be very much a question of fact. Below is a summary of factors which have influenced tribunals; they are not binding.

Blanket policy against job-sharing or part-time work

A blanket policy where no account is taken of individual circumstances may be discriminatory. In *Barrett v Newport Borough Council*[61] management refused to consider an application to work part-time and this was held to be discriminatory. Similarly in *Hicks v North Yorkshire County*

---

58 Even if not preserved by TUPE, continuity of service is preserved by ERA s218.
59 TUPE reg 8.
60 In *DJM International Ltd v Nicholas* [1996] IRLR 76 the EAT held that liability for an act of sex discrimination transferred to the transferee following a transfer, even if the discrimination occurred prior to the transfer.
61 Case No 34096/91, IT.

Council[62] the tribunal found that the council's refusal to allow the applicant to job-share or work part-time were due to an objection which was 'a matter of principle against part-time teachers, nothing less and nothing more' as they had used part-timers freely in the past for cover for absent teachers.[63]

In *Watt v Ballantyne and Copeland*[64] the tribunal held that the refusal to allow a job sharer to return to work on a job-share basis was discriminatory. The tribunal found the employer merely felt it would be more convenient to recruit a full-time employee and this was not enough to show justification.

Job-sharing at supervisory level

In *Given v Scottish Power plc*[65] the applicant (who managed 10–12 team members) was told that it was a policy that at the applicant's grade she could not job-share. The employers justified this on the basis of 'operational' matters and referred to the need for continuity given the importance of handling customer complaints. There was no proper assessment of the applicant's duties and difficulties which might be encountered in job-sharing.[66]

Accommodation and national insurance costs

In *Home Office v Holmes*[67] the Home Office argued that their costs would increase if they took on two part-time workers instead of one full-time worker. The EAT preferred the applicant's evidence that the civil service was losing valuable trained personnel when they left to start families and in some departments efficiency increased when part-timers were introduced.

Requirement to work every day on part-time basis

In *Greater Glasgow Health Board v Carey*[68] the EAT agreed it was reasonable to insist that the applicant, a health visitor, be present every day (for half a day) in order to provide continuity and it was justifiable to refuse to allow her to work a three-day week.

62 COIT 1643/117.
63 See also *Guthrie v Royal Bank of Scotland plc* (1987) 10 March, Case No 31796/86.
64 (1994) 22 August, Case No S/1262/94.
65 (1995) 20 January, Case No S/3172/94. Glasgow IT.
66 The applicant was awarded £5,000 for injury to feelings and £30,000 loss of earnings.
67 [1984] IRLR 299, EAT.
68 [1987] IRLR 484, SEAT.

Maternity rights/Chapter 6

Alternative job on part-time basis not good enough

In *Clay v The Governors, English Martyrs School*[69] a teacher was not allowed to return to work as a job-share but was offered an alternative part-time job. The IT held that although the introduction of a job-sharing scheme causes considerable logistical problems so far as the employer is concerned, there was no evidence that it could be detrimental to the educational interests of the school.[70] However, in *Gill and Oakes v Wirral Health Authority*[71] the IT held that the employers' decision to demote two midwives when they returned to work part-time was justifiable. The higher grade entailed on-going responsibility for patients even when off-duty and they had responsibility for supervising junior staff.

Flexible working hours

In *Wright v Rugby Borough Council*[72] the applicant wanted to have half an hour for lunch and leave half an hour earlier. The council argued this would affect their flexitime policy and set an undesirable precedent. The tribunal rejected this defence.

Other discrimination against part-timers

Failure to promote

In *Gold v London Borough of Tower Hamlets*[73] the tribunal found that, although the employers had an equal opportunities policy, they merely paid lip service to it and the real reason why the applicant had not been put forward for promotion was because she was job-sharing.[74]

Failure to renew part-time fixed-term contract

In *Tickle v Governors of Riverview CF School and Surrey County Council*[75] a part-time teacher did not have her fixed-term contract renewed because the school wanted a full-time teacher. This was held to be indirect discrimination. Although the head said that

---

69 (1993) 8 January, Case No 52319/91, Leicester IT.
70 See also *Roberts and Longstaffe v British Telecommunications plc* (1995) 6 February, Southampton IT. And see n78 below.
71 Case No 16165–6/90.
72 Case No 23528/84.
73 (1991) 9 December, Case No 05608/91/LN/C, London North IT.
74 £6,000 was awarded for injury to feelings.
75 (1993) 24 August, COIT Case No 32420/92, London South IT.

there had been complaints about the fact that children were being taught by two people, the applicant had not been informed of these complaints. The tribunal found that the main reason was financial rather than the emotional and educational needs of the children.

Requirement to work long hours
In *Robinson v Oddbins Ltd*[76] a tribunal held that a term in a branch manager's contract requiring her to work 'such hours as may be necessary' over and above her standard working week was indirectly discriminatory. The applicant usually had to work a 50-hour week. She asked if she could work fixed hours on her return from maternity leave so that she could arrange childcare. The employers argued that it was necessary for one person to do the job and it would not be possible to have fixed hours and thus have a job-share. This was because the post required leadership and motivation of the junior staff; the manager was responsible for recruitment of staff at the branch, and s/he was responsible for stock control and the general running of the business.

The tribunal was impressed by evidence from a representative of 'New Ways to Work' (see Appendix 8) who said that employers are suspicious of job-share schemes until the advantages of retaining qualified staff and motivating the work force are explained to them, as well as the fact that a job-share will not necessarily mean any additional costs or any lack of motivation generally in the workforce. The representative said that very senior jobs had been subjected to work-sharing, including the chief executive of an NHS trust and a ward sister's post in a busy London hospital. She also said that the work of deputy managers at Boots, who are responsible for many more staff than those at Oddbins, had been successfully job-shared. The tribunal held that the employers had failed to justify the condition.

Evidence to support part-time working

The employer should be required to provide good and substantiated reasons why it is not possible to allow a woman to work part-time or job-share. The following should be considered.
- The questionnaire procedure can be used (in discrimination cases) to ask questions about why the employer considers that it is justifiable to refuse to allow a woman to work part-time or job-share (see p251);

76 (1996) 5 January, Case No 4224/95, CDLD No 27.

- General information about the advantages of part-time work and job-sharing is useful. In some cases a representative from New Ways to Work has given very helpful evidence.[77]
- Evidence of other similar jobs which have been done on a job-share or part-time basis will be relevant. In *Barrett v Newport Borough Council* (n61 above) the applicant was a housing officer and produced evidence of other local authorities where housing officers were allowed to job-share.
- Evidence of how the job can be done on a part-time basis will be crucial. In *Given v Scottish Power plc* (n65 above) the applicant successfully rebutted the employer's argument about the need for continuity by saying that if a customer phoned to speak to her the matter could be dealt with by someone else because notes were kept and everything was dealt with under laid-down procedures. Computerisation will make it harder for an employer to justify the need for continuity.
- Sometimes it is argued that there is too much work for a part-time worker; it is always worth exploring whether the employer has considered appointing two people on a part-time or job-share basis.

Options for women not allowed to work part-time

In *British Telecommunications plc v Roberts & Another*[78] the applicants worked full-time. They took maternity leave at the same time. Both women wanted to return to their posts but as job-sharers. They were offered the option of returning full-time or working part-time (which involved unsocial hours plus Saturday working). Neither applicant wanted to lose her job. Therefore one of the applicants opted for part-time working under protest and the other returned to work full-time, also under protest. On appeal, the EAT referred the cases back to the IT to consider the claims of indirect discrimination, having overruled findings of direct discrimination.

Alternatively, the women could have resigned and claimed constructive dismissal. The tribunal would then have had to decide whether the refusal to allow them to work part-time or jobshare was a sufficiently serious breach of contract to entitle the women to resign. If the requirement to work full-time had been

---

77 See also EOC Guidance, *Part-time Workers, not second-class citizens* (1995).
78 [1996] ICR 625.

found to be justified, they would have had no remedy and would also have lost their jobs by resigning.

Remedies

Apart from compensation, the tribunal may make a recommendation. In *Roberts* (above) the tribunal had recommended that the women be allowed to job-share within a month of the decision.

KEY POINTS

Return from maternity leave
- A woman returning from general maternity leave does not need to give any notice; she can simply turn up to work at the end of her leave.
- If she wants to return earlier, she must give seven days' notice.
- There is a statutory prohibition on a woman working within two weeks' of giving birth; a woman working in a factory is not allowed to work within four weeks of the birth; leave will be extended in these circumstances.
- There is limited protection against dismissal for women unable to return to work because of sickness in the four weeks after the end of their leave; a woman who is still sick at the end of the four weeks should be treated like any other employee on sick leave (though the maternity leave period should be ignored).
- As the contract continues during the MLP, the woman is entitled to return to the same job.
- Where a woman is made redundant during her MLP, she must be offered suitable available work.

Return from maternity absence
- The notice provisions must be strictly followed.
- The employer may delay the woman's return by up to four weeks.
- The employee may delay her return for up to four weeks when she is ill; she must give appropriate notice.
- Where a woman is still sick at the end of the four weeks, she may need to go into work in order to go on to sick leave and claim sick pay, though it is arguable that this is discriminatory.

- The woman's return to work may be delayed if there is industrial action.
- Where a woman has a statutory right to return *and* a contractual right to return (a composite right), she can take advantage of whichever right is, in any particular respect, the more favourable.
- The woman is entitled to return to the same job on no less favourable terms and conditions, with preserved seniority, pension rights and other rights; relevant factors are:
  - status and seniority
  - location
  - hours of work.
- Where a woman is made redundant during her maternity absence she is entitled to be offered suitable alternative work.
- There are two exceptions to the right to return:
  - where the employer employs five or fewer employees, and it is not reasonably practicable for the employer to allow the woman to return to her original job and it is not reasonably practicable to offer her suitable alternative work;
  - where it is not reasonably practicable for a reason other than redundancy for the employer to allow the woman to return to her old job and she is offered suitable alternative work.
- There may be a right to return to work part-time or as a job sharer, or on flexible hours; refusal to allow a woman to work part-time must be justified by the employer.

Right not to be unfairly dismissed
- Even where a woman has not complied with the statutory notice provisions or she falls within one of the exceptions, she may still be able to claim unfair dismissal if she is dismissed or not allowed to return.

CHAPTER 7

Unfair dismissal

Introduction

Since 1994 all women employees (irrespective of length of service and hours of work, whether temporary or permanent) are protected from dismissal for reasons connected to their pregnancy, childbirth or maternity leave.¹ Such a dismissal is automatically unfair; it cannot be justified by the employer. These provisions are in addition to the ordinary unfair dismissal protection for all employees with two years' service. Any dismissal connected to a woman's pregnancy, childbirth or maternity leave will generally also be discriminatory.

This chapter sets out the general principles relating to dismissal law, summarises the three main areas of statutory protection from dismissal and looks at how the law operates to protect women in the general maternity leave period, during extended maternity absence, in the exercise of the right to return, from redundancy and in the period immediately after the return from leave; for dismissals during pregnancy see p20. Note that general maternity leave refers to the 14-week period and extended maternity absence to the period at the end of the 14 weeks up to 29 weeks after the beginning of the week of the birth.

General principles relating to dismissals

Two decisions, one from the House of Lords and one from the European Court of Justice, are a useful starting point. In *Brown v*

1 Before June 1994 women with less than two years' service had no protection and in addition an employer could dismiss a woman with two years' service if she was incapable of adequately doing the work which she was employed to do because of her pregnancy, provided the employer had offered her any suitable altertnative vacancy.

Stockton-on-Tees Borough Council,[2] the House of Lords said that:

An employer faced with deciding which of several employees to make redundant must disregard the inconvenience that inevitably will result from the fact that one of them is pregnant and will require maternity leave. If he does not do so and makes that absence the factor that determines the pregnant woman's dismissal, that dismissal will be deemed unfair under [EPCA] s60.[3] Section 60 must be seen as a part of social legislation passed for the specific protection of women and to put them on an equal footing with men. Although it is often a considerable inconvenience to an employer to have to make the necessary arrangements to keep a woman's job open for her whilst she is absent from work in order to have a baby, *that is a price that has to be paid as a part of the social and legal recognition of the equal status of women in the workplace.*[4]

In *Habermann-Beltermann*[5] the European Court of Justice held that it 'is clear that the termination of an employment contract on account of the employee's pregnancy ... concerns women alone and constitutes, therefore, direct discrimination on grounds of sex'. The House of Lords in *Webb v EMO Air Cargo (UK) Ltd (No 2)*[6] followed the ECJ decision, holding that dismissal of a woman because she was pregnant was discrimination in itself, without the need for a comparison with a man in a similar situation (see p176).

What is a dismissal?

A woman can only be dismissed if she has a written or verbal contract of employment. ERA s71 provides that the contract continues during general maternity leave. It may also continue during extended maternity absence (see p98). If there is no contract, there can be no dismissal and a claim for unfair dismissal will then only arise if the employer refuses to allow a woman to exercise her right to return after extended maternity absence (see p103).

Circumstances in which a dismissal occurs include the following:
- where the employer terminates the contract;[7]

---

2 [1988] IRLR 263, HL at 264.
3 Now ERA s99.
4 Emphasis added.
5 *Habermann-Beltermann v Arbeiterwohlfahrt, Bezirksverband Ndb/Opf eV* [1994] IRLR 364, ECJ.
6 [1995] IRLR 645, HL.
7 ERA s95(1)(a).

- where a fixed-term contract is not renewed on the same terms;[8]
- constructive dismissal, ie, where the employee terminates the contract (with or without notice) in circumstances where she is entitled to terminate it without notice because of the employer's conduct;[9]
- deemed dismissal, ie, where the employer does not allow a woman to exercise her right to return after maternity absence.[10]

The exceptions are set out on p14. Women working outside Great Britain and as share fisherwomen are protected if they are dismissed during maternity leave (under ERA s84) or are denied the right to return (under s96), by virtue of ss196(4) and 199(3) respectively.

Fixed-term contract exception

Where an employee is employed under a fixed-term contract of one year or more, and, before its expiry, the employee has agreed in writing to exclude any claim for unfair dismissal, she has no protection against unfair dismissal.[11] A dismissal on pregnancy or maternity-related grounds may still be a breach of the Equal Treatment and Pregnant Workers Directives.

Notice pay

Where either the employer or employee gives notice to terminate the contract at a time when the woman is absent from work because of pregnancy or childbirth, she is entitled to the minimum remuneration during the statutory notice period, provided she has been employed for at least one month. This does not apply where the contract requires the employer to give a period of notice which is at least one week longer than the statutory minimum, in which case the woman will have to rely on her contractual rights.[12] If maternity pay is paid for the period, this can be offset against the notice pay.[13]

8 ERA s95(1)(b); see *Nelson v Western Health and Social Services Board* (1994) 10 October, Case Ref No 887/93SD, Belfast IT, where a woman who had been employed on a series of short-term contracts did not have her contract renewed after she had an ectopic pregnancy (see also p23).
9 ERA s95(1)(c).
10 ERA s96.
11 ERA s197.
12 ERA s86 lays down minimum periods of notice (eg one week's notice where the employee has less than two years service and one week's notice for each year from two up to 12 years). Sections 87–89 lay down the rights of the employee in the period of notice. The details are beyond the scope of this book, but note that where the employee gives notice, she must actually leave to take advantate of them (s88(3)).
13 ERA ss88(2), 89(4).

Maternity rights/Chapter 7
Protection from dismissal: statutory framework

A woman who has been dismissed may have several claims, ie:
- automatically unfair dismissal on pregnancy or maternity-related grounds – for all employees;
- dismissal for assertion of a statutory right;
- dismissal in health and safety cases;
- ordinary unfair dismissal (where the dismissal is not pregnancy-related) – for women with two years' service or more;
- deemed dismissal – where a woman is denied her statutory right to return to work;
- sex discrimination;
- under EU law (Pregnant Workers Directive and Equal Treatment Directive).

Automatically unfair dismissal under ERA s99

It is automatically unfair to dismiss a woman where the reason or main reason for the dismissal is:
a) she is pregnant, or for any other reason connected with her pregnancy;[14] (eg pregnancy-related sickness) (see p20). This is not limited in time and could apply, for example, to dismissal for a pregnancy-related illness arising after the woman has returned to work (see p111);
b) her maternity leave period is ended by dismissal and the reason for the dismissal is that she has had a baby or for any reason connected with the childbirth;[15] this only applies during the maternity leave period (see p97);
c) she was dismissed after the end of her maternity leave period and the reason for the dismissal is that she had taken maternity leave or the benefits of maternity leave;[16] this, like (a), is unlimited in time (see p98);
d) the reason for the dismissal is a requirement or recommendation to suspend the woman on health and safety grounds[17] (see p126);
e) the woman's maternity leave period is ended by dismissal and the reason for the dismissal is that she is redundant and has not been

---

14 ERA s99(1)(a).
15 ERA s99(1)(b).
16 ERA s99(1)(c).
17 ERA s99(1)(d).

offered suitable available employment. This only applies during and up to the end of the maternity leave period;[18] (see pp105 and 107);
f) where:
- the woman told her employer she would be unable to return to work at the end of her maternity leave period; and
- before the end of her maternity leave period she provided the employer with a doctor's certificate stating she was unable to work for health reasons; and
- she was dismissed during the four weeks after the end of her leave while incapable of working and where she has a doctor's certificate for the period; and
- the reason for the dismissal was that she had given birth or for a reason connected to the birth[19] (see p101);
g) a woman with a right to extended maternity absence is denied her right to return because of redundancy and is not offered a suitable alternative vacancy (see p107).[20]

A claim for automatically unfair dismissal under s99(1)(a) (pregnancy-related dismissal) and s99(1)(d) can be made even where the woman has lost her right to maternity leave or absence because of failure to give proper notice.[21]

Written reasons for dismissal

If the woman is dismissed while she is pregnant or where her general maternity leave ends by dismissal, the employer must give written reasons for her dismissal.[22] This applies irrespective of the woman's length of service and regardless of whether she requests a statement. The statement is admissible in evidence.[23]

18 ERA s99(1)(e).
19 ERA s99(3).
20 ERA s99(4).
21 Although the other grounds specifically refer to the 'maternity leave period' (which presupposes that notice has been given) it is arguably automatically unfair to dismiss a woman who had taken maternity absence or time off to have a baby even though this was not 'maternity leave' in the statutory sense. This would be consistent with the House of Lords judgment in *Brown v Stockton-on-Tees Borough Council* (n2 above), when it was made clear that the dismissal of a woman because she took maternity absence (as it then was) was automatically unfair.
22 ERA s92(4); see also PWD article 10(2).
23 s92(5). A woman can complain to a tribunal if the employer unreasonably fails to provide written reasons or the particulars are inadequate or untrue. The tribunal may, if it upholds the complaint, make a declaration about the employer's reasons for the dismissal and make an award of two weeks' pay (s93).

Burden of proof

The woman must prove she has been dismissed. Where the woman has two years' service, the employer must show the reason for the dismissal. In other cases the woman must establish that the reason for the dismissal is related to her pregnancy or maternity leave. If it is, the dismissal is automatically unfair. The principles are similar to those for establishing discrimination (see p179). The employer has no defence so cannot justify the dismissal.[24]

Dismissal for assertion of statutory right

It is automatically unfair to dismiss an employee either for bringing proceedings to enforce a statutory right or alleging that the employer has infringed a statutory right. It is irrelevant if the right has in fact been breached, provided the claim is made in good faith. Statutory rights include, for example, time off for ante-natal care, maternity leave, and health and safety rights.[25]

Dismissal in health and safety cases

It is automatically unfair to dismiss a woman where there is a danger which she reasonably believes is serious and imminent and which she could not reasonably have been expected to avoid where she either:
– left work (or proposed to leave), or
– (while the danger persisted) refused to return to work.[26]
Thus where a woman leaves work because of the employer's refusal to take appropriate steps to deal with health and safety risks, and is dismissed as a result, she may have a claim under these provisions.

General unfair dismissal law

A woman may also have a claim for ordinary unfair dismissal.[27] The legislation limits this right to employees who have worked for the employer for two years. However, this qualifying period may

---

24 Even if the dismissal is not automatically unfair, it may be an ordinary unfair dismissal.
25 ERA s104(1).
26 ERA s100.
27 For detailed discussion see Kibling and Lewis, *Employment Law: An advisers' handbook* (Legal Action Group).

be indirectly discriminatory.[28]

The burden of proof is on the employer to show that the reason for dismissal is a potentially fair one (see below) and the tribunal must decide whether the employer acted reasonably in dismissing the employee (see p95). There are five potentially fair reasons for dismissing a worker:[29]

(1) *Capability* or *qualifications* and
(2) *conduct of the employee*. Both these categories may include lateness or sickness absence, which are common reasons for dismissing pregnant women. Where the employer dismisses a woman because of pregnancy-related sickness it will be automatically unfair (see p21). However, if this is not proved (for example, because the employer was not aware that the woman was pregnant), the dismissal may nevertheless be unfair. The test is the employer's genuine belief held on reasonable grounds. When considering whether to dismiss a woman because of sickness absence, the employer should take account of the length and frequency of absences, the likelihood of future absences, and the effect of the absences on the woman's work. The onus is on the employer to consult the employee to get the relevant information.[30] Account should be taken of the ACAS handbook, *Discipline at Work*.
(3) *Redundancy* (see p105);
(4) *The employee could not continue working without contravening a statutory duty or restriction* (for example, a lawyer struck off will not be able to practice). The provisions relating to health and safety are set out on pp126–127.
(5) *Some other substantial reason*. This may include the following:
a) The most common reason is business reorganisation. Where an employer has a good business reason for a reorganisation, as a result of which s/he terminates the employees' contracts and offers reasonable new ones, an employee who refuses the new agreements may be fairly dismissed. If the employee cannot be employed elsewhere, this may also be 'some other substantial reason' justifying the dismissal.
b) The failure to renew a fixed-term contract where the post is permanently filled may be a substantial reason.[31] The fixed-term

28 *R v Secretary of State for Employment ex p Seymour Smith and Perez* [1995] IRLR 464, CA.
29 ERA s98.
30 *Mitchell v Arkwood Plastics (Engineering) Ltd* [1993] ICR 471 EAT.
31 *North Yorkshire County Council v Fay* [1985] IRLR 247, CA.

contract must have been for a genuine purpose and that fact must have been known to the employee. This would allow an employer not to renew the contract of a maternity locum even though the woman was not going to return from maternity leave or absence. The employer could advertise the post and then fill it on a permanent basis (see also p112).

c) Dismissal of a worker on or after a business has been transferred, where there is an economic, technical or organisational reason entailing changes in the workforce.

Reasonableness test

When deciding whether the employer has shown a potentially fair reason, the question of fairness will depend on whether, in the circumstances, the employer 'acted reasonably or unreasonably in treating it as a sufficient reason for dismissing the employee'. Relevant circumstances will include the employer's size and administrative resources. Account will be taken of the merits of the case and procedural fairness.[32]

There is an important variation of the reasonableness test where there is a deemed dismissal (under ERA s96). The test is whether the employer 'would have been acting reasonably or unreasonably in treating it as a sufficient reason for dismissing the employee if she had not been absent from work'.[33] For example, in *Shirley v Anglian Windows Ltd*[34] the applicant was chosen for redundancy (out of three others) while on maternity absence but was not told until she returned. She was not offered a suitable available vacancy and the IT held that she had been unfairly dismissed. The employer must consider the position of a woman on maternity leave (or absence) when carrying out redundancies or a reorganisation. The test is what would have happened if the woman had been at work.

Deemed dismissal

There will be a deemed dismissal where the employer refuses to allow a woman to exercise her right to return after extended maternity absence (see p103). The dismissal will be for the reason that the woman was not allowed to return.[35]

32 ERA s98(4).
33 ERA s98(5).
34 COIT 1567/205.
35 ERA s96(1).

Sex discrimination claim

A pregnancy or maternity-related dismissal will also be discriminatory and unlawful under the Sex Discrimination Act or Equal Treatment Directive (see chapter 11). Before 1994 this was the only claim available for a woman with less than two years' service.

A sex discrimination claim can be brought by an employee, a self-employed person, independent contractor or contract worker irrespective of length of service. The main advantages of bringing a discrimination claim is that the questionnaire procedure can be used, there is no limit on the amount of compensation and an amount can be awarded for injury to feelings.

Pregnant Workers Directive (PWD)

The Directive provides that:

> whereas the risk of dismissal for reasons associated with their condition may have harmful effects on the physical and mental state of pregnant workers, workers who have recently given birth or who are breastfeeding; whereas provision should be made for such dismissal to be prohibited.

The PWD requires member states to take:

> the necessary measures to prohibit the dismissal of workers ... during the period from the beginning of their pregnancy to the end of the maternity leave save in exceptional cases not connected with their condition which are permitted under national legislation.

The ERA and SDA should be read with this very wide prohibition on dismissal in mind (see p198).

In *Ozkan-Quaynor v Optika (Ltd) Optician*[36] the IT said that, in *Webb* (see p176) the ECJ is:

> approving the directive's view that pregnant women should not be dismissed until after the end of maternity leave, because of the effect this might have on their physical or mental state. This principle clearly applies whatever the ostensible reason for dismissal. The only exception to this according to the directive as approved in the decision, is an 'exceptional case'. If an employer's business had closed down altogether we would regard this as an exceptional case, justifying dismissal of all employees, as would be inevitable.

---

36 (1995) 11 December, Case No: 25564/95/LN/C, London North IT.

The IT held that redundancies could have been made without the applicant being dismissed and the dismissal was a breach of the SDA, read with the PWD. This is a very strict interpretation of the directive, providing greater protection from dismissal than the ERA. It will be interesting to see if it is followed.

Dismissal during maternity leave period

The ERA does not specifically provide that there is a right for a woman to return after her maternity leave period; this is unnecessary as the contract continues throughout the leave.[37] The woman need only present herself for work at the end of the 14 weeks (see p66).

If a woman's maternity leave period is ended by dismissal, the MLP ends at the same time.[38] Thus, she is not entitled to return to work at the end of the 14 weeks. Such a dismissal may be automatically unfair if connected with her pregnancy, maternity leave or childbirth. However, an employer cannot prevent a woman exercising her right to return after maternity absence by dismissing her while she is on maternity leave (or absence) (see p103).[39]

Failure to renew a fixed-term contract (on the same terms) is also a dismissal (see p90). If the reason is because the woman has had a baby or taken maternity leave it will be automatically unfair (see *Caruana v Manchester Airport plc*, p23). If the dismissal is due to redundancy, the woman will be entitled to suitable available work in the same way as a woman on a permanent contract (see p105).

The automatically unfair reasons are set out on p91. An automatically unfair dismissal is likely to be discriminatory. It may also be an ordinary unfair dismissal (see p93).

---

37 ERA s71. As the contract does not necessarily continue during maternity absence ERA s79 provides that women with two years' service have a right to return up to 29 weeks after the beginning of the week of the birth.
38 ERA s73(3).
39 ERA s84. Clearly, this only applies to women entitled to extended maternity absence (see p40).

Dismissal at end of general maternity leave period

Where an employer refuses to allow the woman to return at the end of the maternity leave period, this will be a dismissal.[40] If the reason is related to her pregnancy or the fact that she has taken maternity leave, the dismissal will be automatically unfair (see p91). Thus, if her replacement is kept on in preference to her this is likely to be automatically unfair (see p101). The question to ask is whether 'but for' her pregnancy or absence on maternity leave, she would have been dismissed.

Protection from dismissal for four weeks because of sickness

If a woman is unable to return at the end of her MLP, because of sickness, she should inform her employer and provide a doctor's certificate before she is due to return. She will then be protected from dismissal for up to a further four weeks (see p92). The situation of a woman who fails to return from maternity leave is covered on p69.

Dismissal during extended maternity absence

The dismissal will be automatically unfair where a woman is dismissed after the end of her maternity leave period and the reason (or main reason) is that she took maternity leave or the benefits of maternity leave.[41]

There can, however, be no dismissal if there is no continuing contract during maternity absence (see p89).[42]

Does the contract subsist?

Whether the contract does continue after the end of the MLP will depend on the circumstances. In *Institute of the Motor Industry v Harvey*,[43] the EAT held that if a woman gives notice of intention to take maternity leave, her contract of employment is likely to continue when she goes on maternity leave unless it is terminated by agreement, resignation or dismissal (see also pp56–57).

---

40 The contract continues during the MLP.
41 ERA s99(2)(b).
42 Any claim must be brought within three months of the termnation of the contract
43 [1992] ICR 470, EAT.

A similar conclusion was reached in *Hilton International Hotels (UK) Ltd v Kaissi*,⁴⁴ where the EAT held that the fact that Mrs Kaissi failed to give notice of her intention to return did not mean that her contract was to be treated as terminated. The EAT said that whether or not the contract comes to an end depends, not on the statute, but on the agreement and actions of the parties in each case. The contract may continue if that is what the parties expressly or impliedly agree and neither takes any action to bring it to an end. In Ms Kaissi's case, she was in the position of a person who was off work sick with the tacit permission of the employers. The employers took no action to terminate the contract.⁴⁵

However, in *Crouch v Kidsons Impey*⁴⁶ the EAT held that there is no presumption that the contract remains in existence. It may continue if there is an express agreement or a proper inference, but if the employer merely consents to the employee leaving work and remuneration ceases, the appropriate inference is that there has been an agreed termination.⁴⁷

Crouch is arguably wrong and difficult to reconcile with *Harvey* and *Kaissi* and other EAT decisions. In *Hughes v Gwynedd Area Health Authority*,⁴⁸ the EAT held that the notice of termination must specify the date when the termination is to take effect or at least make it possible for the date to be deduced with certainty. In *Hughes* a statement by a pregnant woman, made three months before she stopped working, that she would be leaving work to have her baby and not returning, was not a notice of resignation but only a

---

44 [1994] ICR 578, EAT.
45 In *Lucas v Norton of London Ltd* [1984] IRLR 86 the EAT found there was an informal agreement that Ms Lucas take maternity absence and an assumption by her that she could return at the end of it. The EAT held that the respondents' refusal to allow her to return to work was a dismissal; the contract was not terminated when her absence began but continued to subsist during her absence. She could therefore pursue a claim that her dismissal was on grounds of pregnancy.
46 [1996] IRLR 79, EAT.
47 The EAT said that where there is no right to return to work, the concept of the continued existence of some sort of 'ghost' contract of employment, where all the ordinary rights or obligations of such a contract have ceased to exist, is a wholly fanciful intention to impute to the parties. The EAT also said there were important distinctions between the facts in *Crouch* and *Kaissi* and the cases were not inconsistent. In Kaissi the fact that the employee was on sick leave and continued to receive sick pay down to the date of birth was said to be 'consistent with the continuation of her contract'.
48 [1977] IRLR 436, EAT.

statement of general intention. It must, therefore, be wrong to assume that the contract comes to an end just because the woman is not at work and not being paid. If unsure of an employee's intentions, the employer can ask the employee if she intends to return.

In other situations, the courts have been reluctant to assume consensual termination where this will deprive the employee of her statutory rights (eg, the right not to be unfairly dismissed).[49]

Finally, there cannot be a presumption that there is a consensual termination when the employee did not consent. Either the employer terminates the contract before or during the maternity leave or the contract continues until such later time as it is terminated. In either case the employer risks a claim by the employee for unfair dismissal (either automatic or ordinary) and for discrimination. An employer can only assume that the employee has resigned if she gives proper notice.

Where the contract does not subsist after the end of the MLP

If there is no contract (because it has been terminated by either employer or employee), there can be no dismissal.[50] However, the contract continues during maternity leave and the woman will have three months from the end of her maternity leave to bring a claim (see p212). If the woman is entitled to maternity absence, she can exercise her right to return (see p103).

Dismissal where contract subsists

Where the contract continues, the woman will be able to make a claim for dismissal (ordinary, automatic or discriminatory) even if she has no contractual or statutory right to return (*Kaissi*). In *Harvey* the applicant was able to bring a claim for constructive dismissal. In *Kaissi* the EAT upheld the tribunal's decision that Ms Kaissi had been unfairly dismissed during her absence as there had been no proper investigation by Hilton of her sickness.

---

49 In *Igbo v Johnson Matthey Chemicals Ltd* [1986] IRLR 215, CA there was an agreement that if the employee failed to return from concessionary leave (to visit her family) the contract would automatically terminate. The Court of Appeal held that contractual agreements which purport to treat the contract as automatically terminated if the employee commits, or fails to perform, a certain act will be void under what is now ERA s203. *Igbo* and *Hughes* were not mentioned in *Crouch*.
50 She will still have the four-week protection from dismissal if she is ill at the end of the MLP (see p92).

In *Rees v Appollo Watch Repairs plc*[51] the applicant was dismissed while on maternity absence because the employers found that her replacement was more efficient. The EAT held that the applicant would not have been dismissed had she not been on maternity absence. Following *Webb*, that meant the dismissal was discriminatory. The EAT said that the protection afforded to women on maternity absence would be drastically curtailed if an employer were able to defeat a complaint of direct discrimination by saying that s/he preferred her replacement; a state of affairs which had arisen solely as a result of her pregnancy and therefore because of her sex.

Sickness after end of MLP

If a woman is ill at the end of her MLP, she is protected from dismissal for a further four weeks provided she gives appropriate notice to her employer (see p92). If she loses this protection (by failing to give proper notice) or if she is still ill at the end of the four weeks, she may still be protected.

If the sickness is related to her pregnancy, she should inform her employer of this; a dismissal in these circumstances is likely to be automatically unfair (see p91). If the dismissal is mainly because the woman has been on maternity leave and the sickness (whether pregnancy-related or not) is the last straw, this will also be automatically unfair (see pp91-92). If the woman is dismissed for unauthorised absence in circumstances where another employee would not be dismissed, there may be an inference that the reason was connected with her maternity leave, in which case it will be automatically unfair. A case from Denmark[51A] has been referred to the ECJ to decide whether the dismissal of a woman, who was absent after the end of her maternity leave, was discriminatory where the absence was caused by an illness which arose during the pregnancy and continued during and after maternity leave.

Even if the illness is unrelated to her pregnancy or childbirth, the dismissal may still be unfair and discriminatory if the employer does not treat the woman like any other employee who is off sick (ignoring the maternity leave). The employer should

---

51 (1996) *Times* 26 February, EAT.
51A *Larsson v Dansk Handel og Service* Case C-400/95 (96/C-46/15).

investigate the sickness, discuss it with the woman and assess how long it is likely to last (see p94).[52]

Failure to return after end of MLP – unauthorised absence
Where a woman does not return to work at the end of the 14 weeks (or any extended period), her contract arguably continues unless terminated by herself or her employer (see pp98ff). It should not be assumed that the woman has resigned because she has failed to return. She should be treated like any other employee who has failed to return from authorised leave. However, unauthorised absence may be a ground for dismissal and if the woman is not sick (so not able to claim the protection set out above) she should negotiate with her employer to extend her leave.

Extension of MLP by agreement
The employer and employee can agree to extend the woman's maternity leave or absence.[53] It is preferable for the agreement to be in writing. If the period is extended, the woman is unlikely to receive contractual sick pay.

What happens if the baby is ill?
There is no provision for extending maternity leave or absence if the baby is sick. A woman can ask for compassionate leave. It could be argued that a woman with a young baby should have the same protected status as a pregnant woman. Thus, to dismiss her because she is unable to work at a time where her young baby is sick is direct discrimination. Babies are particularly vulnerable when they are only a few months old and if the woman is breastfeeding, there may be a health risk. A doctor's letter should be obtained.

It is also arguable that refusing to allow a woman to take sick leave when her baby is sick is indirectly discriminatory (see chapter 13). A requirement to work when the baby is sick has a

52 In the debates on the Trade Union Reform and Employment Rights Act 1993, Patrick McLoughlin said that a woman who could not return to work after her 14 weeks' leave because she was sick would be in the same situation as any other employee who was ill at the end of a period of leave: Hansard (HC) Standing Committee F, 12.1.93, col 376.
53 Though whether she is entitled to the benefit of her contractual terms during the extended period will depend on the contract or what is agreed between the parties.

disproportionate impact on women, who have primary responsibility for children and particularly young babies. The key question is justifiability. If an employee is allowed time off when s/he is sick, should not a child's sickness entitle her to time off – at least taken as part of her sick leave entitlement?

Sickness during and at the end of maternity absence

A woman who is sick at the end of her absence may postpone her return for four weeks (see p92). Alternatively, she may be able to return to work and claim sick pay (see p72). If she is still ill at the end of the four weeks, she should be treated like any other employee who is off sick (but she must have given her notice to return (see p42). It appears she physically has to return to work before she can go on sick leave. If possible it is advisable to do so (see p73).

Dismissal does not destroy right to return

An employer cannot avoid a woman exercising her right to return by dismissing her while she is on maternity leave or absence. She can still exercise her right to return. She will be treated as employed up until the date she notifies her employer she intends to return (see p110 for the advantages of doing this).

Dismissal while exercising right to return

Employees entitled to extended maternity absence have a right to return within this period, whether or not their contract continues during the absence.[54] The woman can choose when she returns provided it is within the 29 weeks.

If the employer does not allow the woman to return, she will be deemed to have been dismissed for the reason that she was not allowed to return.[55] This applies whether she is denied the right to return to the same job or not allowed to return at all. If the woman can show that the reason for the dismissal falls within ERA s99 (ie is related to pregnancy, childbirth or maternity leave), it will be automatically unfair (see p91). For example, if she is not allowed to return because she has had a pregnancy-related sickness, it will be automatically unfair. If the illness is not

54 There are two exceptions which are set out on p79.
55 If she is entitled to extended maternity absence, she will have satisfied the two-year qualifying period necessary to claim unfair dismissal.

pregnancy-related, the woman should be treated like any other sick employee; if she is not, the dismissal may be unfair or discriminatory (see above); and an employee has a right to postpone her return if she is sick (see p70).

If the employee does exercise her right to return, any compensation for unfair dismissal or redundancy payment received for the earlier unfair dismissal is repayable to the employer if the employer so requests.[56]

Failure to give proper notice to return

Under EPCA there were complex statutory provisions which the courts interpreted as preventing a woman claiming unfair dismissal where she had a statutory *and* contractual right to return and failed to give the appropriate notice.[57] In *Crouch v Kidsons Impey* (n46 above) the EAT considered that these statutory provisions had been wrongly interpreted. As these provisions have not been reproduced in ERA, the problem should not arise. A woman who has failed to give proper notice, and so has lost her statutory right to return, should be able to claim ordinary unfair dismissal provided her contract is continuing (see pp93 and 98). Where a woman's contract does not continue during her maternity absence and she has no separate contractual right to return, she will only have her statutory right to return (see p40).

Dismissal on transfer of the business

Where a worker is dismissed (whether by the old or new employer) because of the transfer of the business, the dismissal will be automatically unfair unless the dismissal is for redundancy for a justifiable economic, technical or organisational reason.[57] Even if the dismissal comes within this exception, the employer must show that the dismissal was reasonable (see p95).

---

56 ERA s84.
57 See *Lavery v Plessey Telecommunications Ltd* [1983] IRLR 202, CA.
58 TUPE reg 8.

Redundancy

Introduction

Where a woman has been made redundant while pregnant or when on maternity leave or absence, she will need to consider:
- whether there really is a redundancy situation or whether it is a pretext to dismiss her because of her pregnancy, childbirth, maternity leave or absence;
- whether she has been selected unfairly; and
- whether there is any suitable alternative work which she should have been offered.

The employer must also show that s/he acted reasonably in treating the reason for dismissal – ie, redundancy – as a sufficient reason. The test is whether the employer would have been acting reasonably if the employee had not been absent on maternity leave (see p95).

It is automatically unfair under ERA s105(1) and (2) to select a woman for redundancy for one of the reasons set out in s99 (see p91). In addition, a woman who is made redundant while on maternity leave or absence is entitled to be offered suitable alternative work. This is an absolute right; she should be given priority over other redundant employees (who must also be considered for suitable alternative work under the ordinary redundancy law). Note that this applies even where the woman does not have two years' qualifying service (ERA s108(3)(a) and (b)).

In *Brown v Stockton-on-Tees Borough Council* (n2 above) the House of Lords said that it cannot have been intended that an employer should be able to take advantage of a redundancy situation to weed out his pregnant employees (see p89). The same principles as set out in *Brown* apply if a woman is made redundant for reasons connected with her pregnancy or childbirth while on maternity leave or absence.

What is redundancy?

An employer who dismisses an employee on the grounds of redundancy must show that there is a redundancy situation, ie, that the business is to close, either completely or where the woman works, or that fewer employees are required to carry out the work which the woman is doing.[58] Business includes the business of associated employers.

Duty to consult

The employer has a legal duty to consult a recognised trade union at the earliest opportunity.[59] The aim of the consultation must be to avoid redundancies if possible and to mitigate the effect of any which are unavoidable. In *Polkey v AE Dayton Services Ltd*[60] Lord Bridge said that 'the employer will normally not act reasonably unless he warns and consults any employees affected or their representative, adopts a fair basis on which to select for redundancy and takes such steps as may be reasonable to avoid or minimise redundancy by redeployment within his own organisation.' Failure to carry out consultation with a woman because she is on maternity leave (or absence) may make the redundancy unfair. Where other employees are consulted, failure to consult a woman on maternity leave or absence may also be discriminatory.

In *John Menzies GB Ltd v Porter*[61] the EAT held that the tribunal was entitled to take the view that the failure to consult was particularly blatant because the employee's absence was due to pregnancy (see p109). In *Debenham v Adams Childrenswear Ltd*[62] a tribunal held that a dismissal was automatically unfair because the applicant, who was on maternity leave or absence, had not been considered for alternative posts.

In *Cowan v Western Isles Seafood Co Ltd*[63] a woman who was on maternity absence was informed by letter that she was redundant. There was no consultation. The tribunal held that the respondent failed to warn or consult the applicant, failed to take reasonable steps to avoid her redundancy by redeployment and did not act reasonably in dismissing her. The dismissal was therefore unfair. The tribunal applied the same standards of consultation to an applicant on maternity leave or absence as to an employee at work.

---

58 ERA s139.
59 Trade Union and Labour Relations (Consolidation) Act 1992 s188.
60 [1987] IRLR 503, HL.
61 (1992) 19 February, EAT 644/91.
62 (1995) 20 March, Case No 49552/94; folio No 3106/127.
63 (1994) 26 October, case No S/3439/94 Stornoway.

Redundancy during pregnancy

Where a woman is made redundant because she is pregnant or for a reason connected to her pregnancy (such as pregnancy-related sickness absence), the dismissal will be automatically unfair.

Where there is no unfairness (either automatic or ordinary), she will be entitled, like other employees, to be considered for suitable alternative work. There is no automatic right to be given suitable available work.

Redundancy during general maternity leave

If a woman is selected for redundancy while on maternity leave, the dismissal will also be automatically unfair if related to her pregnancy or the fact that she has taken maternity leave.[64]

Obligation to provide suitable alternative work

A woman who is made redundant during her 14 weeks general maternity leave is entitled to be offered any suitable available vacancy with her employer, his/her successor or an associated employer.[65] Failure to offer suitable available work will make the dismissal automatically unfair. The woman is therefore in a better position than other employees who have a right to be considered, along with others, for any suitable alternative work, but do not have an automatic right.

Redundancy during maternity absence

Selection for redundancy for a reason related to maternity leave or absence is automatically unfair. In *Intelligent Applications Ltd v Wilson*[66] the tribunal found that the applicant's duties were re-allocated simply because she went on maternity absence. Her employment was terminated because the re-allocation became permanent. The EAT held that the tribunal was entitled to find that although there was some over-capacity before Ms Wilson became pregnant, the stimulus for action, by declaring a redundancy, was Ms Wilson's decision to take maternity absence. If she had not gone on maternity absence, there was no certainty that the arrangements would have taken the form that

---

64 *Brown v Stockton on Tees Borough Council* [1988] IRLR 263, HL.
65 ERA ss77 and 81.
66 EAT/412/92 Edinburgh.

they did, and it is at least possible that the other employee would have been made redundant. The dismissal was therefore automatically unfair.

Where initial notice of intention to return has been given
The automatic right to suitable alternative work for women who are made redundant during the maternity absence period applies if the woman has given the initial notice (before going on leave) that she intends to return to work; she need not yet have given the 21 days' notice of the actual date of her return. In *Philip Hodges & Co v Kell*[67] the applicant, a legal secretary, was on extended maternity absence when she was made redundant. The employer had employed another legal secretary two months previously and argued that the right to return (and right to alternative work in the event of redundancy) did not arise until the woman had given the 21 days' notice of the date she intended to return. The EAT held that the applicant was entitled to be offered alternative employment if a suitable vacancy arose at any time during the maternity absence. As the employers had failed to offer the applicant the post, the dismissal was unfair.

Where no notice of intention to return has been given
If the woman has not given notice of intention to return within the appropriate time limit, and so has lost her statutory right to return, and her contract continues during extended maternity absence (see p98), she should be entitled to be considered for suitable alternative employment in the same way as any other employee.

Right to alternative work is absolute
In *Community Task Force v Rimmer*[68] Ms Rimmer was made redundant while she was on maternity absence. The employers did not redeploy Mrs Rimmer into a new job because this would result in a funding cut. The EAT upheld the tribunal finding that failure to offer the post to Mrs Rimmer made her dismissal automatically unfair. The EAT held that if a suitable vacancy was available, the economic (or other) consequences of the employer giving the job to the redundant employee were not relevant.

---

67 [1994] IRLR 568, EAT.
68 [1986] IRLR 203, EAT.

In *John Menzies GB Ltd v Porter*[69] the EAT upheld the tribunal finding that the employers had not given any real consideration to the possibility of offering the applicant alternative employment. That meant the dismissal was automatically unfair.

Suitable alternative work

What is suitable alternative work?

The new employment[70] must take effect immediately on the ending of the existing employment and:
a) the new employment must consist of work which is both suitable in relation to the employee and appropriate for her to do in the circumstances; and
b) the provisions of the new contract (in relation to pay, capacity, location, and other terms and conditions) must not be substantially less favourable than under the previous contract.[71]

Terms and conditions

These must not be substantially less favourable. In *Gillespie v The Stamping Alliance Co Ltd*[72] a woman who had been made redundant during her maternity absence refused alternative work because it was in the middle of the factory and noisy. The tribunal held that the job was suitable and she should have tried it out. She was therefore not entitled to a redundancy payment.

Status of job

If the alternative work is of lower status, it may be unsuitable even if the grade and salary is the same. In *Brown-Williams v Microgen Ltd*[73] Ms Brown-Williams was one of two regional production managers. During her maternity absence the two managers were replaced by a single national production manager. She was not offered this job but only jobs as 'client services representative' and 'enquiry service manager' which were of lower status. The tribunal held that the two jobs were not suitable and failure to offer the applicant the suitable available vacancy (the national production manager) made the dismissal automatically unfair.

---

69 (1992) 19 February, (S)EAT 644/91.
70 Which may be with a successor or associated employer.
71 ERA ss77 and 81.
72 COIT 1142/195.
73 COIT 1415/176.

Increased travelling time
If the alternative work involves an increase in travelling time and additional child-care costs, the offer may be unsuitable.[74]

If there is no suitable alternative work
If there is no suitable alternative work, the dismissal will not be *automatically* unfair (unless the reason for the redundancy or the selection was connected with the woman's pregnancy or maternity leave (see above)). The duty to consult still applies (see p106). If there is no 'unfairness' or discrimination, the woman will only be entitled to a redundancy payment (if she has worked for the same employer for a minimum of two years) and not to compensation for unfair dismissal.

Refusal of suitable alternative work
If the woman unreasonably refuses suitable alternative work, initially or after a trial period, she will not be entitled to compensation for unfair dismissal nor to a redundancy payment.[75] The employee should be consulted on what is suitable alternative work. She may, for example, wish to be redeployed into another job which she considers is more suitable.

Exercising right to return after being made redundant or dismissed

Even if the woman is made redundant or dismissed while on maternity leave or absence, it is still advisable for her to exercise her right to return from maternity absence (by giving the 21 days' notice). There are two reasons:
a) She will be treated as having been continuously employed until the notified day of return and the redundancy payment will be based on continuous service until this date.
b) If the woman is made redundant shortly after the birth and there was no alternative work at that time, it is possible that some months later, when she is due to return, some alternative suitable employment will be available. If it is available, the employer must offer it. If the woman has already received a redundancy payment, she will have to repay it if she returns to work in these circumstances.

74 *Hill v Supasnaps Ltd* COIT 1930/200.
75 ERA ss96(3)and 141(2). The test is subjective, so factors relevant to the individual woman may be taken into account.

Entitlement to redundancy payment

If there is no suitable available work, the employee will be entitled to a redundancy payment (if she has been employed for at least two years). The payment is based on so many weeks' pay for each year of service. For the purposes of calculating a week's pay, the relevant date is the last day she worked immediately before her maternity leave period began.[76]

Where the woman exercises her right to return, the dismissal date will usually be the notified date of return. This does not apply if the employer can show that the employee was, or would have been made redundant had she continued in employment at an earlier date. If the employer proves this, the earlier date is treated as the date of dismissal for the purpose of calculating the redundancy payment.[77] This would only apply, however, if there is still no suitable available work at the date of return.

Dismissal after return to work

The protection against dismissal for reasons connected with either pregnancy[78] or the woman taking maternity leave (or the benefits of leave)[79] is not limited in time. Thus, if a woman is dismissed after she has returned to work for one of these reasons, the dismissal is automatically unfair. It may also be discriminatory (see p96).

However, it is not clear for how long this protection lasts. In *Hertz*[80] the applicant returned to work after maternity leave or absence for six months. She was then absent for a substantial period suffering from an illness arising out of her pregnancy and confinement. She was dismissed because of her repeated absences. Ms Hertz complained that this was a breach of the Equal Treatment Directive. The European Court of Justice held that in relation to an illness which appears after maternity leave or absence, there is no reason to distinguish an illness which has its origin in pregnancy or confinement from any other illness. If

---

76 ERA s226.
77 ERA s137(2).
78 ERA s99(1)(a).
79 ERA s99(1)(c).
80 *Handels-og Kontorfunktionaerernes Forbund i Danmark (acting for Hertz) v Dansk Arbejdsgiverforening (acting for Aldi Marked K/S)* [1991] IRLR 31, ECJ.

sickness absence would lead to dismissal of a male worker under the same conditions, there is no direct discrimination on grounds of sex.

Hertz was a discrimination case under the ETD. However, a claim under the ERA for automatically unfair dismissal may succeed, particularly if the pregnancy-related sickness occurred soon after the end of the 14 weeks maternity leave.

For the purposes of a woman's sickness record, the woman's absence on maternity leave (and probably on maternity absence) should be ignored. Failure to do so would be a breach of ERA s99(1)(c), which makes it unfair to dismiss a woman because she has taken maternity leave. It would also be discriminatory, as it is less favourable treatment on maternity grounds.

The Pregnant Workers Directive only protects women from the beginning of their pregnancy to the end of the maternity leave, though arguably this should also include the period of absence (see p59). A woman who becomes ill after her return to work has no automatic protection. She will have to fall back on the comparative approach in discrimination cases (as in *Hertz*) and, where the sickness is pregnancy-related, on ERA (see p91).

Dismissal of maternity replacement

Where an employer has employed a temporary replacement for an employee on maternity leave or absence (or who has been suspended on health and safety grounds), the dismissal will be for some other substantial reason and fair where:
a) the employer has informed the employee in writing that her/his employment will end when the woman returns to work after maternity leave or absence (or suspension); and
b) the employer dismisses the replacement in order to give the work back to the returning woman.[81]
The IT will still have to consider whether the dismissal was reasonable (see p95). Even if the employer does not comply with (a) the dismissal of the replacement may not be unfair but will depend on the facts.[82]

Where the temporary replacement becomes pregnant, it will still be automatically unfair if she is dismissed because she is pregnant. It may also be discriminatory (see p96).

81 ERA s106.
82 See *Hayes v South Glamorgan County Council* EAT 702/84.

UNFAIR DISMISSAL: KEY POINTS
- All women, irrespective of length of service or hours they work, are protected from dismissal on grounds related to pregnancy, childbirth or maternity leave; they may claim
  - automatically unfair dismissal,
  - deemed dismissal, where a woman is denied her statutory right to return to work,
  - discrimination.
- Women with two years' service may also claim ordinary unfair dismissal.
- The Pregnant Workers Directive prohibits the dismissal of workers from the beginning of their pregnancy to the end of maternity leave, save in exceptional cases not connected with their condition.
- If a woman is dismissed while she is pregnant or on general maternity leave, the employer must give written reasons for the dismissal.

Dismissal while pregnant
- It is automatically unfair to dismiss a woman or make her redundant:
  - because she is pregnant or for any other reason connected with her pregnancy; this would include pregnancy-related sickness. The employer must know she is pregnant;
  - to avoid a health and safety requirement or recommendation.
- A dismissal may also be an ordinary dismissal and/or discriminatory.

Dismissal during general maternity leave
- It is automatically unfair to dismiss a woman or make her redundant:
  - where the reason is that she has given birth or for a reason connected with childbirth,
  - where she has been made redundant but not offered a suitable available vacancy,
  - in the four weeks after the end of her leave when she cannot work for health reasons, provided she has given adequate notice.
- A dismissal may also be unfair and/or discriminatory.

Dismissal during extended maternity absence
- It is automatically unfair to dismiss a woman after the end of

her MLP where the main reason is that she took maternity leave or claimed the benefits of maternity leave.
- However, there can be no dismissal is there is no contract. It is unclear whether the contract continues during maternity absence and will be a question of fact in each case.
- Dismissal does not destroy the right to return after maternity absence.
- If an employer does not allow a woman to return at the end of her maternity absence, it will be a 'deemed dismissal'.
- Refusal to allow a woman to return will be a dismissal.

Redundancy
- It is automatically unfair to make a woman redundant because she is pregnant, has given birth or has taken maternity leave.
- There is a duty to consult employees, including a woman on maternity leave or absence.
- Where a woman is made redundant while she is on maternity leave or absence, she is entitled to suitable alternative work; the terms and conditions must not be substantially less favourable.

Dismissal after return to work
- Dismissal because of sickness absence occurring after the woman has returned to work will not necessarily be discriminatory even if the sickness is connected with the pregnancy or childbirth; the question is whether the woman has been treated less favourably than a man.
- However, dismissal because of pregnancy-related absence occurring after the woman has returned to work may be automatically unfair dismissal under the ERA.

Dismissal of maternity replacement
- An employer can dismiss an employee who has been employed as a temporary replacement for an employee on maternity leave; the employee must be given notice that it is a temporary job.
- Dismissal of a woman for bringing proceedings to enforce a statutory maternity right will be automatically unfair.

CHAPTER 8
Health and safety

Introduction

This chapter looks at the employer's obligations to protect pregnant and breastfeeding women and new mothers from health and safety risks. It briefly summarises the general law and then looks at the changes made in order to implement the Pregnant Workers Directive. As with all maternity rights it is important to bear in mind that if a woman with a health and safety problem is wrongly treated, the unfair dismissal provisions of the ERA and the prohibition of discrimination in the SDA and Equal Treatment Directive come into play.

General duties

An employer has the following duties to protect the health and safety of his/her workers:

- a common law duty of care;
- a statutory duty under the Factories Act 1961, the Health and Safety at Work Act 1974 and other statutes;
- a duty under the Pregnant Workers Directive, the Management of Health and Safety at Work Regulations 1992 SI No 2051 (MHSWR) (as amended by the Management of Health and Safety at Work (Amendment) Regulations 1994 SI No 2865) and other workplace regulations.

Employers' general duty of care to the employee

Employers are under a duty (both in tort and through an implied term in employees' contracts) to take reasonable care for the health and safety of their employees. Employees who are injured as a result of their employer's breach of this duty can sue the employer for damages. This is beyond the scope of this book.

Employers' duties under Health and Safety at Work Act

Employers have a statutory duty, under the Health and Safety at Work Act 1974,[1] to 'ensure so far as is reasonably practicable' their employees' health, safety and welfare at work. Enforcement is generally by the Health and Safety Executive.[2] In summary, the duty is to take reasonable care to lay down safe systems of work, to provide a safe place of work, to provide safe plant and equipment and a safe working environment.[3]

In assessing what steps an employer must take in order to carry out the duty to pregnant workers, account must be taken of:

a) *Current knowledge about reproductive hazards* (such as the hazards set out in Annex I and II of the Pregnant Workers Directive (see appendix 5), advice given by the Health and Safety Executive,[4] and any other advisory material available to the employer for the particular industry). Employers also need to bear in mind the fact that hazards occur before as well as during pregnancy and a pregnant woman is most vulnerable during early pregnancy when she may not be aware she is pregnant. Preventative measures may need to be taken in respect of women of child-bearing age. In *Page v Freight Hire (Tank Haulage) Ltd*[5] the EAT held that the employers were justified in refusing to allow a young female driver to carry loads of a chemical which might be dangerous to women of child-bearing age (see p127).

b) *The extent of the risk*. The more serious the hazard, the more careful the employer must be and the more precautions s/he must take.

c) *The circumstances of the individual employee*. The Health and Safety Executive's advisory leaflet[6] says that 'advice to a pregnant woman that she should or should not continue to work on a particular job depends upon a mixture of social, medical

1 s2(1).
2 s18.
3 s2.
4 For example, in *New and Expectant Mothers at Work – a guide for employers*, and *Occupational Health Aspects of Pregnancy*.
5 [1981] 1 All ER 394; [1981] IRLR 13, EAT.
6 *Occupational Health Aspects of Pregnancy*.

Health and safety 117

and occupational factors which can only be assessed on a case-by-case basis. Moreover, since pregnancy is a dynamic state these factors probably vary in their impact throughout its course. Continual assessment is therefore suggested in cases where difficulties are anticipated.' Thus, for example, a woman with a back problem may be more vulnerable, particularly in the later stages of pregnancy.

Employer's duty and liability towards the child

Where an employer is in breach of her/his duty of care towards a pregnant employee (whether statutory or common law duty) and as a result her child is born with a disability, the child can bring an action for damages against the employer under the Congenital Disabilities (Civil Liability) Act 1976 s1.

The Pregnant Workers Directive (PWD)

The directive's aim is to 'implement measures to encourage improvements in the safety and health at work of pregnant workers and workers who have recently given birth or who are breastfeeding'.

The directive was implemented by regulations which came into force on 1 December 1994. The Management of Health and Safety at Work (Amendment) Regulations 1994 SI No 2865 amended existing regulations[7] and specifically require employers to take particular account of risks to new, breastfeeding and expectant mothers when assessing risks at work. The HSE has issued guidance to employers about the risks to new and expectant mothers (see appendix 6).

Where the workforce includes women of childbearing age, employers are obliged to carry out a risk assessment of any risk to the health and safety of a new or expectant mother, or to that of her baby. If the assessment reveals a risk, the employer must take specified steps to avoid the risk, including the alteration of working conditions, provision of suitable available work or suspension on full pay (see pp122ff).

---

7 The Management of Health and Safety at Work Regulations 1992 SI No 2051 (MHSWR).

The ERA and MHSWR

The ERA provides that a woman (who is pregnant or has recently given birth or is breastfeeding) who is unable to do her job for health and safety reasons is entitled to be offered any available suitable alternative work (s67). If no such work is available, she must be suspended on full pay (ss66 and 68). Dismissing a woman in order to avoid the duty to suspend her is automatically unfair under ERA s99.

Who is protected under the ERA?

The duty on employers to carry out risk assessments[8] applies in relation to risks affecting employees, the self-employed, independent contractors, trainees, apprentices and any other individuals, though many of the specific duties only apply to employees (see below).

Duty to notify employer of pregnancy

The duty to alter the woman's working conditions or hours of work and, if this is not possible, to suspend her on full pay, only applies where the employee has notified the employer of her pregnancy.[9] If the employer makes a written request that the employee provide the employer with a certificate from a doctor or midwife confirming that she is pregnant, the employee must produce this within a reasonable time of the request.[10] The obligations cease once the employer knows that the woman is no longer a new or expectant mother or if the employer cannot establish whether she remains a new or expectant mother.

Exceptions under MHSWR

The regulations do not apply to the master or crew of a sea-going ship or to the employer of such persons.[11] This exception is likely to be in breach of the PWD.

---

8 Under MHSWR regs 3(1) and 13A.
9 MHSWR reg 13C.
10 MHSWR reg 13C(2).
11 MHSWR reg 2.

(1) Employers' duty to carry out risk assessment under PWD

The PWD provides that:

For all activities liable to involve a specific risk of exposure to the agents, processes or working conditions of which a non-exhaustive list is given in Annex 1, the employer shall assess the nature, degree and duration of exposure ... in order to:
- assess any risks to the safety or health and any possible effect on the pregnancies or breastfeeding of workers ...,
- decide what measures should be taken.[12]

Steps required for risk assessment under MHSWR

Under the MHSWR the employer has a general duty to make a 'suitable and sufficient assessment' of 'the risks to the health and safety of his employees to which they are exposed whilst they are at work'.[13] The amended regulations extend the general duty to cover the situation where:

a) there are persons working for her/him who are of childbearing age; and
b) the work is of a kind which could involve risk, by reason of the woman's condition, to the health and safety of a new or expectant mother, or to that of her baby, from any processes or working conditions or physical, biological or chemical agents specified in the Annexes to the PWD.[14]

The risk from any infectious or contagious disease must be such that it is greater than a new or expectant mother may be exposed to outside the workplace.[15]

The type of assessment to be carried out is the same under the PWD and the MHSWR, the latter adopting the main risks set out in the annexes to the PWD. The aim of the risk assessment is to identify the protective or preventive measures necessary to comply with the statutory requirements and prohibitions.

---

12 The duty under the Directive to carry out a risk assessment and associated duties (eg, to adjust working conditions or hours of work and suspension) only apply after the employer has been notified in writing by the employee that she is pregnant, has given birth within the previous six months or is breastfeeding.
13 MHSWR reg 3.
14 MHSWR reg 13A. Note that this duty applies irrespective of whether there actually is a new or expectant mother working in the establishment.
15 MHSWR reg 13A(4).

In *Taylor v Thomas Bee Ltd*[16] the tribunal found that there were very serious shortcomings in the way the risk assessment had been carried out. Thus, the instruction to a pregnant woman to continue working with cleaning material which made her unwell was unreasonable and her dismissal was unfair. In addition, the dismissal was for a reason connected with the pregnancy and so was unfair and discriminatory (see p96).

Types of risk

A non-exhaustive list of agents, processes or working conditions, which employers must assess, is set out in the annexes to the PWD (see appendix 5).

Common risks

There are certain common risks about which employers should be aware. These include risks related to

– too much travelling, which may lead to tiredness;
– extreme temperatures;
– heavy lifting;
– long hours, as pregnant women often suffer from fatigue;
– too much standing (because of varicose veins and haemarrhoids);
– early morning duties (particularly if the woman has morning sickness);
– nauseating smells.

(2) Implementation of review

Requirement for continuing review

Employers are required to review an assessment, and make appropriate changes, where:

a) there is reason to suspect that it is no longer valid; or
b) there has been a significant change in the matters to which it relates.[17]

Duty to record findings of assessment

Where an employer employs five or more employees, s/he must record the significant findings of the assessment and note any

---

16 (1996) 4 January, DCLD No 28, Case No 63877/95.
17 MHSWR reg 3(3).

groups of employees who have been identified as especially at risk.[18]

Duty to implement and monitor preventive and protective measures
The employer has a duty to make appropriate arrangements, having regard to the nature of his/her activities and the size of his/her business, for the effective planning, organisation, control, monitoring and review of the preventive and protective measures.

Duty to inform employees
The employer must provide his/her employees (which include trainees and those on fixed-term contracts) with comprehensible and relevant information on the risks to their health and safety identified by the assessment. This includes any preventive and protective measures taken. The information must be capable of being understood and account should be taken of an employee's training, knowledge and experience. Special consideration should be given to employees with language difficulties.[19]

(3) Where the assessment reveals a risk

Absolute prohibitions
Where the assessment has revealed a risk of exposure which would jeopardise safety or health, there is an absolute prohibition on:

a) pregnant women being obliged to perform duties which involve:
   - work in hyperbaric atmospheres, eg, pressurised enclosures and underwater diving;
   - exposure to toxoplasma or rubella virus (unless the woman has been immunised);
   - exposure to lead and lead derivatives in so far as they are capable of being absorbed by the human organism;
   - underground mining work.
b) breastfeeding women:
   - being exposed to lead and lead derivatives (as above);
   - doing underground mining work (PWD article 6).

---

18 MHSR reg 3(4).
19 See paras 53 – 56 of the approved code of practice.

Maternity rights/Chapter 8

Duty to take preventive or protective measures

Once an assessment has revealed a risk to the safety or health or an effect on the pregnancy or breastfeeding of a worker, the employer must take the necessary measures to ensure that, by temporarily adjusting the working conditions and/or the working hours of the employee concerned, the exposure of that employee to such risks is avoided.[20] This also applies where there is an absolute prohibition on the woman working (article 6).

(a) *Preventive measures.* First, the employer must consider taking action under the relevant statutory provisions in order to avoid the risk. The main statutory provisions are set out in appendix 6.

(b) *Alteration of working conditions or hours of work.* The PWD article 5(1) provides that the employer must take the necessary measures to ensure that, by temporarily adjusting the working conditions and/or working hours of the work concerned, the exposure of that worker to such risks is avoided. This has been implemented by the 1994 Regulations which state that the employer shall, 'if it is reasonable to do so, and would avoid such risks, alter her working conditions or hours of work'.[21]

Reasonableness relates to whether it is reasonable for the woman; the alternative is suspension on full pay. Thus, it would not be reasonable to change the woman's hours to make it impossible for her to continue working.

If the woman's working conditions are adjusted, she should continue to receive the same pay and benefits.

(c) *Suitable alternative work.* If it is not possible to alter the woman's working conditions or hours of work the employer must offer the woman suitable alternative work where this is available.[22] The work must be:
- of a kind which is both suitable in relation to her and appropriate for her to do in the circumstances; and
- where the terms and conditions are not substantially less favourable to her than her existing terms and conditions.

Account should be taken of the following:
- status or grade;
- pay and other remuneration or payments in kind;
- working conditions, hours of work, location;
- travelling time to work.

20 PWD article 5.
21 MHSWR reg 13A(2).
22 ERA ss66, 67.

The woman's condition should be taken into account, so it may be unreasonable to expect her to travel further or work antisocial hours. To this extent at least the test may be different from the test applied in redundancy situations (see p109).

If a woman has been given alternative work, there is no reason why she should not continue doing this right up to the time of the birth (provided she does not have a pregnancy-related absence in the six weeks before the EWC).

If the woman refuses suitable alternative work, she will forfeit her right to be paid while she is suspended.[23]

(d) *Suspension*. If it is not possible to avoid the risk by altering working conditions or hours of work, and there is no suitable alternative work, the employer must suspend the employee from work for so long as is necessary to avoid the risk.[24]

An employee suspended on these grounds is entitled to be paid as though she was working (subject to her not having refused suitable alternative work).[25] She will be entitled to full pay until her maternity leave period begins (see p124).

Calculation of pay during suspension

This is calculated in accordance with ERA ss220ff. A week's pay is based on what the employee would have received if she had been working normally. The calculation date depends on when the suspension occurs. Where the day before the suspension is within the employee's maternity leave or absence period, it is the day before the beginning of the maternity leave period that is relevant. If the suspension take place at any other time, the relevant day is the day before the suspension.[26]

Other contractual terms and conditions should be maintained during the period of suspension.[27]

---

23 ERA s68.
24 ERA s64(2) defines suspension from work on medical grounds as being where an employee is suspended as a result of a relevant requirement or recommendation.
25 Her contractual rights are maintained.
26 ERA s225(5)(b).
27 The government spokesman said, during the debates on the Trades Union Reform and Employment Rights Act 1993, 'the employee's contract continues while she is suspended ... Her contractual rights are maintained. No special provision for that is required.' (Hansard (HC) Standing Committee F, 14.1.93, cols 430-431).

The woman should not have to go on sick leave and lose her pay if the reason for her absence is a health or safety risk. If she is only receiving SSP, this may affect her SMP entitlement (see p132).

Effect of suspension on commencement of maternity leave
Although the position is not entirely clear, it is likely that a woman who is suspended will be treated as absent on account of her pregnancy. She will therefore have to start her maternity leave at the beginning of the six weeks before the EWC (see p37). Her maternity pay period would start at the same time (see p38).

Special provisions relating to nightwork

If a pregnant woman or new mother doing nightwork obtains a certificate from her doctor or midwife stating that it is necessary for her health and safety to avoid such work, the employer must consider offering her suitable alternative work where it is available. If none is available she must be suspended on full pay.[28]

Compulsory leave after the birth

Requirement for minimum of two weeks
An employee who is entitled to maternity leave must not work within two weeks of the birth (see p67).

Prohibition on employment in factory or workshop
It is a criminal offence to allow a woman to work in a factory or workshop within four weeks of the birth (see p68).[29]

Breastfeeding
A woman cannot postpone her return to work because she is breastfeeding. Can the employer refuse to allow a woman to express milk at the office? One company told a woman not to return to work until she had finished breastfeeding. There is no power for an employer to delay a woman's return to work in these

---

28 The PWD has similar provisions. Article 5 states that if the risk cannot be avoided by preventive measures the employer must temporarily adjust the woman's working conditions or working hours. If this is not 'technically and/or objectively feasible or cannot reasonably be required on duly substantiated grounds', the employer must take the necessary measures to move the worker concerned to another job. Failing this, she must be granted leave for the whole of the period necessary to protect her safety or health.
29 Public Health Act 1936 s205 (as amended).

circumstances and a refusal to allow her to return may be unfair and discriminatory (see chapter 7). A refusal to allow a woman to express milk at work, where this does not substantially interfere with her work, may also be discriminatory. If a woman is dismissed as a result, the dismissal may be automatically unfair as it is connected to her pregnancy.

Remedies

Where the employer has failed to pay a woman during her suspension or failed to offer her suitable alternative work, she can complain to a tribunal.[30] The complaint must be lodged within three months from the first day the employer failed to pay her or within three months of the first day of the suspension. The time limit may be extended if it was not reasonably practicable for the complaint to be presented in time (see p214).

The tribunal can make an award of compensation which is 'just and equitable in all the circumstances' having regard to the infringement of the complaint's right by the employer's failure and to any loss attributable to that failure.[31]

If the employer fails to offer the woman available suitable alternative work and does not suspend her, a woman who is injured as a result can sue the employer.[32] If the woman is dismissed for refusing to work because of a health and safety risk, this may be automatically unfair (see p93 and below).

Failure to comply with MHSWR

Where there has been a breach of the regulations, the employee can complain to the Health and Safety Executive.

Civil proceedings

Any breach of a duty owed (under the regulations) to pregnant or breastfeeding women entitles a woman who has been injured to bring civil proceedings in the county court.[33] In addition, any breach should be taken into account in assessing the employer's duty of care.

30 ERA s70.
31 ERA s60.
32 MHSWR reg 15(2).
33 The general exclusion of civil liability does not apply to any duty imposed by the regulations on an employer to the extent that it relates to risks which specifically affect pregnant and breastfeeding women and new mothers (reg 15(2)).

Enforcement through civil proceedings is expensive, time-consuming and depends on the woman having suffered an injury. Arguably, it is an inadequate remedy under the directive, which requires member states to implement measures which enable workers who have suffered by a breach of the directive to pursue their claims by judicial process.[34]

Claiming unfair dismissal

Where a woman is dismissed for refusing to work because of a health and safety risk, this may be automatically unfair (see p91).

It is also automatically unfair to dismiss a woman because of a requirement or recommendation that she be suspended (see p91).[35]

A woman whose employer refuses to comply with the Regulations could resign and claim constructive dismissal. This is often unsatisfactory because the woman will lose her job and it is never possible to predict whether the tribunal will find that she was entitled to resign.

In an IT case, *Anderson v Belcher Food Products*,[36] the applicant, who was a meat packer, was asked to work in very cold temperatures but was moved when she protested because of her pregnancy. She was then told to do a job involving lifting heavy boxes. When she asked to be moved to another line she was told to go home. She took this as being a dismissal. She complained of unfair dismissal and sex discrimination. The IT held that she was dismissed either because she was pregnant or for reasons connected with her pregnancy, ie, her absences and her inability to work on the line which involved lifting heavy boxes. The dismissal was therefore automatically unfair and discriminatory. She could also claim it was automatically unfair because she was dismissed for enforcing health and safety provisions (see p93).

Discrimination

Under the SDA[37] an employer is permitted to discriminate against a woman where the act of discrimination was done in circumstances where it was necessary in order to comply with:

---

34 PWD article 12.
35 ERA s99(l)(d).
36 (1995) 9 August, Case No S/571/95; Glasgow IT. Note that each case will be decided on its own facts and tribunal decisions are not binding.
37 s51. See also Employment Act 1989 s4.

Health and safety

a) an existing statutory provision concerning the protection of women;[38] or
b) the requirement of a relevant statutory provision (within the Health and Safety at Work Act 1974 Part I)[39] and it was done in order to protect the woman;

where, in either case, the provision is necessary for the purpose of protecting women as regards:
- pregnancy or maternity, or
- other circumstances giving rise to risks specifically affecting women.

There is also an exemption from discrimination in the Employment Act 1989 s4. This exempts an act if it was necessary in order to comply with any requirement of any of the provisions specified in Sch 1.

There will, therefore, be no unlawful discrimination where the employer takes action under these provisions provided they are necessary in order to protect women. The appropriate action in respect of pregnant, breastfeeding women or new mothers is to alter working conditions, and, where possible, to consider alternative work and where neither of these are possible, to suspend the woman on full pay.

In *Page v Freight Hire (Tank Haulage) Ltd*[40] the applicant was told that she could not handle a dangerous chemical (DMP) because of the particular potential danger to women of childbearing age. The applicant complained saying that she was aware of and accepted the risks and did not intend to have a child. The EAT held that the company had taken the action in order to comply with the requirements of the Health and Safety at Work Act 1974 and was covered by the exemption under the SDA. There is no entitlement to suspension unless the woman is actually pregnant.

Equal Treatment Directive

The ETD provides that there shall be 'no discrimination whatsoever on grounds of sex ...' The directive, however, exempts 'provisions concerning the protection of women, particularly as regards pregnancy and maternity'. In *Habermann-Beltermann*[41] the appli-

---

38 This includes the Factories Act 1961, and the Offices, Shops and Railway Premises Act 1963.
39 This includes the prohibition on employing a woman in a factory within four weeks of the birth.
40 [1981] IRLR 13, EAT.
41 *Habermann-Beltermann v Arbeiterwohlfahrt, Bezirksverband Ndb/Opf eV* (case C-421/92) [1994] IRLR 364, ECJ.

cant was employed as a night worker. German law prohibited pregnant women working at night and as a result the applicant was dismissed. The European Court of Justice held that the termination of a contract (without a fixed term) on account of a woman's pregnancy cannot be justified on the ground that a statutory prohibition, imposed because of pregnancy, temporarily prevents the employee from performing night work. The court held that to allow an employer to dismiss a woman because of the temporary inability of the pregnant employee to perform night-time work would be contrary to the objective of protecting women.

HEALTH AND SAFETY: KEY POINTS

- Employers have general duties to protect the health and safety of workers, including the common law duty of care and a statutory duty under the Health and Safety at Work Act 1974.
- Employers have specific duties towards pregnant women and new and breastfeeding mothers which include a duty to carry out a risk assessment to assess the risks to the health and safety of a new or expectant mother or that of her baby. If the assessment reveals a risk the employer must:
  - consider whether preventive or protective action can be taken; and if this would not avoid the risk,
  - vary the woman's working conditions to avoid the risk; and if that is not possible,
  - offer the woman suitable alternative work; and if this is not possible,
  - suspend the woman on full pay for as long as necessary to avoid the risk.
- Employees must be informed of any risks.
- Where a pregnant woman or new mother doing nightwork obtains a medical certificate stating that she should avoid such work, the employer must offer suitable available work or suspend her on full pay.
- There is a compulsory period of two weeks' leave after the birth.
- Where an employer fails to offer a woman suitable alternative work, she can complain to a tribunal and the tribunal can award compensation; where a woman is not paid while

suspended, she can claim compensation from a tribunal.
- Where there has been a breach of the management regulations an employee can complain to the Health and Safety Executive.
- The SDA contains an exception relating to statutory provisions concerning the protection of women where the provision is necessary in order to protect women as regards pregnancy or maternity.
- It is automatically unfair and discriminatory to dismiss a woman in order to avoid complying with a health and safety requirement or recommendation or where the woman cannot continue working because of health and safety risks.

CHAPTER 9
Statutory maternity pay

Introduction

This chapter summarises the provisions relating to statutory maternity pay (SMP), including qualifying conditions, notice provisions, calculation method and timing of payment as well as administration by employers.

In the absence of a contractual right, a woman is not entitled to be paid her full salary while on maternity leave[1] (though she may have a claim under the Equal Pay Act if there is a more favourable contractual sick pay scheme, see p54). Whilst on maternity leave, she may be entitled to either SMP or maternity allowance (see chapter 10).

Before October 1994 there was a two-tier SMP system with different rates according to length of service. The system has been simplified so that all women who qualify for SMP now get the same amount, ie, 90 per cent of earnings for the first six weeks and £54.55 per week for the following twelve weeks.[2]

Appendix 7 sets out the SMP tables.

Pregnant Workers Directive

The Pregnant Workers Directive provides that a woman must receive her full pay or be guaranteed an 'adequate allowance'.[3] Under the directive the allowance is deemed adequate if it is at least equal to the amount an employee would receive if off work because of sickness.[4] No mention is made as to whether this is

1 *Gillespie v Northern Health and Social Services Board* [1996] IRLR 214, ECJ.
2 The £54.55 is based on the higher rate of statutory sick pay. The figures increase every year.
3 Article 11(2)(b).
4 Article 11(3).

statutory or contractual sick pay. SMP has been pegged to statutory sick pay. However, it is arguable that if a woman would receive more under a contractual sick pay scheme she should receive this higher amount.

The legislation

The Social Security Contributions and Benefits Act 1992 (SSCBA) and the Statutory Maternity Pay (General) Regulations 1986 SI No 1960 (as amended) (SMP Regs) set out the main provisions.

Eligibility for statutory maternity pay (SMP)

Although SMP is only paid to employees earning more than the lower earnings limit (in the relevant period), it is not a contributory benefit. A woman who does not normally pay national insurance contributions will still be entitled to SMP.

The qualifying conditions for SMP are that the woman must:
a) be an employee or hold an elective office (see p132);
b) have been earning at least the lower earnings limit for national insurance (£61 per week for 1996/97) for the eight weeks or two months immediately before and including the qualifying week;[5]
c) not fall within one of the exceptions (see p136);
d) have 26 weeks continuous service at the qualifying week; the woman must have worked for one day of the qualifying week (see p137);
e) be pregnant and have reached the 11th week before the expected week of childbirth; SMP is not payable before the 11th week unless the baby is born before (see p142);
f) produce medical evidence (see p142);
g) give the required notice to her employer (see p142); and
h) have stopped working (see p143).
Note that:
– SMP is payable by the employer even if the woman does not intend to return to work after the birth and irrespective of whether the contract subsists during the SMP period;
– if the woman resigns, she does not have to repay her SMP;
– if a woman has more than one employer, each must pay her SMP if she qualifies;
– there is no requirement for the woman to be working for a

5 The qualifying week is the 15th week before the expected week of childbirth.

minimum number of hours per week; but the lower earnings limit excludes many part-time women;
- no employers are exempt from paying SMP: small employers must also pay SMP (including private families employing nannies, cleaners etc).
- a week begins on a Sunday.

Stillbirths
Where the woman has a stillbirth after 24 weeks of pregnancy she is still entitled to SMP. If she miscarries earlier than this, SMP is not payable, but she may be entitled to SSP or incapacity benefit.

a) The woman must be an employee[6]
This means that:
- she must be over 16;
- she must be employed under a contract of service or in an office (including elective office).[7] Elective office holders include directors of companies. A women employed under a contract of apprenticeship is entitled to SMP.

Agency workers and seasonal/temporary workers. Provided the worker is an employee of the agency, she will be entitled to SMP from the agency (see p138). Women who have regular work for the same employer may be entitled to SMP (see p139).

Crown employees. Women employed by or under the Crown are entitled to SMP.[8]

b) The woman must be earning not less than the lower earnings limit
The calculation of pay is based on actual gross pay, including overtime, bonuses, sick pay etc. What constitutes pay is dealt with in more detail on p147. It does not matter if pay falls below the lower earnings limit in any one week provided the average pay does not fall below it.

Weekly paid employees. If the woman is paid weekly, she must have been earning (in the eight weeks up to and including the last pay day before the end of the qualifying week) on average enough

6 The DSS Guidance says an employee is a person who pays or is liable to pay Class 1 NI contributions. See SSCBA s171(1) and SMP Regs reg 17.
7 People holding an office would include magistrates, justices of the peace and judges.
8 SSCBA s169; Social Security Act 1990 Sch 6 para 25.

Statutory maternity pay

to pay Class 1 NI contributions – £61 per week for the year 1996/97. The woman's normal weekly earnings are calculated by adding together the pay received for the eight pay days before the end of the qualifying week and dividing by 8. If the woman has been off sick and on SSP, this will count as earnings. However, it may mean that her earnings fall below the lower earnings limit in the relevant period thus making her ineligible for SMP.[9]

For example, if the EWC is 22 December 1996 (the baby being due on 24 December), the qualifying week (QW) is the week commencing 8 September 1996. If the woman is paid every Friday, the relevant paydays will be 13 September and the seven previous Fridays. If the woman was sick during the week of 1 September and so received only £54.55 for this week, but in all other weeks received £63, she will qualify for SMP because her earnings average over £61 per week.

Where the woman's contract specifies a day on which she is paid, the eight-week period runs from the last pay day before the end of the qualifying week.[10] If there is no contractual pay day, the eight-week period runs from the day on which she is normally paid. If there is no 'normal pay day', the period is calculated from the last date the woman was actually paid (before the end of the qualifying week).

Monthly paid employees. If the woman is paid once every month, the average weekly earnings are calculated by:
- adding the gross payments made on the last normal payday falling before the end of the qualifying week and adding any other payments made after (but not including) the last payday which was at least eight weeks before; this will therefore include the last two pay cheques and any other payments in this period;
- multiplying the total by 6 – which gives annual earnings;
- dividing by 52 – to give average weekly earnings.

For example, if the EWC begins on 23 March 1997, the qualifying week will be the week commencing 8 December 1996. If the woman is paid on the last day of each month, the last payday before the end of the qualifying week is 30 November. The payday at least eight weeks before that is 30 September. The intervening payday is 31 October. The calculation is based on the pay received for the two paydays of 30 November and 31 October and any other payments received *after* 30 September.

---

9 This will be the case even though her earnings are usually above the limit.
10 SMP Regs reg 21(2)(3).

Any payments made after 30 November and before the end of the qualifying week are not taken into account. Thus, if the woman received
- £310 on 30 November 1996 and
- £320 on 31 October 1996 and
- a bonus of £250 on 10 October 1996,

her average weekly earnings are £101.54 per week (ie, £880 x 6 divided by 52).

Where payments are made in multiples of a week. Where a woman is paid every month but the calculation is based on a weekly rate, the average weekly earnings are calculated by:
- adding together the gross payments made on the last normal payday before the end of the qualifying week and any other payments made after the payday at least eight weeks before that and
- dividing the total by the number of weeks covered by the payments.

Other forms of payment. Where the woman is paid at other intervals, the employer must:
- add together payments made on the last payday before the end of the qualifying week together with any other payments received since the last pay day to fall at least eight weeks before that pay day;[11]
- divide the total by the number of days the period covers and
- multiply by 7.

This would apply if a woman is paid according to the hours worked, and these varied from week to week. For example, if her EWC is 1 June 1997, the qualifying week would commence on 16 February 1997. If she is paid £300 on 21 February 1997, £400 on 17 January and £200 on 20 December 1996, the relevant period will be 21 December to 21 February inclusive (ie, 63 days). The payment on 20 December does not count, as it is the last payday which was at least eight weeks before. The average weekly earnings are £700 divided by 63, multiplied by 7, ie, £77.78.[11A]

Where the baby is born before the end of the qualifying week. The calculation period will be the eight weeks or two months ending with the last complete week before the week in which the baby is born.

11 This period may well be considerably longer than eight weeks if the gap between payments is longer than one month.
11A SMP Regs reg 4(3).

Statutory maternity pay

Where the woman has more than one contract for the same employer. The employer must usually treat the contracts as one contract for the purpose of SMP. The woman's earnings under both contracts are added together in order to calculate pay.[12] There is an exception where it is not reasonably practicable to aggregate the earnings for the purposes of national insurance contributions. In such a case SMP is payable separately under each contract, but the woman has to earn more than the £61 per week under each contract.[13] The contracts may also be aggregated where the woman works for different but associated employers.

Where, as a result of the establishment of a National Health Service Trust, the woman is treated as having two contracts, she can choose that they be treated as one for the purposes of SMP.[14]

Working for more than one employer. The contracts will not be aggregated where the woman works for two employers. If the woman's earnings are below the lower earnings limit in each employment, she will not be entitled to SMP. If she satisfies the qualifying conditions in each job (including earning above the lower earnings limit), she will be entitled to SMP from both employers.[15]

It is the lower earnings limit in force immediately before the end of the qualifying week which counts.

Lower earnings limit unlawful? It is arguable that making SMP dependent on earning more than the lower earnings limit is a breach of the PWD. There are no exceptions permitted in the PWD; it applies to all pregnant workers. Although article 11(4) says that member states may make entitlement to an allowance conditional on the worker fulfilling conditions of eligibility, arguably this applies to notice provisions and does not allow the exclusion of categories of pregnant workers.

In *Gillespie* (n1 above), the ECJ held that the amount of maternity pay could not be 'so low as to undermine the purpose of maternity leave, namely the protection of women before and after giving birth. In order to assess the adequacy of the amount

---

12 SMP Regs reg 5.
13 Social Security (Contributions) Regulations 1979 SI No 591 reg 11 provides that there will not be aggregation where aggregation is not reasonably practicable because the earnings in the respective employments are separately calculated.
14 The SMP (National Health Service Employees) Regulations 1991 SI No 590.
15 SSCBA s164(3).

payable from that point of view, the national court must take account, not only of the length of maternity leave, but also of the other forms of social protection afforded by national law in the case of justified absence from work.' It is arguable that the exclusion of women earning less than the lower earnings limit *does* undermine maternity leave, as women may feel unable to afford to take leave.

The exclusion of employees earning less than the lower earnings limit from SSP may be indirect discrimination and a breach of article 119 EEC. The vast majority of workers earning below this limit are women. The question is whether the requirement (to be earning at least the lower earnings limit) is justifiable (see p194).

As the PWD provides that maternity pay should not be less than what an employee would receive if off work sick, it is arguable that if the woman would have been entitled to SMP using the SSP calculation period (ie, the 8 weeks immediately before the sickness), she should also receive SMP.

c) Exemptions

The woman must not fall within one of the exceptions:
- a foreign-going mariner employed by a UK employer who pays a special rate of NI contributions;[16]
- employed by a foreign organisation where the employer is not resident or present in Great Britain or does not have a place of business in Great Britain, thus not being liable to pay NI contributions;[17]
- detained in custody or sentenced to imprisonment; this includes detention in prison or a police station, but does not include a suspended sentence. SMP ceases in the week she is detained but does not resume when she is released.

Employees whose EWC begins on 18 August 1996 or later can receive SMP even if they work or go outside the European Economic Area during their MPP.[17A] Before this date they were excluded if they went outside the EEA during their MPP.

---

16 SSCBA s170 and SMP (Persons Abroad and Mariners) Regulations 1987 SI No 418.
17 SMP Regs reg 17(3) and Social Security (Contributions) Regulations 1979 SI No 591 (as amended) reg 119(1)(b).
17A Social Security Contributions, SMP and SSP (Miscellaneous Amendments) Regulations 1996 SI No 777.

d) 26 weeks' continuous service at the QW

The woman must have 26 weeks' continuous service at the qualifying week.

The relevant 'weeks'. The woman must have 26 weeks' continuous service (with the same employer) up until and for at least one day of the qualifying week (ie, the 15th week before the EWC).[18] If the woman started in the 26th week before the EWC, she need only have worked part of that week.[19]

For example, if the baby is due on 4 February 1997, the EWC is the week beginning 2 February. The qualifying week is the week beginning 20 October. Counting back 26 weeks (including the qualifying week) to 28 April 1996, the woman must have been employed for at least one day during the week beginning 28 April, so the latest start date is 4 May 1996. She must still be employed for at least one day during the week beginning 20 October.

Continuous employment. There must have been a contract in existence for the whole period. The contract may be deemed to continue even where the employee is not working.[20] In *Secretary of State for Employment v Doulton Sanitaryware Ltd*[21] the employee left to have a baby and the employers put her on list of 'prolonged absentees'. The EAT held that the contract continued.

However, even where there is no contract in existence, employment will be deemed to be continuous in some circumstances where the woman has left work and then returned to work with the same employer. The rules are similar to those used for calculating an employee's period of continuous employment under ERA ss212ff. The following breaks in the relevant period (ie, the 26 weeks) do not count:
- up to 26 weeks' absence due to sickness or injury;[22]
- where there is a temporary cessation of work because the employer was unable to offer the employee work;[23]
- absence from work in circumstances such that, by arrangement or custom, the woman is regarded as continuing in employment

---

18 SMP Regs reg 11(4).
19 SMP Regs reg 16A.
20 *Satchwell Sunvic Ltd v Secretary of State for Employment* [1979] IRLR 455, EAT.
21 [1981] ICR 477, EAT.
22 SMP Regs reg 11(1)(a).
23 reg 11(1)(b).

(eg, a public holiday or annual shutdown);[24] thus, if the employee worked before and after a week with a public holiday (such as Christmas), that week is treated as a week of employment;
- up to 26 weeks' absence due wholly or partly to pregnancy or childbirth where there is a contract with the same employer before and after the absence;[25]
- absence due to pregnancy or childbirth where the woman exercises her statutory right to return to the same job or suitable alternative work.

In the above situations the woman must return to work for her employer after the absence and before the commencement of maternity leave, otherwise continuity will not be preserved.[26] However, if there was a contract in existence during the absence, the problem does not arise.

Agency workers. Agency workers, like other employees, must have been working for the agency for a continuous period of 26 weeks up to and into the qualifying week. Any periods of interruption in the list above will count towards continuous employment. Thus, if a woman has up to 26 weeks off sick, she will still be treated as continuously employed. If some work was done during any week, it counts as a full week. Continuity is not broken where:
- the agency had no work for the woman in any particular week; or
- the agency offered her work but the woman could not take it because of sickness, injury or pregnancy; if she decided not to accept the work for any other reason, continuity would be broken.

No employment in the qualifying week for agency worker. If there is no work in the qualifying week, the woman can be treated as employed if:

- she was not intending to start her leave at that time and was available for work after the qualifying week, and
- she returns to work for the agency before taking maternity leave.[27]

If she stopped working before the qualifying week because of sickness (but had intended to continue working), she will be treated as working into the qualifying week (and thus be eligible

24 reg 11(1)(c).
25 This is in addition to the maternity leave period where the contract subsists; thus, the whole of the leave/absence period will count towards continuous employment; see reg 11(1) and (3).
26 reg 11(1).
27 see DSS Manual NI 257/1994.

Statutory maternity pay 139

for SMP), but only if she starts work for the agency within 26 weeks. Thus, no decision can be made about entitlement to SMP until after she has returned to work, or registered with the agency.

Where the woman has stopped working for the agency before the qualifying week, she will not be entitled to SMP.

Seasonal workers. There are special rules for seasonal workers which are similar to those for agency workers. A pregnant employee who works spasmodically for fixed periods (such as a supply teacher) may qualify for SMP.

A seasonal or regular temporary worker who is absent because of her pregnancy or is otherwise sick throughout the qualifying week is not required to return to work afterwards. She can be treated as having worked into the qualifying week even though she does not return to work.[28] She must comply with the other conditions, including the earnings rule.

A seasonal worker is one where it is the employer's practice;
- to offer work for a fixed period of not more than 26 consecutive weeks, and
- to offer such work for two or more times a year for periods which do not overlap, and
- to offer the work to the same people.[29]

The requirements to give notice and provide medical evidence apply to seasonal and agency workers.

Birth before qualifying week. Where the baby is born in or before the qualifying week the woman will be entitled to SMP if she would have been employed for 26 weeks by the end of the qualifying week, had the baby not been born early. Thus, if the EWC is 6 to 12 April 1997, the qualifying week commences on 22 December 1996. The woman intended to stop work on 3 March but the baby was born on 10 December. If the woman started work for her employer on or after 6 July 1996, she will qualify.

She must have earned not less than the lower earnings limit in the eight weeks or two months immediately preceding the week of the birth (see pp132ff).[30]

Industrial action and stoppage of work. Where a woman takes part in a strike, the day or week when she does not work will not break her continuity of employment. However, the whole of the

28 SMP Regs reg 11(3A).
29 reg 11(3A).
30 SMP Regs reg 4(2).

week (even if she was on strike for only one day) will be disregarded when working out whether she has worked for 26 weeks.[31] This does not apply if the woman can prove that at no time did she have a direct interest in the trade dispute.[32] Continous employment is not broken by a lockout.

If the woman is dismissed during a stoppage of work, her continuity of employment ceases on the day she stopped work, unless she can prove that at no time did she have a direct interest in the trade dispute.[33]

Lockout. Days when an employee is locked out count towards the 26 weeks' employment.

Return from the armed forces. If a woman returns to her former employer after a period in the armed forces, her previous employment with the former employer will count provided the break is no more than six months.[34]

Dismissal resulting in termination of contract before QW. If a woman is dismissed and her contract terminated before the 15th week (taking account of the notice period during which the contract subsists) she will not satisfy the qualifying conditions. If the dismissal is pregnancy-related she may have a claim for automatically unfair dismissal under the ERA (see p91).

Termination of contract in order to avoid liability for SMP. If the employer terminates the woman's contract in order to avoid liability for SMP, the employer will still be liable to pay SMP if the woman was employed by her/him for a continuous period of at least 8 weeks. The woman will be deemed to have been employed by her/him from the date her employment ended until the end of the qualifying week on the same terms and conditions as those subsisting immediately before her employment ended. Her earnings are calculated by reference to what she was earning in the eight weeks before her contract was terminated.[35]

A woman employed for less than eight weeks who is dismissed by the employer because of his/her liability for SMP will have a claim for unfair dismissal under ERA s99 and for discrimination; she will not have a claim for SMP as such.

31 reg 13(1).
32 reg 13(3).
33 reg 13(2).
34 reg 15.
35 SMP Regs reg 3.

Ordinary unfair dismissal. Where the dismissal is clearly not related to the woman's pregnancy, she will not be able to make a claim under ERA s99. The dismissal may nevertheless be an ordinary unfair dismissal; if it is, the compensation awarded should reflect the loss of SMP.

Reinstatement or re-engagement. Where there has been an order for re-engagement or re-instatement,[36] continuity of employment will be maintained for all weeks between the date the contract was terminated and the date of reinstatement or re-engagement.[37]

Fair dismissal. If the dismissal was fair and not related to pregnancy (for example, if the employee was found to have been dishonest), there will be no entitlement to SMP where the contract has been terminated before the qualifying week.

Termination of contract after qualifying week. Where, for a reason unconnected with pregnancy, a woman is dismissed or leaves her job after the qualifying week (having satisfied the qualifying conditions) she will still be entitled to SMP. SMP Regs reg 23(4) provides that a woman need not comply with the SMP notice provisions where, for a reason wholly unconnected with her pregnancy, she leaves her employment after the qualifying week. This is also the advice given by the DTI.[38]

Insolvency of employer. If the employer has been declared bankrupt, has made a composition or arrangement with his/her creditors, has died or the company has been wound up, the Secretary of State is liable to pay SMP instead of the employer. An adjudicating authority must first determine that the employer is liable to pay SMP and the period for any appeal must have expired (with no appeal having been lodged) or the appeal must have been resolved in the woman's favour.[39]

Transfer of the undertaking. Where the business has been taken over by another employer and this is a transfer of the undertaking,[40] continuity of employment will not be broken. Account must be taken of her continuous employment with the former employer.

36 This includes a compromise agreement or agreement reached with the help of ACAS.
37 SMP Regs reg 12.
38 *Maternity Rights: A guide for employers and employees* (PL958 (Rev1)).
39 SMP Regs reg 7.
40 As defined by TUPE; see reg 14.

Other transfers. Continuity of employment may also be preserved if there are other transfers, such as
- under a statute,
- on the death of the employer, where the personal representatives take over,
- where a teacher moves from one school to another in the same local education authority, or
- where the employee moves to an associated employer.[41]

Suspension for health and safety reasons. A woman who has been suspended for health and safety reasons will be treated as still working.

e) Pregnant at the 11th week

The woman must have reached the 11th week before the EWC or have given birth. She need not be 'employed' until the 11th week; but SMP is not payable before then (unless the baby has been born).

f) Medical evidence

The woman must produce medical evidence (usually a maternity certificate, form MATB1) showing the expected week of childbirth. The form must be signed by a doctor or midwife not earlier than 14 weeks before the week the baby is due. The MATB1 must be given to the employer by the end of the third week of the maternity pay period or, if the woman has a good reason for not providing the evidence earlier, by no later than the end of the 13th week of the maternity pay period (as defined on p144).

If the baby is premature, the woman will also need to provide evidence of the week the baby was born; this will be necessary so that the employer knows when SMP first becomes payable.[42]

g) Notice requirements

The woman must give 21 *clear* days' notice of the date that she intends to stop work because she is pregnant. The notice need not be in writing unless the employer requests it to be. If it is not practicable to give 21 days' notice, because, for example, the baby is born earlier, the woman must give as much notice as possible.[43]

---

41 TUPE reg 14.
42 SMP Regs reg 22(1).
43 SSCBA s164(4)(b).

SMP may be refused if 21 days' notice is not given. If this happens, the woman is entitled to a written statement giving reasons.

Where the woman gives birth before the date given in the notice. The woman must give further notice to her employer stating the date the baby was born and that this is the reason for her absence.[44] This notice must be given within 21 days of childbirth or, if this is not practicable, as soon as practicable. The notice must be in writing if the employer so requests.

Where the baby is born before the qualifying week. The woman must give the employer notice that her absence from work is because of childbirth. Notice must be given within 21 days of the birth or, if that is not practicable (because, for example, she is ill), as soon as reasonably practicable. The notice must be in writing if the employer asks for it to be.[45]

Where the birth is premature, notice contained in a properly addressed and stamped envelope is deemed to be given on the day it was posted – not when it arrives.[46]

Where the woman leaves her job after the qualifying week for a reason unconnected with her pregnancy she does not have to give notice[47] unless she has the baby before the 11th week before the EWC, in which case she must give her employer notice within 21 days specifying the date of the birth. The woman must still provide medical evidence (see p142).

If the woman fails to give 21 days' notice of her leave (and she is not exempt because of premature birth) it is for the employer to decide if it was reasonably practicable for her to have given the full notice. If the employer decides it was reasonably practicable to give 21 days notice, s/he need not pay SMP. The woman is entitled to a written statement of his/her reasons and she may refer the dispute to a DSS adjudication officer (see p149).

b) **The woman must have stopped working**
SMP is not payable until the woman has stopped working.

---

44 SMP Regs reg 23(1).
45 reg 23(1).
46 reg 23(3).
47 reg 23(4).

The maternity pay period

SMP is payable for a maximum of 18 consecutive weeks.[48]

Beginning of maternity pay period (MPP)

The woman must give 21 clear days' notice of the date she intends to stop work, unless this is not possible because the baby is premature (see p33). The MPP cannot start before the 11th week before the expected week of confinement, unless the baby is born before the 11th week. Otherwise the woman can choose when it starts (unless she is forced on to SMP because of a pregnancy-related absence in the six weeks before the EWC). The woman will no longer lose SMP if she works after the sixth week before the EWC. The MPP must start at the beginning of a week, ie, on a Sunday.

SMP usually starts on the Sunday *after* the woman stops working (or gives birth), including the situation:

a) where the woman gives her employer notice that she intends to stop work and does stop work in that week;[49]
b) where she gives birth before the 11th week[50] (this will be before the date notified to the employer – as this cannot be before the 11th week);
c) where she gives birth between the 11th and 6th week before the EWC and before the week she notified to the employer that she intended to give up working;[51]
d) where she is absent because of her pregnancy during the six weeks before the EWC but has either done some work for the employer that week or has been entitled to SSP from her employer in that week.[52]

For example, if a woman, with an EWC of 18 May 1997, has a pregnancy-related absence (which could include childbirth) after the 6th week before the EWC (ie, the week beginning 6 April) and has worked or claimed SSP that week, her SMP will start the following Sunday. So if she is sick (because of her pregnancy) between 8 to 11 April 1997 (ie, the Tuesday to Friday), her MPP will start on 13 April 1997. She will be entitled to SSP for the period 8 to 11 April subject to complying with the qualifying conditions.

48 reg 2(2).
49 reg 2(1).
50 reg 2(3)(a).
51 reg 2(3)(b).
52 reg 2(5).

Statutory maternity pay

However, where the woman stops working because of a pregnancy-related absence during the six weeks before the EWC and she has not worked for her employer for that week nor been entitled to SSP, the MPP starts at the beginning of the week.[53] Thus, if the woman is absent with a pregnancy-related sickness on Monday 7 April (using the above example), her MPP would start on the previous Sunday, 6 April.

These rules only apply to pregnancy-related absence. Other sickness does not trigger the start of the MPP and the woman can choose when her SMP period starts.

The latest the MPP can start is the week following the week in which the baby was born. Thus, if the woman works until the birth, and the baby is born on a Tuesday, SMP is payable from the following Sunday. SSP is not payable in the intervening period, so the woman will have to rely on savings or means-tested benefits.

Where employment ends after qualifying week

If the employee leaves after the qualifying week, SMP will be payable on whichever date is the later of:
- the 11th week before the EWC; or
- the start of the week after employment ends.

End of maternity pay period

The MPP lasts for 18 weeks. A woman who is only entitled to 14 weeks' maternity leave will therefore lose out on 4 weeks SMP, unless she chooses not to return to work at all or her leave is extended because of a late birth or sickness during the four weeks immediately after the end of the 14 weeks (in which case she will receive SMP and not SSP).

Sickness during maternity pay period

If a woman is sick between the 11th week and the EWC, she can claim statutory sick pay, providing she is not getting SMP. The only exception is where it is a pregnancy-related sickness occurring in the six weeks before the EWC, when she will automatically be transferred on to SMP and will not be entitled to SSP (see p144).

It will often be difficult to judge whether the sickness is pregnancy-related. The Benefits Agency Medical Services has produced guidance[54] which divides diagnoses into three categories:

---

53 reg 2(4).
54 Available from local Contributions Agency offices.

a) pregnancy-related conditions;
b) conditions where it is reasonable to accept that pregnancy is not a significant contribution to the absence;
c) where it is not clear if the condition is due to pregnancy.

Where a woman is unable to work in the four-week period after her MLP, she may be entitled to contractual sick pay.

Working in the maternity pay period

SMP is not payable for any week where, during any part of that week, the woman works for the employer liable to pay SMP.[55]

If a woman continues to work after the MPP has started, she will lose SMP, at the lower rate first, for every week she works. The MPP will not be extended to compensate for the weeks in which the woman has worked. She will lose SMP for the whole week even if she only works for a few hours during the week. Thus, if a woman starts her MPP in the 11th week before the EWC and is absent from work during that week, but works for part of the following week, she will lose one week's SMP. If she were, unusually, to work for 13 weeks (because the baby was born late), she would lose 12 weeks at the lower rate and 1 week at the higher rate.

Working for another employer

If a woman works for an employer not liable to pay SMP before the baby is born, it does not affect her entitlement to SMP from any other employer who is liable to pay. If the woman works for another employer after the birth and during the MPP, her entitlement to SMP ceases from the week she starts work, *unless* she was working for that employer in the qualifying week and the employer is not liable to pay SMP.[56] She must, within 7 days of starting work, inform the employer who is paying her SMP.[57]

Calculation of maternity pay

90 per cent of full pay is paid during the first six weeks. This is based on the pay during the eight weeks or two months ending with the qualifying week (see pp132ff) (ie, the same period as used for assessing whether the woman's earnings are above the lower

---

55 SSCBA s165(4).
56 SSCBA s165(6) and SMP Regs reg 8.
57 SMP Regs reg 24.

Statutory maternity pay

earnings limit). There is no upper limit on pay for assessing SMP.

Pay

Pay is defined as earnings on which national insurance contributions are payable. The gross figure is used. It includes:
- gross earnings;
- any profit from the woman's employment in the eighth week period, including bonuses or overtime;[58]
- contractual sick pay or payments for injury;[59]
- statutory sick pay;[60]
- arrears of pay under an order for reinstatement or re-engagement;[61]
- pay which is paid under an order under ERA for the continuation of a contract of employment;
- pay in pursuance of a protective award.

Pay does not include:
- payments on account;[62]
- holiday payments, where the sum is from a fund to which more than one employer pays;[63]
- tips and gratuities paid directly to the employee;[64]
- payments in kind or board or lodging or other services or facilities;[65]
- pension payments;[66]
- fees to a minister of religion which are not part of her salary or stipend;[67]
- travelling expenses for disabled women under Disabled Persons (Employment) Act 1944 s15;[68]
- payments from profit-sharing schemes;[69]
- sick pay derived from contributions made by the woman into a sickness fund;[70]

---

58 reg 20(2). A bonus paid during the eight-week period will be included even if it relates to earnings over a longer period.
59 reg 19(b).
60 reg 20(4)(d).
61 reg 20(4)(a).
62 reg 20(2)(a).
63 reg 20(2)(b).
64 reg 19 and Social Security (Contributions) Regulations 1979 reg 19B.
65 reg 20(2)(d).
66 reg 20(2)(f).
67 reg 20(2)(g).
68 reg 20(2)(h).
69 reg 20(2)(i).
70 reg 20(3).

- redundancy payments;[71]
- payments or contributions to a woman's expenses for the purpose of her carrying out her employment.[72]

Pay rise after qualifying week

In *Gillespie* (n1 above), the ECJ held that a woman on maternity leave should receive the benefit of any pay rise which occurred after the period used to calculate maternity pay (ie, the qualifying week for SMP) and before the end of paid maternity leave.[73] As from 12 June 1996 new regulations provide that if there is a pay rise backdated to the qualifying period, the earnings-related part of the employee's SMP must be increased to reflect this increase.[74] This does not include a pay rise which only applies to a period after the qualifying week. It is likely, therefore that the UK law is still in breach of article 119, which requires any pay rise effective from the qualifying week up to the end of the earnings-related SMP period to be taken into account and reflected in maternity pay.

Where a woman is receiving maternity allowance (because she earns less than the lower earnings limit in the relevant period) but, as a result of a backdated pay increase, she becomes entitled to SMP, the employer need only make up the difference (between maternity allowance and SMP payable).

How SMP is paid

SMP is usually paid in the same way as contractual pay.[75] It is rounded up to the nearest penny.[76] Tax and national insurance contributions are payable on SMP. However, If the woman is only receiving £54.55 (which is the lower rate of SMP), she will not be liable to pay national insurance contributions, as these are not payable on earnings under £61 per week. She should write to the local Benefits Agency office and ask for national insurance credits

---

71 reg 20(6)(a).
72 reg 20(6)(b).
73 It would only apply where the rise took place while the woman was receiving earnings-related pay.
74 Statutory Maternity Pay (General) Amendment Regulations 1996 SI No 1335.
75 SMP Regs reg 27.
76 reg 28.

Statutory maternity pay   149

for the maternity pay period. This is important in order to protect her future entitlement to benefits and old age pension. She may also be entitled to a tax rebate and should contact the Inland Revenue.

Overlap with contractual maternity pay

The employer is not obliged to pay both contractual maternity pay and SMP. SMP will usually be offset against contractual maternity pay. However, if in any week the SMP exceeds contractual maternity pay, then the difference must be paid.[77]

Refusal of the employer to pay SMP

The woman should first ask the employer for the reasons why s/he will not pay. An employer who refuses to pay SMP must give the employee written reasons in the form SMP1. A woman who disagrees with this decision can then ask the adjudication officer at the local Benefits Agency office to review the decision.[78] If an order is made against the employer and s/he still fails to pay and does not appeal, the Secretary of State will pay.[79] There is a further right of appeal to the Social Security Appeals Tribunal.[80]

Employer's insolvency

If the employer becomes insolvent, the woman should contact the Benefits Agency, which will become responsible from the date of the insolvency.

No contracting out of the SMP scheme

Any agreement between an employer and employee to exclude, limit or modify the statutory provisions relating to SMP or to require an employee to contribute to the costs is void. Deductions may be made from SMP where the employer is authorised to make deductions from the contractual pay.

Effect on other benefits

SSP and SMP are mutually exclusive. An employee who is entitled

---

77 SSCBA s13 and Sch 3 paras 1 and 2.
78 Both parties will be asked for written observations and supporting evidence.
79 SMP Regs reg 7.
80 There is a further appeal on a point of law to a Social Security Commissioner. On appeals procedure see *Rights Guide to Non-Means-Tested Benefits*, Child Poverty Action Group, annual.

to SMP cannot get SSP for 18 weeks from the beginning of the SMP period. Nor can the woman get SSP for the same period if she is entitled to maternity allowance.

Where the woman is not entitled to SMP or MA, she cannot get SSP for 18 weeks starting with the earlier of:
- the date of the birth, or
- the start of the sixth week before the EWC if she is by then absent because of her pregnancy.

SMP is not income for the purposes of calculating family credit but it is counted in full for income support. SMP has no effect on guardian's allowance, disability living allowance or widow's benefits.

Administration of SMP by employers

The employer must keep, for three years after the end of the tax year in which the MPP ends, a record of:
a) the notified date of absence (because of pregnancy or confinement) and, if different from the actual date she was first absent, the date of her first absence;
b) the weeks in which SMP was paid (in each tax year) and the amount paid each week; and
c) any week within the woman's maternity pay period when no SMP was paid and the reasons no payments were made.[81]

The employer must also keep for three years any medical certificate or other evidence relating to the EWC or the childbirth. Where the woman needs the medical certificate back, the employer should keep a copy[82] and the employer should only keep a copy of the birth certificate, not the original.

There are standard forms (available from the local Contributions Agency office) for SMP purposes:
- *SMP1:* this must be sent to an employee employed in the qualifying week but who is not eligible for SMP;
- *SMP2:* this is a record sheet designed to help small businesses operate the scheme;
- *SMP3:* this provides information about how to pay, record and recover SMP.

---

81 SMP Regs reg 26(1).
82 reg 26(3).

Statutory maternity pay 151

Recovery of SMP by employers

All employers can recover payments of SMP by making a deduction from their national insurance contributions. There is a different rate of recovery according to the size of the employer.

Small employers

Where the employer's NI and tax contributions payments for the previous tax year do not exceed £20,000, the employer can deduct 100 per cent of the gross SMP paid to employees. S/he can also deduct an additional 5.5 per cent of the total gross SMP paid.[83]

Other employers

All other employers can recover 92 per cent of the total gross SMP they have paid in the tax month by deducting it from their NI contributions and tax.[84]

STATUTORY MATERNITY PAY: KEY POINTS

- Women are not entitled to full pay during maternity leave unless the contract provides for it.
- An employed woman will be entitled to SMP where she:
  - has been earning at least the lower earnings limit for national insurance (£61 per week for the year 1996/97) during the 8 weeks (or 2 months) before the end of the qualifying week;
  - has 26 weeks' continuous service into the qualifying week;
  - is pregnant (or has given birth) at the 11th week before the EWC; she need only be employed up until the week qualifying before the EWC;
  - has given 21 clear days' notice to the employer of the date she intends to stop working and has produced the required medical evidence (usually a MAT B1);
  - has stopped working; and
  - does not come within the limited exemptions.
- SMP is payable even if the woman does not intend to return to work after the birth. It is not repayable.
- There is no requirement that the woman must have been

---

83 SMP (Compensation of Employers) and Miscellaneous Amendment Regulations 1994 SI No 1882. This is to compensate small employers for the employers' NI contributions on SMP.
84 SMP (Compensation of Employers) and Miscellaneous Amendment Regulations 1994 SI No 1882.

working a minimum number of hours per week.
- No employers are exempt from paying SMP.
- Where an employer dismisses a woman to avoid paying her SMP, she will be deemed to have been employed until the end of the qualifying week and the employer will have to pay SMP.
- The woman can choose when SMP is payable except that:
  - it cannot be paid before the 11th week, unless the baby is born before then;
  - it is not payable while she is still working;
  - if she has a pregnancy related absence in the 6 weeks before the EWC her SMP will start the following Sunday (or in some circumstances, the previous Sunday);
  - if the baby is premature, SMP will be paid from the following week.
- Where a woman is off sick at any time during pregnancy but before her MPP starts, she will be entitled to SSP and any contractual sick pay provided the sickness is not pregnancy-related.
- SMP is 90 per cent of full pay for the first six weeks and £54.55 for the following 12 weeks; there are detailed provisions for the calculation of pay.
- SMP is paid in the same way as wages and tax and national insurance are payable.
- SMP will usually be offset against contractual maternity pay.
- Where an employer refuses to pay SMP, the woman should ask for reasons. The employer should provide her with a form SMP 1; if she is dissatisfied she can ask the adjudication officer to review the decision.
- Employers are obliged to keep records of SMP payments.
- Employers can recover SMP by deductions from NI contributions and tax; small employers can recover 100 per cent + an extra 5.5 per cent; other employers can recover 92 per cent.

CHAPTER 10
Maternity allowance and other benefits

Introduction

If a woman is not entitled to statutory maternity pay (because, for example, she has recently changed jobs, become self-employed or has given up work), she may be entitled to maternity allowance. Maternity allowance is paid weekly by the Benefits Agency.[1]

This chapter looks at entitlement to maternity allowance, how to claim, and the effect of maternity allowance on other benefits. It also looks, in brief, at entitlement to other benefits during pregnancy and maternity leave or absence, such as statutory sick pay, income support and free prescriptions.

The relevant statute for maternity allowance is the Social Security Contributions and Benefits Act 1992 (SSCBA). The main regulations are the Social Security (Maternity Allowance) Regulations 1987 (MA Regs).[2] References are to these provisions unless otherwise stated. Definitions of 'week', 'birth' etc are set out on pp9ff. See also appendix 4.

Maternity allowance
Qualifying conditions

In order to qualify for MA, the woman must:[3]
- be pregnant and have reached the 11th week (or have given

---

1 The Benefits Agency has produced a guide to maternity benefits (NI 17A, November 1994) which sets out the maternity allowance provisions.
2 SI No 416, as amended by the Social Security (Maternity Benefits and Statutory Sick Pay) (Amendment) Regulations 1994 SI No 1367.
3 SSCBA s35.

birth) before the expected week of confinement;[4] she no longer still has to be working at the 11th week but the allowance is not payable before the 11th week (see p155); and
- have been working (either employed or self-employed) for at least 26 weeks in a 66-week period ending immediately before the week the baby is due (previously the contribution period was 52 weeks); and
- have paid 26 weeks Class 1 NI contributions in the 66-week period.[5]

For example, if the baby is due on Tuesday 15 October 1996, the woman must have paid NI contributions in respect of at least 26 weeks in the period between 9 July 1995 and Saturday 12 October 1996.

The amendments introduced in 1994 mean that it is now easier for a woman to qualify for maternity allowance. If a woman has not paid 26 contributions by the 11th week, she can continue working up to the birth in order to qualify.[6]

Irregular income

There are special rules where a claimant is paid otherwise than weekly.[7] Where
a) in respect of any week she did not pay NI contributions, but
b) her earnings were such that, had she been paid weekly, she would have been required to pay Class 1 contributions, and
c) she has not elected to pay reduced contributions (widows and married women),
she will be treated as having paid weekly contributions.[8]

Women working abroad

There are special provisions for women who are ordinarily resident in Great Britain but who have worked abroad in the 12 months immediately before the end of the qualifying week.[9]

4 Maternity allowance is payable if the baby is stillborn after the 24th week of pregnancy, but not if she miscarries earlier than this.
5 SSCBA Sch 3 Pt I para 3. The following contributions do not count: the woman's husband's NI contributions; credited contributions – except credited contributions for weeks of holiday and/or sickness; reduced-rate contributions which some married women and widows pay.
6 Provided she is not absent because of her pregnancy in the six weeks before the EWC (see p156).
7 SSCBA 1992 Sch 3.
8 SSCBA Sch 3 para 3(2).
9 Social Security (Maternity Allowance) (Work Abroad) Regulations 1987 SI No 417.

Disqualification

There are three grounds for disqualification:
a) where a woman works during her maternity allowance period (MAP), she will be disqualified for the days she worked and for such part of the MAP as is reasonable;
b) if during the MAP the claimant fails without a good reason to take due care of her health and answer reasonable inquiries concerning it;
c) if, before the birth, the woman fails without good cause to attend a medical examination, she may be disqualified for a reasonable period.[10]

Maternity allowance is not payable to women in prison nor in legal custody.

Maternity allowance is not usually payable for a period when the woman is outside the EU (unless there is a reciprocal agreement). However, it may be paid during a temporary absence where the absence is for treatment of an illness or the claimant had been incapable of work (for a reason unrelated to pregnancy) for 26 weeks at the date of departure and is still incapable of work.

Rates of maternity allowance

There are two rates of maternity allowance:
a) the *higher rate* of £54.55 (1996/97 rates), payable to women who are employed in the 15th week before the EWC; and
b) the *lower rate* of £47.55 (1996/97 rates), payable to women who are self-employed or unemployed in the 15th week before the EWC.

Adult dependant

An increase of maternity allowance may be paid for an adult dependant spouse or partner. The amount is currently £28.55.

Payment period

The payment period (the MAP) is the same as for SMP – 18 weeks.[11] Payment can begin at the 11th week before the EWC (but not earlier unless the woman has already given birth). The latest

---

10 MA Regs reg 2.
11 SSCBA 1992 s35(2).

it can start is the beginning of the week following the week of the birth. It lasts for a continuous period of 18 weeks. Maternity allowance is not payable while the woman is working nor while she is in receipt of SMP.

Where the woman is unemployed at the 11th week before EWC
A woman's MAP will start at the beginning of the 11th week where at the 11th week she is unemployed.

Where the woman is working or in employment
A woman's MAP may, if she chooses, start later than the 11th week if, at the 11th week, the woman is:
– still working, or
– receiving SSP from her employer, or
– still employed but claiming incapacity benefit, or severe disablement allowance,
unless she is absent from work because of her pregnancy in the six weeks before the EWC (see below). The MAP will then start from the Sunday after the week in which the woman stops work.

Premature birth
If the birth occurs before the date the woman intended to start her leave, maternity allowance is automatically payable from the week after childbirth.[12]

Late birth
If the baby is born later than expected the MAP will not change.

Pregnancy-related absence in the six weeks before the EWC
Where a woman is, because of her pregnancy, absent from work after the sixth week before the expected week of confinement, she will automatically be transferred onto maternity allowance.[13] The allowance will be payable from the Sunday of the first week she is absent.

To assist in deciding whether an absence is pregnancy-related, the Department of Social Security has published a guide to pregnancy-related illness.[14] There is an alphabetical list of common diseases divided into three groups:

12 MA Regs reg 3(2).
13 MA Regs reg 3.
14 NI 200, August 1994.

Maternity allowance and other benefits

Definite: where the illness is definitely pregnancy-related, such as morning sickness;
Possible: where the illness could be pregnancy-related, such as back pain, or urinary tract infections;
None: where the illness has no relationship to the pregnancy, such as flu.

Where entitlement to MA arises after beginning of 11th week

Where a woman is not entitled to maternity allowance at the 11th week before the EWC (because she has not paid the required contributions) but subsequently becomes entitled before giving birth, the maternity allowance period will be the 18 weeks commencing with the week after she stopped work.[15] She must, of course, work up until the time she satisfies the contributions test.

How to claim maternity allowance

If the woman is working, she should first claim SMP from her employers. If she is not entitled to SMP, the employer must give her a form SMP1 within one week of refusal of SMP. The woman must then complete the MA1 form and submit this with SMP1 to the Benefits Agency.

When to claim

A claim cannot be made before the 14th week before the EWC.[16] It is advisable to claim as soon as possible after the 14th week. This applies even if the woman is still working.

Claiming after the birth

Failure to make a claim before the baby is born may result in a loss of some benefit unless there is a good reason for the delay.[17]

Good cause for late claim

Maternity allowance may be backdated (but not earlier than the week after the birth) where the woman has a good cause for her failure to claim. If a claim is not made within 12 months of the birth, the woman may lose all her benefit.

---

15 MA Regs reg 3(2A).
16 Social Security (Claims and Payments) Regulations 1987 SI No 1968 reg 14.
17 See MA Regs reg 3.

How to claim

The following forms must be taken or sent to the woman's local social security office:

a) Form MA1[18] which is an eleven-part form requesting information about the date of the birth, national insurance contributions, work, benefits claimed etc;
b) Form MAT B1, signed by the doctor or midwife; this states the week the baby is due; if the baby has been born the birth certificate should also be sent;[19]
c) If the woman is working for an employer, she must send form SMP1, which is the form on which the employer states why the woman is not eligible for SMP (see p157);
d) If the woman has been getting SSP she must also send form SSP1 which is the form on which the employer will state that the woman is no longer getting SSP.

If the claim is made before the woman stops working, the social security office will send her a form (BM25A) notifying her of her entitlement and asking to be informed of the date she stops working.

Payment of maternity allowance

MA is paid through a book of weekly orders which can be cashed each Friday at the post office. Any dependant's allowance will be included.

Loss of entitlement

Women taken into custody or who go outside the European Economic Area will lose their entitlement to maternity allowance. Maternity allowance is not usually payable in any week when the woman works.

Tax and national insurance

Tax and national insurance are not payable on maternity allowance. NI contributions will usually be credited for each week the woman receives maternity allowance.

---

18 Available from a social security office or maternity clinic.
19 Social Security (Medical Evidence) Regulations 1976 SI No 615 reg 2(3) and Sch 2, Pt I.

Effect of MA on other benefits

Statutory sick pay

A woman who is sick before the beginning of her MPP or MAP (and her maternity leave) can claim SSP from her employer. Entitlement to SSP depends on the woman having earned an average of £61 per week (for 1996/97) during the eight weeks immediately before the period of entitlement. SSP is not payable during the 18-week MPP or MAP.[20] This applies whether or not the woman is actually entitled to SMP or MA.[21]

As the MPP or MAP can start at any time from the 11th week before the EWC up to the week after the birth, SSP is payable during this period if the woman has not chosen to start her MPP or MAP. Women who are absent for a pregnancy-related reason in the six weeks before the EWC will move into their MPP or MAP and lose entitlement to SSP.

Where a woman is claiming SSP when she reaches her MPP or MAP, the employer should give her form SSP1(T) stating that she is not entitled to SSP.

A woman will be entitled to SSP (if she otherwise qualifies) after the end of the 18-week MPP or MAP if she is sick after she has returned to work. However, she is unlikely to have earned enough in the previous eight weeks (see above). She should also be entitled to contractual sick pay (see p69).

Jobseekers' allowance (previously unemployment benefit)

Jobseekers' allowance (which replaced unemployment benefit in October 1996) is not payable at the same time as SMP or MA. If the woman is claiming jobseekers' allowance at the 11th week, her MAP will start immediately. If she is not entitled to SMP or MA, she can continue to claim jobseekers' allowance as long as she is available for and capable of work.

Incapacity benefit

Incapacity benefit (which was introduced on 13 April 1995 to replace sickness benefit) may be payable if there is no entitlement to SMP or MA. The woman has to have sufficient NI contributions in earlier tax years.[22] Where a claim is made for MA, and is unsuccess-

---

20 SSCBA 1992 s153(2)(d) and (12) and Sch 11.
21 Statutory Sick Pay (General) Regulations 1982 SI No 894 reg 3(4) and (5) (as amended by the Social Security Maternity Benefits and Statutory Sick Pay (Amendment) Regulations 1994 SI No1367).
22 For three years previously. The details are outside the scope of this book.

ful, the claim should automatically be considered for incapacity benefit, but it is necessary to check. The MAT B1 should be sent as with maternity allowance. It can be paid from six weeks before the baby is due until two weeks after the baby is born,[23] but is not paid for any week that the woman works. If the claim is made after the birth, incapacity benefit will only be payable from the date of the birth. The amount for the year 1996/97 is £46.15 per week.

Income support or means-tested jobseekers' allowance

Income support is for anyone over 18 who is not working and is not obliged to sign on for work or who works less than 16 hours per week and is on a low wage. Women aged 16 or 17 can claim income support (if they satisfy the severe hardship test) for the last eleven weeks of pregnancy or after the birth if they have no other income and are not supported by a spouse or partner.

Income support is means-tested and the income of spouses and cohabitees is aggregated. Once the woman is within her maternity allowance period (ie, expecting a baby in the next 11 weeks), she can claim income support (if she satisfies the severe hardship test) without having to be available for work (provided her spouse or partner is not earning or is on a low wage and working less than 16 hours per week and seeking work).[24] SMP and maternity allowance will be taken into account when calculating income support. The amount payable depends on circumstances.[25]

Other benefits

Family credit

Family credit is payable to families (including lone parents) with at least one child where one parent works 16 or more hours per week and has a low wage. It cannot therefore be claimed before the first baby is born.

Housing benefit and council tax benefit

Both these benefits are means-tested and paid to those on income support (or means-tested jobseekers' allowance) or a low income. Housing benefit helps to pay the rent. Council tax benefit covers all or some of council tax.

23 And on any other day when working would cause a serious risk to the health of the woman or baby.
24 SSCBA 1992 s166(2) and (4).
25 The rules are complicated and this is only a very brief summary.

Maternity allowance and other benefits 161

Child benefit and one-parent benefit
These benefits are not means-tested. Child benefit is paid to all parents at the rate of £10.80 per week for the eldest (or only) child and £8.80 for each other child in the family. Lone parents can also get one parent benefit, which is £6.30 per week. Claims are made from the Benefits Agency and claim forms are also available in the 'bounty bag' from the postnatal ward after the woman has had her baby.

Maternity expenses payments
If the woman or her partner is claiming income support, means-tested jobseekers' allowance, family credit or disability working allowance, she is entitled to a maternity expenses payment of £100 for each child. This includes an adopted child aged less than 12 months. Any capital over £500 will reduce the payment.

The claim should be made on form SF100 and can be made in the 11 weeks before the baby is due until three months after the birth. If the claim is made before the baby is due, the MAT B1 or a note from the doctor or midwife must be submitted. If the claim is made after the birth, a maternity birth or adoption certificate must be provided.

Other social fund payments
In addition to a maternity expenses grant, the social fund provides discretionary grants and loans.

Prescription charges and free dental treatment
All women are entitled to free prescriptions and free dental treatment during their pregnancy and for the year after the birth of the baby. The woman's GP will issue her with a form FW8 which is sent to the Family Health Services Authority for an exemption certificate. Children under 16 are also entitled to free prescriptions.

Free milk and vitamins
Women on income support (or means-tested jobseekers' allowance) can get tokens to exchange for milk while they are pregnant. Children under five years whose family receives income support can also get milk tokens. The tokens can be exchanged for seven free pints (or 4 litres) per week or, where the baby is under one, for dried milk formula. There is also concessionary dried milk for a woman getting family credit who is caring for a child under one.

Expectant and breastfeeding mothers and mothers of children under five who are on income support (or means-tested jobseekers' allowance) can get free vitamins (two bottles every three months). These are available from the antenatal or child health clinic.

Help with fares to hospital
Women on income support (or means-tested jobseekers' allowance), family credit or on a low income can get help with fares to the antenatal clinic or hospital. The claim form (AG1) can be obtained from the doctor, dentist, hospital or Benefits Agency.

Free dental treatment
Pregnant women and women who have given birth within the last 12 months are entitled to free NHS dental care.

Disputes

Adjudication officer

Disputes about entitlement to maternity allowance can be referred to an adjudication officer, who should make a decision within 14 days.

Appeals

There is an appeal from the adjudication officer to an independent social security appeals tribunal. There is a further appeal on a point of law to the social security commissioners.

MATERNITY ALLOWANCE AND OTHER BENEFITS: KEY POINTS
- Women who are not entitled to SMP may be entitled to maternity allowance which is paid by the Benefits Agency.
- Qualifying conditions for maternity allowance: the woman must
  - be pregnant and have reached the 11th week before the EWC;
  - have been working (either employed or self-employed) for at least 26 weeks in the 66 weeks immediately before the week the baby is due;

- have paid 26 weeks' Class 1 NI contributions in the 66 week period.
- Maternity allowance is not payable for any day when the employee works.
- There are two rates:
  - the *higher rate* (£54.55), payable to women who are employed in the 15th week before the EWC;
  - the *lower rate* (£47.55), payable to women who are self-employed or not working (in the 15th week).

  An increase may be paid for an adult dependant.
- Maternity allowance is payable for 18 weeks.
- Maternity allowance will not be paid before the 11th week (unless the woman has already given birth); it may start later, depending on the woman's circumstances.
- Where a woman has a pregnancy-related absence in the six weeks before the EWC, her maternity allowance will start immediately.
- A claim for maternity allowance should be made as soon as possible after the 26th week of pregnancy. A claim made after the birth may result in loss of benefit.
- Maternity allowance is claimed from the local Benefits Agency and is payable by weekly orders at the post office.
- SSP is not payable during the maternity allowance period.
- A woman may be entitled to other benefits, such as income support, incapacity benefit, family credit, housing benefit and council tax benefit, or maternity expenses payment. She is entitled to free prescriptions and dental treatment. Women on income support get free milk and vitamins.

CHAPTER 11
Discrimination and equal pay claims

Introduction

Although the ERA provides for most maternity rights, there may be circumstances when the discrimination and equal pay law provides greater protection. In addition, under the Sex Discrimination Act 1975 there is no limit on the amount of compensation and an award can be made for injury to feelings.

Treating a woman less favourably because she is pregnant, has taken maternity leave or had a baby will usually be discriminatory. This chapter summarises the protection provided by the Sex Discrimination Act, Equal Pay Act and European law. For further detail see Palmer, *Discrimination at Work* (Legal Action Group).

The Sex Discrimination Act 1975 (SDA) and Equal Treatment Directive (ETD) provide protection against discrimination on the grounds of sex. This is additional to the protection against dismissal on pregnancy and maternity-related grounds under the ERA. The SDA prohibits direct and indirect discrimination in defined circumstances. Discrimination against married people is also unlawful, whether direct or indirect (SDA s3).

The Equal Opportunities Commission has issued a Code of Practice for 'the elimination of discrimination on the ground of sex and marriage and the promotion of equal opportunity in employment'. Failure to observe the code is not itself unlawful but is admissible in evidence and, if relevant, will be taken into account by the tribunal.[1]

The Equal Pay Act 1970 (EqPA) entitles a woman to the same contractual terms and conditions as a man (in the same employment) doing like work, work rated as equivalent under a

---

1 SDA s56A(10).

Discrimination and equal pay claims 165

job evaluation scheme or work of equal value, provided there is no 'material factor' defence (see p171). The EqPA covers all contractual terms, not just pay.

Article 119 EEC and the Equal Pay Directive (EPD) provide for equal pay for work of equal value. They only cover 'pay', which, however, is widely defined (see p172). It is irrelevant whether the entitlement is contractual or non-contractual.

Sex and marital discrimination

Direct discrimination

Direct sex discrimination occurs when a woman is or would be treated less favourably than a man on the ground of her sex.[2] Less favourable treatment of a woman (or man) because she is married is also unlawful.

In *Webb v EMO Air Cargo (UK) Ltd*[3] the House of Lords and European Court of Justice held that less favourable treatment of a woman because she is pregnant or has recently given birth was unlawful discrimination in itself; there was no need to prove that she had been treated less favourably than a man in a similar situation (see chapter 12).

Indirect discrimination

Indirect discrimination is concerned with practices which have the effect, without necessarily the intention, of discriminating against women, in that a woman would find it more difficult (in a particular case or on average) to comply with a job requirement, generally because of women's primary responsibility for the family (see chapter 13).

Victimisation

It is unlawful to victimise (ie, treat less favourably) a person for:
a) making a complaint under the SDA;
b) giving evidence or information in connection with proceedings; or
c) doing anything else under or by reference to the SDA; or
d) making allegations against the discriminator that s/he has acted

---

2 SDA s1(1)(a). Discrimination against men is also prohibited.
3 [1994] IRLR 482, ECJ; [1995] IRLR 645, HL.

unlawfully under the Acts,
or if the discriminator knows that the person victimised intends to do any of the above or suspects that she has done, or intends to do, any of them.[4] The detailed provisions are outside the scope of this book.

Who is protected?

Job applicants and employees are protected. The definition of 'employee' under the SDA[5] is wider than under the ERA.[6] 'Employee' includes women working under a contract of service or of apprenticeship or a contract personally to execute any work or labour. This covers the self-employed and independent contractors. Barristers and advocates are also protected, though the provisions are different.[7]

The EAT has said that:

> the concept of a contract for the engagement of personal work or labour lying outside the scope of a master-servant relationship is a wide and flexible one, intended by Parliament to be interpreted as such ... [T]hose who engage, even cursorily, the talents, skill or labour of the self-employed are wise to ensure that the terms are equal as between men and women.[8]

There are no maximum or minimum age limits[9] or minimum length of service requirements to qualify for protection against discrimination.

Discrimination by whom?

The SDA prohibits discrimination by employers (s6), business partners (s11), trade unions and organisations of employers (s12), qualifying bodies (s13), persons concerned with provision of vocational training (s14) and employment agencies (s15). Individuals working for or as agents of such bodies may also be liable.

(1) Prohibited sex discrimination by employers

Discrimination in the following circumstances is prohibited:
a) in the arrangements made by an employer for determining who

4 SDA s4.
5 s82(1).
6 ERA s223(5).
7 SDA ss35A and 35B.
8 *Quinnen v Hovells* [1984] IRLR 227, EAT; see also *Mirror Group Newspapers Ltd v Gunning* [1986] IRLR 27, CA.
9 SDA s5(2).

Discrimination and equal pay claims 167

should be offered employment (eg, selection procedures, advertising)[10] (see p25);
b) in the terms and conditions on which a person is offered a job, (eg, if a woman is offered shorter holidays, fewer perks, lower pay)[11] (see p25);
c) by refusing or deliberately omitting to offer a woman a job[12] (see p25);
d) by refusing or not giving a woman the same opportunities for transfer, training or promotion[13] (see p27);
e) by giving women fewer or less favourable benefits, facilities or services (eg, if free travel were provided for the families of men but not of women);[14]
f) by dismissing a woman on the ground of her sex[15] (see chapter 7);
g) by subjecting a woman to any other detriment (ie, by treating a woman less favourably in any other way – provided such treatment is not excluded by the Act).[16]

The first three situations apply only to job applicants and the last four apply to women already employed. Dismissal under (f) includes the expiry of a fixed-term contract which is not renewed on the same terms and constructive dismissal.[17]

Exclusions

Exclusions relevant to maternity provisions are only summarised in brief (for further detail see *Discrimination at Work*).
a) The provision of special treatment for women relating to pregnancy, childbirth and maternity leave.[18] Men cannot, for example, claim that failure to give them paternity leave is unlawful;
b) Women working, wholly or mainly, at an establishment abroad.[19] Women working on British-registered ships, or on aircraft or hovercraft registered in the UK and operated by someone whose main place of business or ordinary residence is in the UK, will be protected unless the employee works wholly outside

10 SDA s6(1)(a).
11 s6(1)(b).
12 s6(1)(c).
13 s6(2)(a).
14 s6(2)(a).
15 s6(2)(b).
16 s6(2)(b).
17 s82(1A).
18 s2(2).
19 ss6 and 10.

Great Britain.
c) Where sex is a genuine occupational qualification;[20] this covers, for example, jobs which need to be held by a man (or woman) to preserve decency or privacy.
d) Certain discriminatory acts, in relation to employment and vocational training, contained in legislation passed before the SDA; this applies, for example, to health and safety legislation restricting women's employment (see p126 for provisions).[21]

Armed forces

Until 1990 the armed forces had a policy of dismissing women when they became pregnant. The SDA s85 used to exempt the armed forces but the policy was in breach of the ETD. The armed forces were brought within the scope of the SDA from 1 February 1995, though there is still an exception where the discriminatory act is done for the purpose of ensuring 'combat effectiveness'.[22]

Vicarious liability

An employer is liable for discrimination carried out by a worker in the course of his/her employment, whether or not it was done with the employer's knowledge or approval, unless the employer can prove that s/he took such steps as were reasonably practicable to prevent it.[23]

(2) Prohibited sex discrimination by partners

It is unlawful for a firm of partners to discriminate in relation to recruitment, terms of the partnership, access to benefits, exclusion from the partnership or any other detriment. Thus, a partner (or applicant for partnership) should not be treated less favourably because she is pregnant, has given birth or has taken time off to have a baby, though she may not be entitled to receive the same share of the profits while away from work.

---

20 SDA s7.
21 Note that pregnant women and new mothers, who are prevented from working for health and safety reasons, are entitled to be suspended on full pay (see pp123-124).
22 Sex Discrimination Act (Application to Armed Forces etc) Regulations 1994 SI No 3276.
23 SDA s41.

Discrimination and equal pay claims 169

(3) Prohibited sex discrimination by vocational training bodies

It is unlawful for a person who provides, arranges or facilitates vocational training to discriminate in relation to access to and terms of training, termination of training and by subjecting a woman to any other detriment.

(4) Prohibited sex discrimination by employment agencies

It is unlawful for an employment agency (which includes any person who provides services for the purpose of finding employment for workers or supplying employers with workers) to discriminate on the ground of sex:
– in the terms on which the agency offers its services; or
– by refusing to provide its services; or
– in the way it provides its services.[24]

This does not apply if it would be lawful for the employer to refuse to employ the person, ie, if the discrimination fell within one of the exceptions.

For example, if an employment agency refuses to provide work to a woman because she is pregnant or about to go on maternity leave, this will be unlawful discrimination. The questionnaire procedure may be used to find out how other (non-pregnant) workers have been treated in order to show that the reason for failure to provide work was the woman's pregnancy.

(5) Discrimination against contract workers

Contract workers are individuals working for a person (the principal) who are not employed by the principal but by a third party who supplies them under a contract with the principal. Thus, a temporary secretary would be employed by the agency but work for the principal. It is unlawful for the principal to discriminate against a contract worker:[25]
a) in the terms on which s/he allows her to work; or
b) by not allowing her to continue to work;[26] or

24 SDA s15.
25 SDA s9. Where the general employer is an employment agency s/he will be liable under s15 (see above).
26 Unless the genuine occupational exception applies.

c) in the way s/he affords her access to any benefits, facilities or services or by refusing such access; or
d) by subjecting her to any other detriment.

In *BP Chemicals Ltd v Gillick and Roevin Management Services Ltd*[27] the EAT held that a contract worker could bring a complaint against her principal that he had discriminated against her by not allowing her to return to work after time off having a baby.

Where the general employer is an employment agency s/he will be liable under SDA s15 (see above).

There are also general exceptions for discrimination by other bodies than employers.

Discrimination under EU law: the Equal Treatment Directive

The directive provides that there should be no discrimination whatsoever on the grounds of sex, either directly or indirectly by reference (in particular) to marital or family status, in
– access to employment
– training
– working conditions
– promotion
– dismissal.

Exceptions to the Directive are:
a) Occupational activities for which, by reason of their nature of the context in which they are carried out, the sex of the worker constitutes a determining factor;[28]
b) Provisions for the protection of women, particularly as regards pregnancy and maternity;[29]
c) Promotion of equal opportunity;[30] this covers measures to promote equal opportunity for men and women and to remove existing inequalities.

The effect of EU law is set out in chapter 14.

Equal pay law: Equal Pay Act 1970

The EqPA provides that where a woman is employed on:
a) similar work; or

27 [1995] IRLR 128 EAT.
28 This is similar to the genuine occupational qualification exception in the SDA.
29 ETD article 2(3).
30 Article 2(4).

Discrimination and equal pay claims

b) equivalent work under a job evaluation scheme; or
c) work of equal value,

if any term of her contract is less favourable (whether concerned with pay or not) than a term of a similar kind in the man's contract, the woman's contract shall be modified to be not less favourable.[31] An equality clause is implied into the woman's contract unless the employer proves that the difference is genuinely due to a 'material factor' which is not the difference in sex. This might cover, for example, market forces, geographical differences (such as London weighting), experience, unsocial hours.

The definition of pay is similar to that in European law (see below). EqPA applies to contractual terms which include not only pay but also any other benefits under the terms of the contract, whether express or implied.

The EqPA protects those working under a contract of service (ie, employees) or of apprenticeship or a contract personally to execute any work or labour.[32] Like the SDA, the Act applies irrespective of the age, hours of work or length of service of the worker.

Exceptions

The EqPA does not apply to the armed forces (as at August 1996),[33] nor to women working wholly or mainly outside the UK.[34] There is special treatment for women in connection with pregnancy or childbirth,[35] and certain provisions relating to retirement and pensions.[36]

Relationship between SDA and EqPA

The SDA and EqPA are mutually exclusive – ie, there is no overlap between the Acts. The EqPA applies only if there is a 'comparable man' (meaning a man doing like work, work rated as equivalent under a job evaluation scheme or work of equal value). If the

---

31 EqPA s1(2).
32 s1(6)(a).
33 s1(9). The Armed Forces Act 1996 will (when·implemented) bring the armed forces within the EqPA, though it is likely that a complainant will first have to go through the internal complaints procedure. The Act also provides that a woman cannot bring a claim unless she has been employed for nine months ending with the date she presents her claim.
34 The provisions are the same as under the SDA s10.
35 EqPA s6(1)(b).
36 s6(1A)(b).

172 *Maternity rights/Chapter 11*

matter complained of is not in the contract or if there is no 'comparable man', only the SDA applies. Discrimination which falls outside the EqPA (such as recruitment, training and promotion) may be covered by the SDA. If it falls outside both it may be covered by EU law. If in doubt it is advisable to claim under both Acts and EU law.

Article 119 and the Equal Pay Directive

Article 119

Article 119 EEC and the Equal Pay Directive (75/117/EEC) provide that 'men and women should receive equal pay for equal work'.

Pay is defined as 'the ordinary basic or minimum wage or salary and any other consideration, whether in cash or kind, which the worker receives, directly or indirectly, in respect of his employment from his employer'. It includes:
- wages and salary,
- maternity pay,
- payments towards an occupational pension scheme,[37]
- redundancy pay,[38]
- contractual and statutory sick pay[39] and other analogous payments (such as guarantee payments),
- payments for time off for union duties,[40]
- (probably) compensation for unfair dismissal[41] and
- other 'perks' which are payable, directly or indirectly, by the employer as a result of the employee's employment.

---

37 *Barber v GRE Assurance Group* [1990] IRLR 240 ECJ.
38 *Hammersmith and Queen Charlotte's Special Health Authority v Cato* [1987] IRLR 483, EAT; *Secretary of State for Scotland and Greater Glasgow Health Board v Wright and Hannah* [1991] IRLR 187, SEAT; *Barber v Guardian Royal Exchange Assurance Group* [1990] IRLR 240, ECJ.
39 *Rinner-Kühn v FWW Spezial-Gebäudereinigung GmbH* [1989] IRLR 493, ECJ.
40 *Arbeiterwohlfahrt der Stadt Berlin eV v Botel* [1992] IRLR 423 ECJ.
41 *Mediguard Services Ltd v Thame* [1994] IRLR 504, EAT, but see *R v Secretary of State for Employment ex p Seymour Smith and Perez* [1995] IRLR 464, CA.

The Equal Pay Directive

This directive was principally designed to facilitate the practical application of the principle of equal pay outlined in article 119 and does not alter the content or scope of that principle as defined in the Treaty.[42]

The directive provides that the 'principle of equal pay' means equal pay for the same work or work to which equal value is attributed and for the elimination of all discrimination on grounds of sex with regard to all aspects and conditions of remuneration.

It is important to consider *all* the above provisions when advising on maternity rights (see p6). In some situations European law provides more comprehensive rights; in most cases it overrides UK law (see p200).

DISCRIMINATION AND EQUAL PAY CLAIMS: KEY POINTS
- Direct and indirect sex and marital discrimination and victimisation are prohibited in defined situations.
- Less favourable treatment relating to a woman's pregnancy, childbirth or maternity leave is discriminatory.
- Both men and women are protected, except that men have no right to the equivalent of maternity leave.
- Protected workers are:
  - job applicants
  - employees
  - the self-employed
  - apprentices
  - independent contractors
  - trainees
  - contract workers
  - barristers, trainee barristers, advocates.

  Most Crown employees are protected, including the armed forces.
- Discrimination is unlawful by:
  - employers
  - partners
  - persons concerned with the provisions of vocational training

---

42 *Pickstone v Freemans plc* [1988] IRLR 357, HL; *Barber v GRE Assurance Group* [1990] IRLR 240, ECJ.

- employment agencies.
- Discrimination in the following situations is prohibited:
  - in the arrangements made for deciding who should be offered employment;
  - in the terms and conditions on which a person is offered a job;
  - by refusing or omitting to offer a woman a job;
  - by not giving a woman the same opportunities for transfer, training or promotion;
  - by giving women fewer benefits, facilities or services;
  - by dismissing a woman;
  - by subjecting a woman to any other detriment.
- There are various exclusions, though most are not relevant to maternity rights.
- There is a very wide prohibition against discrimination under the Equal Treatment Directive.
- The exceptions under EU law are narrower.
- Under the Equal Pay Act a woman can claim the same pay and contractual terms as a man working for the same employer if she is doing:
  - like work
  - work rated as equivalent under a job evaluation scheme, or
  - work of equal value

  provided there is no material factor defence.
- Article 119 of the Treaty of Rome provides that 'men and women should receive equal pay for equal work'; pay is widely defined and includes sick pay, redundancy pay, unfair dismissal compensation (probably) and maternity pay. Note that full pay is not payable during maternity leave/absence.
- The SDA and EqPA are mutually exclusive, though they should be construed as a 'harmonious whole'. If in doubt both should be pleaded as well as EU law.

CHAPTER 12
Direct discrimination

Less favourable treatment

Less favourable treatment of a woman because she is pregnant or has given birth will usually be unlawful under the Sex Discrimination Act 1975 (SDA) and the European Equal Treatment Directive (ETD). It is important to consider claims under the SDA and ETD because, unlike under the ERA, there is no limit on compensation and compensation may be awarded for injury to feelings.

Definition

The SDA[1] provides that a person discriminates against a woman if 'on the ground of her sex he treats her less favourably than he treats or would treat a man'. It is unlawful for an employer (and certain other bodies) to discriminate on the ground of sex in relation to recruitment, promotion, training, dismissal, sexual harassment and 'any other detriment' (see pp166–167).

Comparing like with like

When comparing the treatment of a woman and man the SDA provides that the relevant circumstances of the woman and man must be the same or similar.[2] This means that like must be compared with like; the comparison is between a man and a woman in a similar situation.

The problem with the statutory definition in the context of maternity rights is that it presupposes a comparison between a woman and a man in similar circumstances and there is clearly no male equivalent of a pregnant woman. For many years the UK

1 s1(1)(a).
2 SDA s5(3).

courts compared a pregnant woman with a sick man.

In *Dekker*[3] the ECJ held that it was a breach of the Equal Treatment Directive for an employer to refuse to appoint a suitable female applicant on the ground of the possible adverse consequence for him arising from employing a pregnant woman. The ECJ said that 'as employment can only be refused to women because of pregnancy, such a refusal is direct discrimination on grounds of sex'. Thus, there was no need to show a male comparator had been treated more favourably.[4] The woman, being pregnant, has in effect a special 'protected' status.

In *Hertz*[5] the ECJ held that:

> The dismissal of a female worker because of her pregnancy constitutes direct discrimination on grounds of sex, in the same way as does the refusal to recruit a pregnant woman. Therefore, a woman is protected from dismissal because of her absence during the maternity leave from which she benefits under national law.

The conflict between UK and EU law was clarified, to some extent, in *Webb v EMO Air Cargo Ltd (No 2)*.[6] Mrs Webb was employed to cover for a pregnant employee, though she had a permanent contract and was expected to stay on after the maternity period. Mrs Webb then became pregnant herself and she was dismissed. The IT, EAT, and Court of Appeal held that a man absent for a similar period would also have been dismissed, so there was no discrimination. The House of Lords first decided that where the dismissal of a pregnant woman was not simply on the grounds of her pregnancy but because of the consequences of the pregnancy (ie, she was unable to work), then it was not unlawful if a man in the same circumstances (ie, unable to work) would have been dismissed.

The Lords referred the case to the European Court of Justice to decide whether, under the Equal Treatment Directive, the less favourable treatment of a pregnant woman was itself discrimination, without the need for a comparison to be made with a man in similar circumstances.

---

3 *Dekker v Stichting Vormingscentrum voor Jonge Volwassenen (VJV-Centrum) Plus* [1991] IRLR 27, ECJ.
4 In *Dekker* there was no male comparator.
5 *Handels-og Kontorfunktionaerernes Forbund i Danmark (acting for Hertz) v Dansk Arbejdsgiverforening (acting for Aldi Marked K/S)* [1991] IRLR 31, ECJ.
6 [1995] IRLR 645, HL.

The ECJ held[7] that:
a) there can be no question of comparing the situation of a woman who is unable to work because of her pregnancy with that of a man similarly incapable for medical or other reasons;
b) dismissal of a pregnant woman recruited for an indefinite period cannot be justified because she is unable to work for a temporary period because of her pregnancy.

The ECJ held that the protection given by European law to a woman during pregnancy and childbirth could not depend on whether her presence at work was essential to the proper functioning of the undertaking. Any less favourable treatment of a woman because she is pregnant or because of the consequences of pregnancy is discrimination.

The case was then referred back to the House of Lords[8] which, applying the ECJ judgment, held that it was unlawful to dismiss a woman who had been employed for an indefinite period where she was temporarily unavailable for work as a result of pregnancy.

In a judgment which is difficult to understand, the Lords stated that 'in a case where a woman is engaged for an indefinite period, the fact that the reason why she will be temporarily unavailable for work at a time when to her knowledge her services will be particularly required is pregnancy is a circumstance relevant to her case, being a circumstance which could not be present in the case of a hypothetical man'. This obscure judgment appears to mean that where there is a circumstance, such as pregnancy, which only applies to women, there is automatically sex discrimination where a woman is treated less favourably because of those circumstances. There is no need for a comparison to be made with a man in a similar situation, nor should a distinction be made between pregnancy itself and the consequences of pregnancy. Thus, a woman has a 'protected' status when she is pregnant.[9]

The House of Lords suggested that there was a distinction between permanent and short fixed-term contracts. They said *obiter* (ie, in words which are not binding) that if a woman was employed on a fixed-term contract and would, because of her pregnancy, be absent for the *whole* of the contract, then it may not be unlawful to dismiss her. Nor would it be unlawful to fail to appoint a pregnant woman in these circumstances.

7 [1994] IRLR 482, ECJ.
8 *Webb v EMO Air Cargo (UK) Ltd (No 2)* [1995] IRLR 645, HL.
9 See also *O'Neill v Governors of St Thomas More RCVA Upper School and Bedfordshire County Council* [1996] IRLR 372, EAT.

However, in *Caruana v Manchester Airport plc*,[10] the EAT firmly rejected the idea that the European Court of Justice or the House of Lords in *Webb* considered there were any exceptions to the principle that less favourable treatment of a pregnant woman is discrimination other than the 'possibility of a distinction between an indefinite contract and a case where the employee will be absent for the whole of the fixed term'. Even then, this would only apply where the woman had never been employed, not where she already had a fixed-term contract. It was, therefore, unlawful discrimination for the employer to fail to renew a fixed-term contract because of the applicant's pregnancy. As the EAT said,

> to disqualify Mrs Caruana from the protection of the ECJ's ruling would be a positive encouragement to employers to offer or to impose, not a continuous and stable employment relationship, but a series of short-term contracts, with the object or collateral advantage of avoiding the impact of the discrimination laws. We are confident that neither the ECJ nor the House of Lords did or would support such an approach.

The principles laid down in *Webb* (and *Caruana*) will also apply to less favourable treatment of a woman because she is on, or has taken, maternity leave or for any reason connected with maternity leave.

Relevance of the comparative approach after Webb

There will still be some situations where the less favourable treatment of a pregnant woman is not, in itself, unlawful discrimination. It will then be necessary to show that a man in a similar situation would have been treated more favourably. For example, a woman who has a pregnancy-related illness after her return from maternity leave or absence may have lost her 'protected' status. If so, the question is whether a man with a 'comparable' illness would be treated more favourably (see *Hertz* on p111).

No comparison between woman on maternity leave and person at work

Logically, if pregnancy is a relevant circumstance (being a circumstance which could not be present in the case of the hypothetical man) and discrimination on grounds of pregnancy is unlawful in itself, arguably the same reasoning should apply to a

---

10 [1996] IRLR 378, EAT.

Direct discrimination 179

woman on maternity leave. Absence on maternity leave is, like pregnancy, clearly a circumstance only relevant to women.

However, this was not the approach adopted by the European Court of Justice in *Gillespie and Others v Northern Health and Social Services Board*,[11] where it was held that it was not possible to compare the special situation of a woman on maternity leave with a man or woman actually at work.[12] There was no requirement, therefore, that women should receive full pay during maternity leave. Thus, less favourable treatment of women on maternity leave or absence (compared with employees at work) is *not* unlawful (at least in respect of pay), whereas less favourable treatment of pregnant women who are still at work (or on sick or other leave) is unlawful.

In *Gillespie* the ECJ also made the distinction between 'pay', which is not payable during maternity leave or absence, and the benefit of a pay rise, which a pregnant woman should be awarded while on maternity leave. *Gillespie* could be restricted to its facts – in other words all that it decided was that women on maternity leave or absence were not entitled to full pay, only maternity pay (either statutory or contractual). The only way of reconciling these two limbs of the decision, if this is possible, is to distinguish between a benefit which is linked to the woman actually being at work (such as her basic pay) to which she is not entitled during her leave or absence, and benefits which are paid regardless of whether the employee is 'at work', which should be provided (see pp58-59).

Although *Gillespie* was an ECJ decision under article 119 EEC, it is possible that the same interpretation would be given to a claim under the EqPA. A woman on maternity leave should still be able to compare herself with the treatment of a man who is *not* at work. The ECJ, in *Gillespie*, was never asked to consider this. A comparison between maternity provisions and sick pay provisions may still possible (see p55).

Establishing a pregnancy-related reason for discrimination

Employers may deny that the less favourable treatment is connected to the woman's pregnancy and allege instead that she

11 [1996] IRLR 214, ECJ.
12 The ECJ said that there is only discrimination where there is the 'application of different rules to comparable situations or the application of the same rule to different situations'.

was incompetent, that she had a bad sickness record, or that there was a redundancy situation. It is a question of fact in each case and the burden is on the applicant to prove that the less favourable treatment is to do with her pregnancy or childbirth and is therefore unlawful. Note, however, that under EU law the emphasis is on *transparency*, in this case the employer showing why s/he treated the applicant less favourably.[12A] The general principles which apply to all sex discrimination cases apply and these are set out below.[13]

What is less favourable treatment?
The denial of a choice to the applicant which is valued by her (whether or not it can be shown to be better) is less favourable treatment. For example:
- If a woman is told that she has to apply for voluntary redundancy before she goes on maternity leave, whereas other employees affected have a longer time to decide whether to apply, that may be less favourable treatment.
- If a woman is denied access to training because she is about to go on maternity leave that may be less favourable treatment.

'On the ground of sex'
The reason for the less favourable treatment must be the complainant's sex. If the reason is due to her pregnancy or childbirth or maternity leave, that will be sufficient to prove that the reason is sex-based (following *Webb*).

The employer must be aware of the employee's pregnancy for the less favourable treatment to be 'on the grounds of sex'. For example, the dismissal of a pregnant woman will not be discriminatory if the employer was unaware that she was pregnant (see p21). It may, however, still be unfair.

'But for' test
A useful question to ask is: 'Would the woman have been treated in the same way *but for* the fact that she was pregnant, had given birth or taken maternity leave?'[14]

12A *Handels-og Kontorfunktionaerenes Forbund i Danmark v Dansk Arbejdsgiverforeniging (acting for Danfoss)* [1989] IRLR 532, ECJ.
13 For more detail see chapter 2 of *Discrimination at Work*.
14 This test was established in the House of Lords cases of *R v Birmingham City Council ex p Equal Opportunities Commission* [1989] IRLR 173, and *James v Eastleigh Borough Council* [1990] ICR 554. It was followed by the EAT in *O'Neill* (n9 above).

Direct discrimination 181
Pregnancy need not be the only reason

In a race discrimination case,[15] the EAT held that where there were mixed 'motives', not all of which constitute discrimination, the unlawful discrimination must be an important factor. Thus, if one reason for the dismissal is incompetence and another is pregnancy-related sickness absence, the absence must be of sufficient weight in the decision-making process to be a cause of the dismissal.

In *O'Neill v Governors of St Thomas More RCVA Upper School* (see p24) the EAT said that the basic question is what is the 'effective and predominant cause' or the 'real and efficient cause' of the act complained of. The EAT said that the event or fact which is said to have caused the discrimination 'need not be the only or even the main cause of the result complained of' but 'it is enough if it is an effective cause'. Thus, where pregnancy is a factor without which the less favourable treatment would not have happened, this should be enough to establish discrimination.

Stereotyping

Preconceptions that women possess or lack certain characteristics are discriminatory. Thus, an assumption that a woman's work will become less important after childbirth will, if acted upon, be discriminatory.[16]

Motive or purpose is irrelevant

Once it has been shown that the less favourable treatment was related to the woman's pregnancy, it is irrelevant that the employer may have a 'good' motive, such as a desire to protect the woman.[17] This was reiterated in *O'Neill* when the EAT stressed that the test was not subjective – ie, about intentions, motives, beliefs or subjective purposes – but an objective test of 'causal connection'.

Proving discrimination by inference

In *King v Great Britain-China Centre*[18] the Court of Appeal laid down guidelines for proving discrimination. These have been widely adopted by tribunals. They are as follows:

15 *Nagarajan v Agnew* [1994] IRLR 61, EAT.
16 See *Hurley v Mustoe* [1981] IRLR 208, EAT.
17 *James v Eastleigh Borough Council* [1990] IRLR 288, HL.
18 [1991] IRLR 513, CA; this was a race discrimination case but the same principles apply to sex discrimination cases.

a) it is for the applicant to prove her case on the balance of probabilities;
b) the tribunal should bear in mind that it is unusual to find direct evidence of discrimination. Few employers will be prepared to admit such discrimination, even to themselves. In some cases the discrimination will not be ill-intentioned but merely based on an assumption that 'he or she would not have fitted in';
c) the outcome of the case will therefore usually depend on what inferences it is proper to draw from the primary facts found by the tribunal. These can include inferences from an evasive reply to a questionnaire;
d) a finding of discrimination and a finding of a difference in sex will often point to the possibility of sex discrimination. In such cases the tribunal will look to the employer for an explanation;
e) if no explanation is forthcoming from the employer, it will be legitimate for the tribunal to infer that the discrimination was on grounds of race or sex;
f) there is no need to shift the burden of proof. The tribunal should make findings on the primary facts and draw such inferences as it considers proper from those facts.

What kind of evidence is relevant?

Gathering evidence is crucial to proving a claim and full use should be made of the questionnaire procedure and tribunal procedure (see chapter 15). Examples of behaviour from which an inference may be made are given below.

Where a woman has not been appointed or promoted

- Questions at an interview about intention to have a family, or domestic arrangements for children (see p26);[19]
- an assumption that women with young children are not reliable (see *Hurley v Mustoe*);[20]
- comments that the employer could not afford to pay maternity pay or hire and train a replacement.

Where a woman has been dismissed

- Dismissal occurring soon after the pregnancy is announced;
- change of attitude by the employer to the woman;

19 See *Smith v North Western Regional Health Authority* (1987) 15 January, Case No 29270/86.
20 [1981] IRLR 208, EAT.

Direct discrimination 183

- lack of evidence to support employer's case that the dismissal was due to incompetence or misconduct, particularly if there is a disciplinary procedure which has been breached.

Statistical evidence of past discrimination against women, and, in particular, pregnant women and those who have taken maternity leave, may be relevant.[21] This can be obtained through discovery (see p217). Where, for example, a disproportionate number of men are promoted and there are equally qualified women, the employer may be required to provide an explanation.[22]

Can direct discrimination be justified?

There is no provision in the SDA for justifying direct sex discrimination; this is limited to indirect discrimination.

DIRECT DISCRIMINATION: KEY POINTS

- Less favourable treatment of a woman because she is pregnant, has given birth or taken maternity leave will be unlawful discrimination under the SDA and European law.
- The treatment must be on the ground of sex (which includes grounds of pregnancy, childbirth, maternity leave). The question is whether the woman would have received the same treatment as the man *but for* the fact that she is a woman (or pregnant etc).
- There is no longer any need to compare a pregnant woman with a sick man in order to prove discrimination. While pregnant she has a special 'protected' status.
- Nor can a distinction be made between the less favourable treatment of a woman because she is pregnant and less favourable treatment because of the *consequences* of her pregnancy (ie, because she is unable to work).
- The comparative approach may still be relevant where the less favourable treatment is not, in itself, discrimination.
- Less favourable treatment of a woman on maternity leave or absence than an employee at work is not in itself discriminatory; it may become so where a woman on

---

21 See *West Midlands Passenger Transport Executive v Singh* [1988] IRLR 186, CA.
22 See *Handels-og Kontorfunktionaerernes Forbund i Danmark v Dansk Arbejdsgiverforening (acting for Danfoss)* [1989] IRLR 532, ECJ, where the ECJ stressed the importance of transparency in the employer's decision-making process.

maternity leave is treated less favourably than an employee on other leave.
- The employer must be aware of the woman's pregnancy for the less favourable treatment on grounds of pregnancy to be sex discrimination.
- It is not necessary to show that sex or pregnancy was the *only* ground for the less favourable treatment – though it must be an important factor.
- The intention or motive of the discriminator is irrelevant.
- Direct discrimination can be proved by inference.
- Direct discrimination cannot be justified by the employer.

CHAPTER 13
Indirect discrimination

Introduction

Indirect discrimination is concerned with practices which have a disproportionate effect on women because of social conditions, mainly childcare responsibilities. Women with primary responsibility for children (and particularly babies) are less likely to be able to work long and/or anti-social hours and are less likely to be able to comply with mobility requirements. Many women would like to return to work (from maternity leave or absence) on a part-time or job-share basis. Refusal to allow them to do so may be indirectly discriminatory (see also p81).

Indirect discrimination may be on the ground of sex or being married. A practice which has a disparate impact on women may also to have a disparate impact on married people. For example, a requirement to be free from childcare responsibilities would impact on both women and married people.

The ECJ has held that less favourable treatment of part-time workers, who are predominantly women, is indirect discrimination and in breach of the Equal Treatment Directive if there is no objective justification.[1]

This chapter looks at how to prove indirect discrimination, concentrating on the maternity context, that is in relation to part-time work, job-sharing and flexible working hours.

Definition of indirect discrimination

Indirect discrimination on ground of sex occurs when a person applies to a woman a:

1 *Bilka-Kaufhaus v Weber von Hartz* [1986] IRLR 317, ECJ; *Rinner-Kühn v FWW Spezial-Gebäudereinigung GmbH* [1989] IRLR 493, ECJ and *Arbeiterwohlfahrt der Stadt Berlin eV v Botel* [1992] IRLR 423 ECJ.

186 *Maternity rights/Chapter 13*

requirement or condition which applies or would apply equally to a man but:

(i) which is such that the proportion of women who can comply with it is considerably smaller than the proportion of men who can comply with it, and
(ii) which the person cannot show to be justifiable irrespective of the sex to whom it is applied, and
(iii) which is to the her detriment because she cannot comply with it.

(SDA s1(1)(b))

Definition of indirect discrimination under EU law

There is a much broader definition under EU law. In *Bilka Kaufhaus v Weber von Hartz* (n1 above) the European Court of Justice held that the exclusion of part-time workers from an occupational pension scheme was discriminatory where that exclusion affected a far greater number of women than men unless the exclusion was based on objectively justified factors unrelated to sex discrimination. Thus, a practice which has a disparate impact must be justified by the employer. Claims under the SDA may fail because of the technical nature of the definition. It is therefore always important to consider EU law, which may provide a remedy where none exists under the SDA (see chapter 14).

Proving indirect discrimination (UK law)

There are seven main questions which relate to the definition of indirect sex discrimination:
1) Has the respondent applied any requirement or condition to the applicant?
2) When was the requirement or condition applied to the applicant?
3) Identify the relevant population within which the proportionate comparison has to be made (the pool);
4) Establish disparate impact;
5) Has the employer justified the requirement or condition?
6) Can the applicant comply with the requirement or condition?
7) Has the applicant suffered a detriment?

(1) Has the respondent applied any requirement or condition to the applicant?

What does 'requirement or condition' mean?
There is a substantial overlap between 'requirement' and 'condition'. The EAT, in *Clarke v Eley (IMI) Kynoch Ltd*,[2] said that the words should be interpreted widely.[3] In *Clarke v Eley*, the employer argued that a procedure whereby part-time workers were dismissed first could not be a requirement, as a requirement meant that the person had to do a certain act. The EAT disagreed, saying that requirement meant a provision which a person has to fulfil to obtain a benefit.

In *Home Office v Holmes*[4] the EAT held that:

> Words like 'requirement' and 'condition' are plain, clear words of wide import fully capable of including any obligation of service, whether for full or for part-time, and we see no basis for giving them a restrictive interpretation in the light of the policy underlying the Act. ...

Unfortunately, in *Clymo v Wandsworth LBC*,[5] the EAT adopted a much narrower interpretation of 'requirement', holding that the employers had not 'applied' a requirement or condition of full-time working; full-time working was a requirement of the terms of employment but was not something which the employers had positively 'applied' to the applicant when they had offered her employment. The EAT made a distinction between different types of jobs, saying that if a cleaner is required to work full-time, it would clearly be a 'requirement' or 'condition', whereas for a managing director it would be in the nature of the appointment and not a 'requirement' or 'condition'.

Clymo was not followed by the Northern Ireland Court of Appeal in *Briggs v North Eastern Education and Library Board*,[6] where the court held that the fact that the nature of the job requires full-time attendance does not prevent there being a 'requirement'. *Clymo* is also inconsistent with European law (see below).

---

2 [1982] IRLR 482, EAT.
3 The EAT said that the purpose of the draughtsmen in using both words must have been to extend the ambit of what is covered so as to include anything which fairly falls within the ordinary meaning of either word and should not be given a narrow construction.
4 [1984] IRLR 299 EAT.
5 [1989] IRLR 241, EAT.
6 [1990] IRLR 81, NICA.

There is no ECJ case which supports the interpretation of 'requirement' adopted in *Clymo* and it is now generally disregarded as an authority. In *Bilka-Kaufhaus v Weber von Hartz* (n1 above) the ECJ held that a practice which in fact affects more women than men infringes article 119 EEC unless the employer can prove that the measure is objectively justified. It is doubtful, therefore, whether under European law it is necessary to show that a requirement has actually been 'applied' at all (see *Enderby v Frenchay Health Authority and Secretary of State for Health*).[7]

Examples of 'requirements' and 'conditions'
– The requirement to work full-time;
– the requirement to work anti-social hours, such as late at night or early in the morning;
– the requirement to work rigid, inflexible hours;
– the requirement to be mobile, ie, move workplace;
– length of service requirements.

Requirements and conditions may be explicit or implicit and may be found in a job description, contract of employment, collective agreement, notice, letter, or custom and practice.

Is the requirement or condition an absolute bar?

In *Perera v Civil Service Commission and Department of Customs and Excise*[8] the Court of Appeal held that the applicant must establish that the requirement is an absolute bar in the sense that failure to comply would disqualify the applicant. It was therefore not enough to show that factors taken into account by the employer merely weigh against the applicant.[9] *Perera* is arguably wrong and in a sex discrimination case such a restrictive interpretation could be challenged as a breach of the Equal Treatment Directive. The ETD provides that there shall be no discrimination whatsoever, whether direct or indirect. The fact that the employer expresses a *preference*, instead of a *requirement*, for a full-time worker does not mean there is no discrimination; if

---

7 [1993] IRLR 591, ECJ; but see also *Bhudi and Others v IMI Refiners Ltd* [1994] IRLR 204, where the EAT held that there was no obligation on a UK court to construe SDA s1(1)(b) in such a way as to disregard the express provision relating to proof of a 'requirement or condition', even after *Enderby*).
8 [1983] IRLR 166, CA.
9 See also *Meer v Tower Hamlets LBC* [1988] IRLR 399, CA and *Brook v London Borough of Haringey* [1982] IRLR 478, EAT.

a female applicant is rejected because her inability to work full time is taken into account, this is surely less favourable treatment.

(2) When was the requirement or condition applied to the applicant? (the material time)

The test is whether the applicant could comply with the requirement or condition at the time when it was applied to her. At different times she might have been able to comply with the requirement or condition; that is not relevant.

In *Clarke v Eley* (n2 above) the employers argued that one of the part-time workers could, in the past, have transferred to full-time work.[10] The EAT held that the relevant time was when the redundancies were taking place and it was irrelevant that she could have transferred to full-time work in the past.

The timing is important for women wishing to return to work part-time. A request to work part-time on return from maternity leave is often made before the woman goes on leave. The request clearly relates to the date when she is due to return and this should be the 'material time'. However, according to the EAT decision in *Cast v Croydon College*[11] the time limit for bringing a claim is within three months of the date the employer first refused the employee's request to return to work part-time. This is arguably wrong, as the act of discrimination (as defined by the Act) is not complete until the employee is not able to comply with the requirement (see p195). In addition, it could be argued the discrimination continues throughout the woman's absence.

(3) The 'relevant circumstances' and the pool

Indirect discrimination is concerned with the differential impact of requirements or conditions on women and men. The relevant circumstances in each case must be the same or similar. Thus, the comparison is between groups of men and women – those in the pool – as defined by 'the relevant circumstances'.

This is one of the most difficult points to demonstrate, as the impact of a requirement or condition may depend on the groups of men and women compared. The comparison may be between

10 Though she could not have done so at the time that the redundancies were being negotiated and the requirement that part-time workers go first was applied.
11 Unreported EAT/161/95, June 1996. Leave to appeal has been sought.

men and women in the labour market, men and women who are qualified for the job, or men and women in the particular workforce.

In *Pearse v City of Bradford MC*[12] the applicant challenged an employer's requirement that only full-time employees could apply for a post. She chose as the pool all the staff at the college where she was employed but the IT held that the pool should be restricted to those qualified for the post. As the applicant had produced statistical evidence relating only to the entire staff, as opposed to the qualified staff, her claim was dismissed.

In *Jones v University of Manchester*[13] the Court of Appeal held that the pool should consist of those otherwise qualified for the post, excluding the discriminatory requirement.

In *London Underground Ltd v Edwards*[14] Mrs Edwards, a single parent with a young child, worked as a train driver between about 8 am and 4 pm every weekday with Saturday as a rest day. In 1991 her employers announced a new flexible shift system, under which she would sometimes have to work from 4.45 am and all day on Sundays (when she had previously only worked the early turn). The tribunal took the pool to be all lone parent drivers.[15]

On appeal by London Underground, the EAT held that the tribunal had chosen the wrong pool. The correct pool for comparison was all train drivers to whom the new rostering arrangements applied; the proper question was whether the requirement relating to availability for rostering was such that a considerably smaller proportion of women qualified as train drivers than of men so qualified could comply.

When the case returned to the tribunal, it still upheld the applicant's complaint.[16]

It is important to ensure that discrimination is not incorporated into the pool. In *Kidd v DRG (UK) Ltd*,[17] where the applicant challenged as discriminatory a redundancy procedure whereby part-time workers were dismissed first, the EAT said that

12 [1988] IRLR 379, EAT.
13 [1993] IRLR 218, CA.
14 [1995] IRLR 355, EAT.
15 It still found that a considerably smaller proportion of female single parents than male single parents could comply with their requirement to work non-social or extended hours and found in favour of the applicant.
16 *Edwards v London Underground Ltd (No 2)* (1996) EAT DCLD 27 COIT Case No 04813/93. It is now being appealed again.
17 [1985] IRLR 190, EAT.

Indirect discrimination 191

the pool was the section of the population living in households needing to provide childcare to an extent that would normally be incompatible with acceptance of full-time employment. By defining the relevant circumstances as the need to provide care for children, the EAT restricted the pool to those who largely could not comply with the requirement to be a full-time worker, omitting all those who could comply with it, thus making it very difficult to show disparate impact as between members of that pool. Although this case was not further appealed, it must be wrong to limit the pool by the very factors (such as childcare responsibilities) which gave rise to the applicant's inability to comply with the requirement. The whole point is to compare the effect of a requirement on an 'advantaged' and 'disadvantaged' group, not between two sections of the 'disadvantaged' group.

Applicants should take great care in their choice of pool where there is a dispute. It is advisable for this to be decided by the IT as a preliminary point so that appropriate statistics can be obtained.

Obtaining the evidence

It will often be difficult to obtain evidence of the impact of a requirement on men and women in the identified pool. In *Greater Manchester Police Authority v Lea*[18] the EAT said that the pool does not have to be a statistically perfect match of persons who would be interested in and capable of filling the post offered. The IT was not wrong to accept that the economically active population was an appropriate pool of persons for the purpose of determining the proportion of men and women who could comply with a condition of not being in receipt of an occupational pension, even though the statistical base was wider than perfection would have dictated.

If, for example, a woman applies for a job asking to work part time, the appropriate pool may be men and women in the surrounding area who are qualified for the job in question. Yet how is this information to be obtained? It could be the actual applicants for the post but this may have a distorting effect, as many women might not apply if the job was advertised as a full-time one.

Tribunals are often prepared to take account of the 'ordinary behaviour' of men and women and accept that women are much more likely to want to work part-time than men. In *Meade-Hill*

---

18 [1990] IRLR 372, EAT.

and *National Union of Civil and Public Servants v British Council*,[19] where the challenge was to a mobility clause, the Court of Appeal said that it was common ground that because a higher proportion of women than men are secondary earners, it is more difficult for them to move house and therefore a considerably greater proportion of women than men could not in practice comply with a direction to move house. That was something of which judicial notice could be taken.

Where statistics are available these should be presented. Where, for example, a woman is seeking to return to work part-time, the questionnaire procedure can be used to find out how many men and women in the organisation work part-time. In *Greater Glasgow Health Board v Carey*[20] the EAT held that the tribunal was entitled to draw an adverse inference from the failure of the employers to answer questions relating to the number of health visitors who failed to return to their employment after maternity leave because of the employers' policy of refusing to allow them to job-share or work half weeks.

General statistics can be obtained from the *Labour Force Survey*, Equal Opportunities Commission, Income Data Services and the *Employment Gazette*.

(4) Establishing disparate impact

The test under the SDA is whether the *proportion* (not number) of women who can comply is smaller than the proportion of men who can.

The proportionate comparison is calculated by:
a) taking the number of women in the pool;
b) taking the number of women in the pool who can meet the challenged requirement; and
c) dividing (b) by (a); this gives the proportion of women in the pool who can satisfy the requirement.

The same calculation is then done for men and the comparison is then between the two fractions or percentages.

A variation of this test was adopted in *R v Secretary of State for Employment ex p Seymour Smith and Perez*,[21] where the

---

19 [1995] IRLR 478, CA.
20 [1987] IRLR 485, EAT.
21 [1995] IRLR 464, CA (on appeal to the House of Lords).

challenged requirement was the two-year qualifying condition for claiming unfair dismissal. The Court of Appeal said that the test under EU law was that:

> ... there must be a considerable difference in the number or percentage of one sex in the advantaged or disadvantaged group as against the other sex.

In *Seymour Smith* the Court of Appeal said that, following *Jones v Chief Adjudication Officer*,[22] the court should first predict what proportion of the women in the pool should be able to comply with the requirement and how many not, and second, compare the predicted result with the actual result. The steps to be taken were to:

a) identify the requirement or condition;
b) identify the relevant pool, comprising all those who satisfy the other criteria for selection (eg, qualified train drivers);
c) divide the relevant pool into:
  – those who satisfy the challenged criterion (eg, those who can comply with a requirement to work anti-social hours) and
  – those who do not satisfy it;
d) predict statistically what proportion of each group should consist of women; this should reflect the proportion of women in the pool;
e) work out what the actual male/female balance in the two groups is; and
f) compare the actual with the predicted balances.

If women are considerably under-represented in the group which can comply with the requirement and considerably over-represented in the group which cannot, disparate impact is proved.

In *Seymour Smith* the Court of Appeal was impressed by the persistence and consistency of the figures over a six-year period. Between 1985 and 1991 the ratio of women to men with two years' service or more ranged only from 85.6 per cent to 87.5 per cent. Between 72 per cent and 77.4 per cent of men had two or more years' service, compared to between 63.8 per cent and 68.9 per cent of women.

---

22 [1993] IRLR 218, CA.

Extent of disparity

There is no rule as to when one proportion should be viewed as 'considerably' smaller than another.[23] In *Seymour Smith* the Court of Appeal accepted that the test is whether there is a 'considerable' difference. It was pointed out that the ETD provides that there shall be 'no discrimination whatsoever on grounds of sex'; thus the weight to be attached to the word 'considerable' must not be exaggerated. In *Seymour Smith* the Court of Appeal held that disparate impact had been proved.

(5) Can the employer justify the requirement or condition?

Once the complainant has shown disparate impact of the requirement or condition, it is then up to the employer to prove that it is justifiable. The employer must give reasons for any difference of treatment. A mere assertion is insufficient.

In *Bilka* (n1 above), which has been followed in other cases, the ECJ said that the measures chosen (which had a disparate impact) must:

a) correspond to a real need on the part of the undertaking;
b) be appropriate with a view to achieving the objectives pursued; and
c) be necessary to that end.[24]

In *R v Secretary of State for Employment ex p EOC*,[25] where the exclusion of part-time workers from certain employment rights was successfully challenged, the House of Lords said that the aim of the qualifying thresholds was to bring about an increase in the availability of part-time work. The purpose was said to be to reduce the costs to employers of employing part-time workers. The Lords pointed out that the same result would follow from paying part-time workers a lower basic rate than full-time workers. This would be a 'gross breach of the principle of equal pay' and could not possibly be regarded as a suitable means of achieving an increase in part-time employment. Nor did the House of Lords accept that there was any evidence that the threshold provisions had actually resulted in greater availability of part-time work than would have been the case without them.

---

23 *McCausland v Dungannon District Council* [1993] IRLR 583, NICA.
24 See also *Rinner-Kühn v FWW Spezial-Gebäudereinigung GmbH* [1989] IRLR 493, ECJ.
25 [1994] IRLR 176, HL.

Indirect discrimination 195

It is clear from the *EOC* case and *Rinner-Kühn* that generalised statements should not be sufficient to show justification.[26]

In *Hampson v Department of Education and Science*[27] the Court of Appeal said it was necessary to strike a balance between the discriminatory effect of the requirement or condition and the reasonable needs of the person who applies it. In *Jones v University of Manchester* (n13 above) the court said that it was necessary to consider how many of the 'disadvantaged' groups were likely to suffer as a result of the discriminatory requirement or condition and the extent of the damage.

Examples of grounds for justification (which have been accepted by ITs, so are not binding) are summarised in chapter 6, pp81ff.

(6) Can the applicant comply with the requirement or condition?

'Can' means 'can in practice' or can consistent with social conditions. In *Price v Civil Service Commission*[28] the EAT said 'it is relevant in determining whether women can comply with the condition to take into account the current usual behaviour of women in this respect as observed in practice, putting aside behaviour and responses which are unusual'.

However, in *Clymo* (n5 above) the EAT upheld the IT decision that the applicant could comply with the requirement to work full-time. The IT said that:

> At this level of income, and most particularly in the London area, with child minding facilities readily available, people of these qualifications and this combined income and with a professional career both behind and ahead of them could certainly conduct their family arrangements on less old-fashioned bases than the less qualified and more lowly paid.

---

26 Although the ECJ accepted generalised statements in two German cases (*Nolte v Landesversichherungsanstalt Hannover* [1996] IRLR 225 and *Megner and Scheffel v Innungskrankenkasse Vorderpfalz* [1996] IRLR 236), the ECJ later (in *Küraatorium für Dialyse und Nierentransplantation eV v Johanna Lewark* 9.2.96) and *Edith Freers, Hannelor Speckmann v Deutsche Bundespost* (7.3.96) reiterated the *Bilka* test – ie, whether the legislation was suitable and necessary for achieving its stated purpose. In the latter cases the ECJ left this question for the national court to decide.
27 [1990] IRLR 302, HL.
28 [1977] IRLR 291, EAT.

This, however, ignores all the factors which make it difficult for women to combine full-time work and childcare. The decision is inconsistent with several House of Lords decisions and this very restrictive interpretation is almost certainly a breach of the ETD.

(7) Has the applicant suffered a detriment?

A woman cannot complain of a requirement being indirectly discriminatory unless she herself cannot comply with it at the time the requirement is imposed. The Northern Ireland Court of Appeal has pointed out that the verb 'can' in 'cannot comply with' must be given the same interpretation as the verb 'can' in the term 'can comply with'. The two subparagraphs are reverse sides of the same test, in so far as they refer to being able to comply.[29] It is irrelevant if at some time in the past or future the woman might not have been able or would not be able to comply with the requirement.[30]

INDIRECT DISCRIMINATION: KEY POINTS

- Indirect discrimination is concerned with practices which have a disparate impact on women; in the maternity context this is because of their family commitment.
- There are seven questions to address:
(1) There must be a requirement or condition. These terms should be broadly defined. The courts have held that the requirement or condition must be an absolute bar rather than a preference. This may be contrary to EU law.
(2) The question is whether the applicant could comply with the requirement or condition when it was applied to her.
(3) The relevant circumstances must be the same or similar, thus the comparison is not between *all* men and women but between, say, qualified men and women. The pool may be

---

29 *Briggs v North Eastern Education and Library Board* [1990] IRLR 181, NICA.
30 In *Clymo*, the EAT refused to accept that a requirement to work full time was to the applicant's detriment because she could not comply with it. The EAT said that 'in trying to fit society into the framework of the statute and the statute into our society, in every employment ladder there will come a stage at which a woman who has family responsibilities must make a choice'. This statement is contrary to the underlying purpose of the SDA and should not be followed. It was doubted by the Northern Ireland Court of Appeal in *Briggs*.

restricted to men and women in the area or in the particular workforce. Where there is doubt about the identity of the pool, it should be resolved as a preliminary issue, or the case should be argued on the basis of different pools; failure to identify the correct pool may be fatal to the case. Care must be taken to ensure that there is no discrimination in the 'relevant circumstances' or choice of pool.

(4) The comparison is proportionate, not absolute. The court should predict what proportion of the women in the pool should be able to comply with the requirement and how many not, and then compare the predicted result with the actual result. The test is whether there is a considerable difference and the persistence and consistency of statistics will be important. Tribunals may take judicial notice of 'ordinary behaviour', particularly in part-time work cases.

(5) Once disparate impact has been proved, the employer will have a defence if s/he can prove that the requirement or condition is justifiable. The employer should be required to provide evidence that the requirement is justified.

(6) Could the applicant comply with the requirement? Theoretical but impractical possibilities should be disregarded; current usual behaviour, such as women's childcare responsibilities, must be taken into account.

(7) The applicant must show that she suffered a disadvantage or detriment because of her inability to comply with the requirement at the time it is imposed. Generally only a victim can bring a claim of discrimination.

CHAPTER 14

European Community law

Introduction

The influence of European law on UK discrimination law and maternity rights has been enormous and is continuing. Amendments to EPCA (now the ERA) were forced on a reluctant government in 1994 by the obligation to implement the Pregnant Workers Directive.

In many cases, as in *Webb v EMO Air Cargo* (see p176), the UK courts have been obliged to interpret UK law in the light of the more liberal EU law and ECJ decisions. In all sex discrimination and maternity rights cases, applicants, respondents and advisers should consider the parallel provisions of EU law. European law often offers more protection to women than UK law. Unlike the tightly defined rights provided under the SDA and the maternity provisions of the ERA, EU law lays down broad principles.

European Communities Act 1972

The European Communities Act 1972 s2(1) provides that rights and obligations under EU law, which are sufficiently clear and precise, must be recognised and can be directly enforced in the UK.[1] The ECJ has said that the UK courts must set aside any national legislation which prevents a person from relying on directly effective EU law.

Although the European Communities Act 1972 s2(4) and the

---

1 Section 2(1) provides that all 'rights, powers, liabilities, obligations and restrictions' arising by or under Community law which, under EU law 'are without further enactment to be given legal effect or used in the UK shall be recognised and available in law, to be enforced, allowed and followed accordingly'. Section 2(4) provides that '...any enactment passed or to be passed ... shall be construed and have effect subject to the foregoing'.

caselaw would suggest that EU law should, in all cases, take precedence over UK law, in practice the implementation of this seemingly straightforward principle has not been so simple.

This chapter sets out a brief summary of the relevant European provisions and how they can be enforced in different situations.[2]

EU legislation

Treaty of Rome and article 119

The Treaty of Rome was one of the three treaties which set up the EU. The Treaty comprises many articles, one of which, article 119, provides that 'men and women should receive equal pay for equal work'. This is further explained by the provisions of the Equal Pay Directive (see p173).

The Pregnant Workers Directive

The provisions of this Directive are summarised on p11.

The Equal Treatment Directive

The Equal Treatment Directive provides that there shall be no discrimination whatsoever on the ground of sex, either directly or indirectly, nor by reference to marital or family status. It covers all aspects of employment (see p170). This was interpreted very broadly by the ECJ in *P v S and Cornwall County Council*,[3] a case which established that transsexuals are protected by the ETD. The Advocate General (who provided a legal opinion on the case for the court) stressed 'the true essence of that fundamental and inalienable value which is equality'. He expressed his 'profound conviction that what is at stake is a universal fundamental value, indelibly etched in modern legal traditions ...: the irrelevance of a person's sex with regard to the rules regulating relations in society.'

The Parental Leave Directive

The UK has refused to adopt this directive, which provides for three months' parental leave and time off to care for sick dependants.

---

2 For a more detailed analysis see *Discrimination at Work*.
3 [1996] IRLR 347.

EU law in UK courts and tribunals

EU law applies in tribunals as well as courts. The EAT has rejected the argument that as tribunals are creatures of statute they have no power to apply EU law.[4] However, they have no inherent or general jurisdiction to hear cases under Community law other than under specific domestic statutes. In *Biggs v Somerset County Council*[5] the EAT said that tribunals only had jurisdiction to apply and enforce Community law to claims within their jurisdiction as defined by statute. The statutes include ERA 1996, EqPA 1970 and SDA 1975.

Interpreting UK law to comply with EU law

Where possible UK law should be interpreted so as to conform with EU law.[6] In *Webb v EMO Air Cargo (UK) Ltd*[7] the House of Lords held that:

> it is for a United Kingdom court to construe domestic legislation in any field covered by a Community directive so as to accord with the interpretation of the directive as laid down by the European Court, if that can be done without distorting the meaning of the domestic legislation.... That is so whether the domestic legislation came after or, as in this case, preceded the directive ...

Thus, where the meaning of UK law is quite clear and it conflicts with more favourable EU law, UK law cannot be distorted so as to accord with EU law.[8]

Where there is a conflict between UK and EU law

The principle is that national courts must apply EU law (including case law) irrespective of what national legislation says.[9] They must if necessary refuse to apply any provision of national legislation

---

4 *Secretary of State for Scotland and Greater Glasgow Health Board v Wright and Hannah* [1991] IRLR 187, EAT.
5 [1995] IRLR 452, EAT. The decision was upheld on appeal: [1996] IRLR 203, CA.
6 *Garland v British Rail Engineering Ltd* [1982] IRLR 111, ECJ.
7 [1993] IRLR 27, HL.
8 See also *Porter v Cannon Hygiene Ltd* [1993] IRLR 329, NICA.
9 The ECJ has stated that 'every national court must, in a case within its jurisdiction, apply Community law in its entirety and protect rights which the latter confers on individuals and must accordingly set aside any provision of national law which may conflict with it, whether prior or subsequent to the Community rule'.

where it conflicts with EU law.[10] However, this principle is not easy to apply in practice. Different principles apply according to whether:
– the complainant is relying on article 119 or on one of the directives, and
– in the case of directives, whether the complainant is working for a public-sector or private-sector employer.

Article 119

Article 119 is directly applicable and directly effective where its terms are unconditional and sufficiently precise. This means that, even where there is a conflict between UK and EU law, the latter may be relied on by private and public-sector employees in tribunals and courts.[11] Article 119 can, effectively, be treated as being part of UK law, subject to matters of interpretation being referred to the ECJ.

The directives

Private-sector employees

Private sector employees cannot rely on the provisions of a directive. A directive is only binding on the member state, ie, the government. Thus an employee working for a private individual or company cannot enforce the provisions of a directive against her employer.[12]

Public-sector employees

A public sector employee can rely on the provisions of a directive provided they are clear, precise and not subject to any exceptions which would require the intervention of the national authorities in order to be enforceable.[13] The rationale is that a public body should not be able to take advantage of the government's failure

---

10 This applies even if the national law was adopted subsequently, and it is not necessary for the court to request or await the prior setting aside of such provisions by legislative or other constitutional means: *Amministrazione delle Finanze dello Stato v Simmenthal SpA* [1978] CMLR 263, ECJ.
11 *Pickstone v Freemans plc* [1988] IRLR 357, HL.
12 *Marshall v Southampton and South-West Hampshire Area Health Authority* [1986] IRLR 140, ECJ.
13 *Marshall* (above); *Griffin and Others v South West Water Services Ltd* [1995] IRLR 15, ChD.

to implement the directives.

In *Marshall v Southampton and South-West Hampshire Area Health Authority (No 2)*[14] the European Court of Justice held that the limits on compensation in the SDA were a breach of the Equal Treatment Directive. Article 6 of the directive provides that 'Member States shall introduce into their national legal systems such measures as are necessary to enable all persons who consider themselves wronged by failure to apply to them the principle of equal treatment ... to pursue their claims by judicial process ...' The ECJ held that this article meant that compensation must enable the loss or damage actually sustained as a result of the discriminatory dismissal to be made good in full. As a result of this decision the limit on compensation contained in the SDA was removed.

It should be noted that the Pregnant Workers Directive article 12 is almost identical. Following the principles laid down in *Marshall (No 2)*, the limit on compensation for pregnancy-related dismissals under the ERA is almost certainly a breach of the Pregnant Workers Directive.

It is often appropriate to bring a claim under both article 119 and all the directives. For example, a challenge to the 'triggering' provisions (whereby women are forced on to maternity leave if they have a pregnancy-related absence in the six weeks before their EWC) may be made under article 119 on the basis that they have been denied sick pay (whether statutory or contractual), which is 'pay' under article 119. There may also be a breach of the Equal Treatment Directive because the women have been refused sick leave. In addition the provisions may be contrary to the Pregnant Workers Directive because there has been a derogation of existing rights (see p12). All women can rely on article 119, but only women working for a public-sector employer will be able to rely on the directives. A woman working for a private sector employer will need to consider proceedings against the government, either through judicial review or a *Francovich* challenge (see below).

What is a public-sector worker?
Public-sector employers include the government, local authorities, health authorities and the police. A privatised water company has

---

14 [1993] IRLR 445, ECJ.

been held to be a public employer on the basis that the public service in question is under the control of the state.[15] The governing body of a voluntary aided school is not a public employer, though it is likely that governing bodies of LEA schools would be classified as public bodies.

Enforcement of directives through judicial review against the government

In *R v Secretary of State for Employment ex p Equal Opportunities Commission and Another*,[16] the EOC, together with an individual, brought judicial review proceedings in the High Court against the Employment Secretary, alleging that the exclusion of part-time workers from protection under the old EPCA was indirectly discriminatory and in breach of the Equal Treatment Directive. The House of Lords held that judicial review was available for the purpose of securing a declaration that UK primary legislation is incompatible with European Community law. In the *EOC* case, the court made a declaration that the provisions regarding length of service before a part-time worker could bring a claim for certain employment rights were incompatible with Community law. As a result, the law was changed.

In *R v Secretary of State for Employment ex p Seymour Smith and Perez*[17] the applicants successfully challenged, by way of judicial review, the two-year qualifying period for bringing an unfair dismissal claim. The Court of Appeal granted a declaration that the two-year qualification period was incompatible with the principle of equal treatment enshrined in the ETD. During the relevant period (1985–1991) a considerably smaller proportion of women than men could comply with the qualifying conditions (see p193).

Either an individual, an official body such as the EOC, a trade union or a voluntary organisation with sufficient interest may bring judicial review proceedings against the government for failure to implement the Pregnant Workers Directive or the Equal Treatment Directive.[18] These can only be brought in the High Court, not an industrial tribunal.

15. *Griffin v South West Water Services Ltd* [1995] IRLR 15, ChD.
16. [1994] IRLR 176, HL.
17. [1995] IRLR 464, CA. This case is being appealed to the House of Lords (due to be heard in October 1996).
18. *R v Secretary of State for Social Services ex p CPAG* [1989] 3 WLR 1116, QBD.

Francovich proceedings

An individual who has suffered financial loss because of the failure of the state to implement a directive may be able to recover compensation from the state. This principle was established by three ECJ decisions.[19] There are three conditions which must be satisfied:

a) the directive must confer identifiable rights on individuals (the Equal Treatment Directive and Pregnant Workers Directive clearly provide rights for individuals);

b) the breach must be sufficiently serious. The test is whether the member state manifestly and gravely disregarded the limits on its discretion. Relevant factors include:
   - the clarity and precision of the rule breached,
   - the measure of discretion left by that rule to the national authorities,
   - whether the infringement and damage caused was intentional or involuntary,
   - whether any error of law was excusable,
   - the adoption or retention of national measures or practices contrary to EU law.

   In other words, the remedy will depend on the extent to which the member state was at fault.

c) there must be a causal link between the failure by the member state to implement the directive and the damage suffered by the individual.

There have been surprisingly few cases following *Francovich*.

Francovich proceedings should be brought against the Attorney General in the High Court. They cannot be brought in an IT.[20]

Challenging UK law through the European Commission

An individual or interested organisation can request the European Commission to take proceedings against the government for failing to implement a directive. The Commission can take action against the UK government if it considers that the UK has not fulfilled its obligations under EU law. Initially the Commission will attempt to reach a settlement, failing which it may bring infringement proceedings in the ECJ.

19 *Francovich v Italian Republic* [1992] IRLR 84; *Brasserie du Pecheur SA v Federal Republic of Germany* [1996] All ER (EC) 301; [1996] IRLR 267, ECJ and *R v Secretary of State for Transport ex p Factortame Ltd and Others* [1996] IRLR 267. (The last two cases were considered by the ECJ together.)
20 *Secretary of State for Employment v Mann and Others* [1996] IRLR 4, EAT.

Reference to the ECJ

The Treaty of Rome article 117 gives the ECJ power to make preliminary rulings on the proper interpretation of EU law, which must then be followed in the UK. A national court (or tribunal) may refer a question of interpretation, if necessary, to the ECJ, and *must* do so if there is no remedy under national law, unless the question is irrelevant, has already been answered by the ECJ or the answer is clear.[21]

A tribunal or court may, either if requested by a party to proceedings or of its own volition, refer a question of interpretation of EU law to the ECJ. The House of Lords, in *Webb v EMO Air Cargo (UK) Ltd*,[22] felt it was appropriate to make a referral to the ECJ as the ECJ had not considered whether it would be discriminatory for an employer to dismiss a female employee who because of her pregnancy would be unable to carry out her job.

Referral to ECJ by an individual

Individuals can bring a direct action by writing to the ECJ with details of the dispute, grounds for application and some evidence. This is outside the scope of this book.

Powers of the ECJ

The ECJ cannot decide the case at issue. It will only answer the questions of law put to it and refer the case back to the tribunal or court to apply the law to the facts of the case. Thus the ECJ will not generally decide on justifiability in indirect discrimination cases, though guidelines may be laid down. Usually, it is for the national court to decide whether a requirement is justified.

Sufficient remedy under UK law is a bar to an EU claim

In *Blaik v The Post Office*[23] the EAT held that 'if there is a sufficient remedy given by domestic law, it is unnecessary, and, indeed, impermissible to explore the same complaint under the equivalent provisions in the Directive.' It is only if there is a disparity between the two that it becomes necessary to consider whether the provisions in EU law are directly enforceable by the complainant in her proceedings against the respondent.

---

21 See *Pickstone v Freemans plc* [1988] IRLR 367, HL and *Johnstone v Chief Constable of the Royal Ulster Constabulary* [1986] IRLR 263, ECJ for guidance as to when to refer a case to the ECJ.
22 [1993] IRLR 27, HL.
23 [1994] IRLR 280, EAT.

Time limits under EU law

The ECJ, in *Emmott v Minister for Social Welfare*,[24] held that, in the absence of Community rules, it is for each member state to decide the procedural conditions governing claims under EU law, provided:
- such conditions are not less favourable than those relating to similar actions; and
- the conditions are not framed so as to make it virtually impossible to exercise EU rights.

Thus, national time limits will generally apply to claims under article 119 or one of the directives.[25]

However, where a directive (but not article 119) has not been properly implemented by the member state, time will run from the date the directive was implemented. In article 119 cases the Court of Appeal has said that, as article 119 is directly effective, national time limits apply.[26] Thus the time limit for bringing an unfair dismissal claim based on article 119 is within three months of the date of dismissal. (For time limits generally, see chapter 15.)

Backdating of claims

A national rule which limits the period within which compensation can be backdated is not in breach of EU law.[27] Thus in order to challenge the two-year period (prior to issuing proceedings) for claiming arrears of pay under the EqPA it must be shown that such a limitation would 'render virtually impossible the exercise of rights conferred by community law' or is less favourable than for similar claims.[28]

Usefulness of EU law

The broad principles laid down by EU law, which apply to a wide range of discriminatory acts, are in stark contrast to the tightly

---

24 [1991] IRLR 387, ECJ.
25 See also *Johnson v Chief Adjudication Officer (No 2)* [1995] IRLR 157, ECJ.
26 In *Biggs v Somerset County Council* [1996] IRLR 181 the Court of Appeal held that a part-time worker could have brought an unfair dismissal claim in 1976 (relying on article 119), even though at the time the national law excluded certain part-time workers from unfair dismissal protection.
27 *Steenhorst-Neerings v Bestuur van de Bedrijfsvereniging voor Detailhandel* [1994] IRLR 244, ECJ.
28 *Levez v T H Jennings (Harlow Pools) Ltd* [1996] IRLR 499, EAT. The latter point was held and referred to the ECJ by the lay members, overruling the President.

defined provisions in the SDA, EqPA and ERA. There are no exceptions to the Pregnant Workers Directive and few in the Equal Treatment Directive. It is likely that EU law will continue to provide protection where none exists under UK law.

EC LAW: KEY POINTS

- Relevant EU legislation is:
  - article 119, which provides that men and women should receive equal pay for work of equal value,
  - the Equal Pay Directive, which explains article 119,
  - the Equal Treatment Directive, which provides there shall be no discrimination in all aspects of employment, and
  - The Pregnant Workers Directive, which lays down minimum maternity rights.
- The effect of EU law in UK courts;
  - ITs have the same jurisdiction to apply EU law as the courts.
  - UK law must, where possible, be interpreted so as to conform with EU law.
  - UK courts and tribunals must set aside any national legislation which prevents a person from relying on directly effective EU law.
  - If there is a clear and direct conflict between UK and EU law, the latter's effect depends on whether it is directly effective (enforceable without further implementation) and directly applicable (enforceable by public-sector employees).
  - Article 119 is directly applicable *and* directly effective where its terms are sufficiently precise.
  - Where their provisions are sufficiently clear and precise, the directives can be relied on by public sector employees (without further implementation by the UK government) but not by private-sector employees; this means that where a directive provides greater rights than UK law, a public sector-employee can rely on the EU right in UK courts and tribunals.
- The directives, where they have not been implemented (or inadequately implemented), may be enforced through legal proceedings against the government.

- An individual can request the European Commission to take enforcement action against her or his government for failing to implement a directive.
- An individual who has suffered financial loss because of the failure of the state to implement a directive may be able to recover compensation from the State in a *Francovich* action.
- An IT or court can refer a question of interpretation to the ECJ and must do so in certain circumstances. Individuals can bring a direct action by writing to the ECJ with details of the application.
- There are no procedural rules under EU law, but the parallel domestic procedures apply, including time limits.
- Applicants should always consider bringing an action under EU law as it is of much wider application than UK law.

CHAPTER 15
Procedure and remedies

Introduction

This chapter contains a summary of the practice and procedure in tribunals for unfair dismissal and discrimination and describes the remedies. References to rules are to those in the Industrial Tribunals (Constitution and Rules of Procedure) Regulations 1993 SI No 2687 Sch 1 unless otherwise stated.

Tribunal procedure is meant to be informal and accessible to litigants in person. For example, there are no strict rules of evidence and the tribunal has a wide power to regulate its own procedure.[1] Despite the intended informality, tribunal procedure is becoming increasingly technical, particularly where the parties are represented.[2]

Framework

Industrial tribunals

ITs have no powers other than those given to them by statute, eg, the ERA, the SDA and the European Communities Act 1972 (see p200). Tribunal decisions are persuasive but not binding.

Appeals

An appeal from an IT (on a point of law) lies to the Employment Appeal Tribunal (EAT). EAT decisions are binding on ITs and county courts. There is a further appeal to the Court of Appeal and House of Lords. A tribunal or court can refer a question about the interpretation of European law to the European Court of Justice (see p205).

---

1 r13(1).
2 For a detailed analysis see McMullen and Eady, *Employment Tribunal Procedure* (Legal Action Group 1996). See also the EOC guide, *Your Rights: A step-by-step guide to presentation of cases at an industrial tribunal*.

Financial help and legal advice

Legal aid is not available for representation in tribunals. The preparation of the case may be covered by the 'green form' scheme for those on a low income with little capital. Legal aid is available (for those who come within the income and capital limits) for an appeal to the EAT or to the higher courts, provided that the case has sufficient merit.

Unions sometimes provide legal help for complainants, either through local branch officers or stewards or national officers and legal departments.

Law centres, citizens advice bureaux or other advice agencies in the area may offer legal advice and/or representation (see appendix 8).

The Maternity Alliance offers free legal advice on maternity rights and benefits, but is not usually able to provide legal representation.

The Equal Opportunities Commission (EOC)

The EOC can give advice or financial assistance under the SDA or EqPA. It has no power to grant assistance for claims under the ERA. However, most maternity-related claims will also include a discrimination claim under the SDA. Assistance may include giving advice, negotiating a settlement, and arranging for assistance or representation.[3]

Initial steps in bringing a claim

Whom to name as respondent

The employer should be named. If there is any doubt about the identity of the employer, it is advisable to name all the alternatives. Dismissal by a school with a delegated budget is deemed to be a dismissal by the governing body, though any compensation will be payable by the local education authority.[4]

Letter before action

Before issuing proceedings, it is usually advisable to write a letter

---

3 SDA s75.
4 Education (Modification of Enactments Relating to Employment) Order 1989 SI 1989/901, arts 4, 6(3).

to the employer setting out the broad nature of the claim. It is important that the information contained in the letter is absolutely accurate, as it may otherwise be used by the respondent at the hearing to show up inconsistencies in the case.

Duty to mitigate

In recruitment and dismissal cases, an applicant should take steps to find alternative employment. Evidence of such steps will be required, so it is important to keep a record of job applications, interviews, visits to the job centre and any other measures taken to find work. The costs of taking such steps are recoverable (provided that evidence is available).

If re-employment or reinstatement is sought, the employer should be informed as soon as possible so as to try and avoid the respondent employing a replacement.

The questionnaire procedure

In cases under the SDA (but not the ERA) the employee can ask the employer questions by using the questionnaire procedure.[5] There are standard forms.[6] The purpose of this procedure is to help a complainant decide if she should start proceedings, and, if so, to help her present her claim in the most effective way.

The questionnaire may be served on the employer at any time up to three months from the act of discrimination or, if served after proceedings have been commenced, within 21 days of their commencement. Otherwise the permission of the tribunal is required. It is possible, with leave of the tribunal, to serve a further questionnaire if, after receiving a reply to the first, further questions need to be asked. The EAT has approved this, saying it is a 'sensible and necessary part of the procedure'.[7]

The questions and replies are admissible in evidence.[8] If the employer deliberately or without reasonable excuse fails to reply or is evasive or equivocal, the tribunal can draw any inference it thinks appropriate, including one that the employer has discriminated unlawfully.[9] If the employer refuses to reply to a question in the questionnaire, it may be possible to ask questions again in a request for written answers (see p216).

5 SDA s74.
6 Sex Discrimination (Questions and Replies) Order 1975 SI No 2048. See Tamara Lewis, *SDA Questionnaires* (Central London Law Centre 1996).
7 *Carrington v Helix Lighting Ltd* [1990] IRLR 6, EAT.
8 SDA s74(2)(a).
9 SDA s74(2)(b).

The questions depend on the nature of the case but in a pregnancy dismissal claim, for example, it would be useful to ask about:
- the reasons why the woman was dismissed;
- details of other employees dismissed in similar circumstances;
- what procedure should have been followed and whether it was;
- how the work of the applicant was to be done, by whom and the qualifications and experience of the replacement employee (see p249).

Time limits for bringing a claim

Unfair dismissal claims

An application claiming unfair dismissal must be made within three months of the date the contract was terminated. Where a woman is denied the right to return after maternity absence, her effective date of termination is the notified date of return.[10]

SDA claims

A sex discrimination claim must be made within three months (ie, three months less one day) from the act of discrimination. If the claim relates to a discriminatory dismissal, the time limit runs from the date when the contract was terminated, not when notice was given.[11]

A deliberate omission is treated as done when the person decided on it.[12]

If the discrimination is continuing, time starts from the last act of discrimination.[13] In *Owusu v London Fire and Civil Defence Authority*[14] the EAT held that an act extends over a period of time 'if it takes the form of some policy, rule or practice, in accordance with which decisions are taken from time to time.' This might apply, for example, to a policy on job-sharing. However, where, before she goes on maternity leave, a woman makes a request to return to work part-time, the time limit will run from the date the employer first refuses her request.[15] This is arguably wrong as the act of discrimination is not complete until the woman is unable to

---

10 ERA s97(6).
11 *Lupeti v Wrens Old House* [1984] ICR 348, EAT.
12 SDA s76.
13 SDA s76(6)(b).
14 [1995] IRLR 574, EAT.
15 *Cast v Croydon College*, unreported, EAT/161/95, June 1996.

comply with the requirement – and this is the date she wants to *start* working part-time.

In *Gledhill v Employment Service*[16] the employers had a policy whereby all returners from maternity leave had a four-week deferral of the date on which they would return on their giving three weeks notice. The tribunal held that this policy was a continuing act of discrimination which did not end until the woman returned to work. As her complaint was presented within three months from the date she returned, it was in time.[17]

Where the unlawful act is the inclusion of any unfair term in a contract, the act is treated as extending throughout the duration of the contract, so time does not start to run until the end of the contract.[18]

Equal pay and redundancy claims

An equal pay claim must be brought within six months of the employee leaving a job or the last date when the pay or contractual term was not equal.[19] The same time limit applies to claims for a redundancy payment. Where the redundancy is unfair or discriminatory, the three-month limit applies.

Claim for wrongful deduction of wages

This claim (which used to be under the Wages Act) must be made within three months of the last deduction of wages.[20]

Breach of contract

There is a six-year time limit for bringing a claim for breach of contract in the county court. Proceedings may be brought in an IT where there is a claim outstanding or which arises at the end of the woman's employment, but the time limit for bringing a claim in the IT is only three months from the effective date of termination.[21]

---

16 (1994) 24 May, Case No 2546/94, Leeds IT.
17 See also *Owusu v London Fire and Civil Defence Authority* [1995] IRLR 574, EAT.
18 SDA s76(6)(a).
19 EqPA s2(4).
20 ERA s23(3).
21 Industrial Tribunals (Extension of Jurisdiction) (England and Wales) Order 1994 SI No 1623 reg 7.

Out-of-time claims

An application may sometimes be made outside the time limit. The test is different under the ERA and SDA.

Under ERA

For unfair dismissal claims the three months run from the effective date of termination or 'within such further period as the tribunal considers reasonable in a case where it is satisfied that it was not reasonably practicable for a complaint to be presented' within the three months.[22] Examples where time has been extended include those where the applicant has a physical or mental illness, and has no adviser acting for her, postal delays, ignorance of rights or mistaken belief as to essential matters. A young pregnant woman was allowed to claim out of time after she was wrongly advised by a CAB.[23]

Once the tribunal has found that it was not reasonably practicable for the complaint to be presented in time, it must then decide whether the claim was brought within a reasonable period. The longer the delay, the less likely is it than an application for an extension will be granted.

Under the SDA

A court or tribunal may consider any complaint which is out of time if 'in all the circumstances of the case, it considers that it is just and equitable to do so'.[24] Factors that will be taken into account include those set out above and, in addition:
- any prejudice that might be caused to the respondent;
- the health of the applicant; this might include, for example, a difficult birth or subsequent postnatal illness;
- the merits of the case;
- any other relevant circumstance.

In *Faulkner v Fuller Foods International plc*[25] the tribunal allowed an out-of-time claim because of the stress the applicant suffered after a miscarriage.

In *Hancock v Lloyd*,[26] however, the tribunal refused to allow an out-of-time application, finding that the applicant had not had a particularly difficult pregnancy, had had discussions with ACAS

---

22 ERA s111(2).
23 *Cheshire v Intasave Travel and Shipping Ltd* S/2642/89.
24 SDA s76(5).
25 (1995) 1 March, Case No 64704/94, Leeds IT.
26 (1995) 10 February, Case No 56417/94, Shrewsbury IT.

and agency advisors, though they gave her confusing advice, and she had obtained a leaflet which referred to a sex discrimination claim. The IT followed the EAT decision in *Berry v Ravensbourne National Health Service Trust*,[27] where it was held that relevant matters were:
- the date on which the applicant became aware of the event giving rise to the claim,
- the lapse of time between this date and presentation of the complaint, and
- reasons for the delay.

There is no power to extend time for applications under the EqPA.

Although most late claims are barred, there is nothing to lose by making the claim.

How to apply

All claims for unfair dismissal, sex discrimination and equal pay must be lodged with the office of industrial tribunals specified on the IT1 form for the postal district concerned or with the Office of the Industrial Tribunals and the Fair Employment Tribunal in Northern Ireland.

The first step is to submit a letter or form IT1, available from the local job centre, employment office or advice agency. The following information must be given:
- the name and address of the applicant,
- the name and address of the respondent, and
- the grounds for the claim.

In *Dodd v British Telecom plc*,[28] the EAT said that the other requirements on the IT1 were directory, not mandatory. The written application need contain only sufficient information to identify who is making it, against whom, and what sort of complaint it is.

Content of application

The main incidents on which the applicant will rely should be set out. In maternity cases it is often advisable to make a claim under UK law (ERA, SDA and possibly EqPA), under EU law (Equal Treatment Directive, Pregnant Workers Directive, article 119) and for breach of contract (see pp6-7).

27 [1993] ICR 871, EAT.
28 [1980] IRLR 16, EAT.

Stages before the hearing

Amendment
The tribunal can allow amendments which may change the basis of the claim, from say unfair dismissal to discrimination, but it may be allowed only if the facts set out in the claim would also give rise to a claim of discrimination. The test is whether hardship or injustice would be caused to either party by granting or withholding permission to amend.[29]

The employer's response: notice of appearance (IT3)
The secretary of the tribunal will send a copy of the IT1 to the respondent. The employer has 21 days[29A] from receipt of the IT1 to reply, though the time limit can be extended and usually is.

The notice of appearance should set out:
- the respondent's full name and address;
- whether or not the respondent intends to resist the application; and
- the grounds of resistance.

Further particulars of IT1 and IT3
Either party can ask for further details about the other's case. This can be done by letter. If answers are not forthcoming, the tribunal may, on application, order the provision of further particulars.[30] A tribunal may also, of its own accord, ask for further details of either party's case.

Written answers
A tribunal may also make an order that written answers be given to specific questions.[31] These are similar to interrogatories in the High Court or county court. The test is whether the tribunal considers:
a) that the answer of the party to that question may help to clarify the issues likely to arise for determination in the proceedings, and
b) that it would be likely to assist the progress of the proceedings for that answer to be available to the tribunal before the hearing.

---

29 *Cocking v Sandhurst (Stationers) Ltd* [1974] ICR 650, NIRC.
29A Increased from 14 days by Industrial Tribunals (Constitution and Rules of Procedure) (Amendment) Regulations 1996 SI No 1757.
30 r4(1)(a).
31 r4(3).

Discovery

Documentation can be crucial to a maternity or pregnancy discrimination case. If the applicant is aware that the employer has particular documents, she should make a specific request for these, as well as a request for all other relevant documents. There is no duty on the parties to disclose documents unless the tribunal has made an order for discovery.[32] The test to be applied in deciding whether disclosure or production of the documents should be ordered is whether they are material and relevant to the issues in the proceedings. The tribunal can refuse to order discovery if it is not necessary either for disposing fairly of the action or matter or for saving costs.[33]

The Court of Appeal has set out important guidelines for discovery in discrimination cases in *West Midlands Passenger Transport Executive v Singh*.[34] Where the document is confidential the tribunal should inspect the document to decide whether disclosure is necessary.[35] Names and addresses can be blanked out.

It is usually preferable to ask for a list of all relevant documents as well as copies, as this will avoid any dispute over whether a document has been disclosed.

Agreed bundle of documents

It is usual for there to be an agreed bundle of documents for the hearing.

Power to strike out

The tribunal has power to strike out the whole or part of the IT1 or IT3 if a party does not comply with a tribunal order, or if there has been inordinate and inexcusable delay which might cause serious prejudice, or where a claim is scandalous, frivolous or vexatious.

Witnesses

Both parties can call witnesses and the tribunal can order a witness to attend and produce relevant documents. Application for a witness order is made by letter to the secretary of the

---

32 r4(1)(b).
33 The power to make the order under r4(1)(b) is the same as for a county court under CCR Order 14 r8(1).
34 [1988] IRLR 186, CA.
35 See also *Science Research Council v Nasse; Vyas v Leyland Cars* [1979] IRLR 465, HL.

tribunals, with an explanation as to why the evidence is relevant and giving reasons why the witness may not otherwise attend.

Tribunals now encourage the parties to prepare written statements and exchange them before the hearing. However, there is no power to order the making of such statements or their exchange. The witness statement is then usually read aloud by the witness at the hearing. The witness can usually give supplementary oral evidence.

Directions hearings

A tribunal may give directions about any matter in relation to the proceedings. Directions may be given at a hearing or by letter. Common directions relate to clarification of the issues, discovery, further and better particulars, and estimated length of the hearing.

Pre-hearing review

A tribunal has a discretion, either on the application of a party or of its own motion, to hold a pre-hearing review to determine whether the application or arguments of either party have any chance of success.

Preliminary hearings

There may be a preliminary hearing:
- to hear any issue relating to the entitlement of a party to bring or contest proceedings (eg, whether the applicant has satisfied the two-year qualifying period to bring an ordinary unfair dismissal claim), or
- to determine an issue of law, or
- to decide whether a reference should be made to the ECJ for a preliminary ruling.

Adjournments, extension of time

The tribunal has power to grant an extension of time or adjourn a hearing. An adjournment may be granted if the applicant is ill, about to give birth or has recently given birth, where a witness is ill, or where there are proceedings pending in the High Court or county court.

Equal value cases

There are special rules for equal value cases. These are outside the scope of this book (see *Discrimination at Work*).

The hearing

This will be in public. At least 14 days' notice of the hearing date must be given.

In unfair dismissal cases the burden of proof is on the employer to show the reason for the dismissal and s/he will open the case. In constructive dismissal cases where the employer claims that the employee resigned, the burden of proof will be on the employee, who will go first. In discrimination cases the burden is on the applicant and she will usually go first. Where the claim is for an unfair dismissal and discrimination the applicant will usually open.

The tribunal has a very wide discretion as to how the proceedings are conducted. There is a duty on tribunals to 'make such enquiries of persons appearing before it and witnesses as it considers appropriate'.

Evidence

Hearsay evidence is often allowed in tribunals though is not as good as first hand evidence. In discrimination cases, events which took place both before and after the discrimination may be used in evidence 'if logically probative of a relevant fact'.[36] Evidence used to challenge a witness's credibility or character will not usually be allowed.

The decision

The decision can be a majority one. It may be given at the end of a hearing or at a later date. Reasons must be given in extended form in discrimination cases; in other cases the decision may be given in summary form. The decision will then be registered and is open to inspection.

Costs

Costs can only be awarded against the opposing party where:
a) a party has 'in bringing or conducting the proceedings acted frivolously, vexatiously, abusively, disruptively or otherwise unreasonably';
b) an adjournment is necessary because the employer has failed to adduce evidence as to the availability of a job where:

---

36 *Chattopadhyay v Headmaster of Holloway School* [1981] IRLR 487, EAT.

- there was a request for reinstatement in an unfair dismissal case, or
- the employer failed to permit a woman to return to work after an absence due to pregnancy or confinement.[37]

Review of decisions

A tribunal has power to review its decision on specified grounds. An appeal to the EAT can be made at the same time as a review.[38]

Remedies

The remedies are different for unfair dismissal claims under the ERA, sex discrimination claims under the SDA and the ETD and equal pay claims under the EqPA or article 119. Because there is no limit on the amount of compensation which can be awarded under the SDA and under Article 119 and the European Directives, it is always worth making a discrimination claim.

Settlements

The Advisory, Conciliation and Arbitration Service (ACAS)

Where a complaint is presented to an IT under the ERA, SDA or EqPA, a copy is sent to an ACAS conciliation officer. ACAS has a duty, if requested to do so by both complainant and respondent or if it thinks that there is a reasonable chance of achieving a settlement, to try to promote a settlement. Any settlement reached through ACAS is binding on the parties.

Other settlements

If the parties agree a settlement without ACAS, the agreement will only be valid if:
- the agreement is in writing,
- the agreement relates to the specific complaint,
- the employee has received independent legal advice from a qualified lawyer who is insured to give such advice,
- the agreement identifies the lawyer, and
- the agreement states that the conditions regulating compromise agreements are satisfied (ERA s203).

---

37 r12(5).
38 For distinction between grounds for review under r11 and appeal see *Trimble v Supertravel Ltd* [1982] IRLR 451, EAT.

Procedures and remedies

Consent orders

If the applicant has been claiming jobseeker's allowance or income support it is advisable for any agreement to be in the form of a 'Tomlin order' in order to avoid benefit being recouped from the money (see p223). A Tomlin order is an order that proceedings are stayed upon terms scheduled in the order. It is also easier to enforce if the settlement terms are not honoured.

Remedies for unfair dismissal

Where the tribunal makes a finding that the applicant has been unfairly dismissed, it must make a declaration to this effect. The tribunal must then explain to the complainant that an order for reinstatement or re-engagement may be made and ask if she wishes for such an order. If no order for reinstatement or re-engagement is made, the tribunal must award compensation for unfair dismissal.

Reinstatement

Reinstatement is an order that the employee returns to her job on the same terms and conditions as if she had not been dismissed.[39]

The IT1 form (see p215) asks if the applicant wishes to be reinstated and this section should be completed if reinstatement is sought. Failure to do so means that the tribunal may take into account the fact that the employer has employed a permanent replacement and so refuse to make an order.

Re-engagement

Re-engagement is where the tribunal orders that the complainant be employed by the employer (or a successor or associated employer) in similar employment or other suitable employment.[40]

Where there is an order for reinstatement or re-engagement, the tribunal must specify the back pay and benefits to be awarded from the date of termination to the date of reinstatement or re-engagement and any rights to be restored.[41] Where there is a deemed dismissal (ie, a woman is denied her right to return after maternity absence), the date of termination is her notified date of return.[42]

39 ERA s114.
40 ERA s115.
41 ERA ss114(2) and 115(2).
42 ERA ss114(5) and 115(4).

Compensation

Compensation for unfair dismissal consists of:

a) a *basic award* (based on a week's pay up to a maximum of £210); this is calculated according to length of service and age;[43] and

b) a *compensatory award* which includes compensation for the financial loss suffered as a result of the dismissal, including expenses incurred and loss of benefits.[44]

The maximum limit for the compensatory award is £11,300. The maximum for the basic and compensatory awards combined is £17,600 (from 27 September 1995). This, and the maximum week's pay, is subject to annual review.

Loss of wages. This includes regular overtime and bonuses. It is calculated from the effective date of termination until the hearing date, less tax and national insurance.

Future loss of earnings. The woman must provide evidence of future loss. The IT will estimate how long the worker is likely to remain unemployed and how much she would have earned in the old job. Factors taken into account when assessing how long the woman is likely to be unemployed include her age, personal characteristics, the availability of work in the area and how long she might have remained in her old job. The likelihood of her returning after maternity leave will be taken into account. If she has a new job at a lower rate of pay the IT will assess how long she is likely to be earning less and award the difference.

Where a woman who is entitled to extended maternity absence is dismissed during or after her maternity leave period, but not when she is exercising her right to return under her contract, compensation is assessed without regard to her right to return.[45] In other words, compensation should be awarded on the assumption that she will not be returning.

Calculation date for week's pay in deemed dismissal cases

Where there is a deemed dismissal the calculation date for a week's pay is the last day on which the employee worked under

---

43 ERA ss118(1)(a) and 119–122.
44 ERA ss118(1)(b) and 123–124.
45 ERA s127.

her contract immediately before the beginning of her maternity leave period.[46]

Loss of benefits and statutory rights
Account will be taken of:
– entitlement to holiday pay;
– any gratuitous payments, bonuses etc;
– loss of a company car;
– subsidised loans;
– subsidised accommodation;
– medical insurance;
– loss of maternity rights;
– loss of pension rights (this could be one of the most valuable losses).

The award can be reduced if the woman has not mitigated her loss by failing to look for alternative work.[47] All efforts to seek work should be produced.

Additional award
If, in an unfair dismissal case, the employer fails to comply with a reinstatement or re-engagement order, the IT must make an additional award of between 26 to 52 weeks' pay in discrimination cases and between 13 and 26 weeks' pay in other cases.[48] The maximum weekly sum is £210.

Recoupment
The tribunal must deduct jobseeker's allowance and income support from the compensatory award.[49] This does not apply if the case is settled by a Tomlin order before the hearing (see p221).

Remedies under the Sex Discrimination Act

The following remedies are available:
a) a declaration;[50]
b) compensation;[51] and
c) an action recommendation.[52]

46 ERA s226(3)(a).
47 ERA s123(4).
48 ERA s117.
49 Employment Protection (Recoupment etc) Regulations 1977 SI No 674.
50 SDA s65(1)(a).
51 SDA s65(1)(b).
52 SDA s65(1)(c).

Declaration

This is a statement declaring the rights of the complainant and respondent. It is not enforceable, so if the employer chooses not to comply with it, nothing can be done.

Compensation

There is no limit on the amount of compensation which can be awarded.[53] Compensation is assessed on the basis that the applicant must be put in the position she would have been in if the discrimination had not been committed (ie, in the same way as in an action in tort).[54] The applicant can claim for any pecuniary loss attributable to the unlawful discrimination.[55]

Compensation is broken down into different heads:
- *actual losses* which can be quantified, such as loss of earnings up to the date of the hearing;
- *future losses*, including loss of earnings, pension etc; and
- *injury to feelings*.

Principles in assessing compensation in pregnancy dismissal cases

The EAT considered principles relating to assessment of compensation in two pregnancy dismissal cases against the Ministry of Defence. Two women brought proceedings against the Secretary of State for Defence, which conceded that its policy of dismissing women because they were pregnant was a breach of the Equal Treatment Directive. As a result about 5,000 women issued sex discrimination claims for compensation.

Guidelines were laid down by the EAT in *Ministry of Defence v Cannock* (n54 above) and *Ministry of Defence v Hunt*.[56] Although these were cases decided on their facts, the guidelines will be relevant for all pregnancy dismissals and other sex discrimination cases.

Assessment of chance of woman returning and for how long. The EAT held that tribunals should assess the chances of a woman

---

53 The Sex Discrimination and Equal Pay (Remedies) Regulations 1993 SI No 2798 repealed SDA s65(2), which set a limit on the amount of compensation which could be awarded.
54 *Ministry of Defence v Cannock and Others* [1994] IRLR 509, EAT.
55 *Coleman v Skyrail Oceanic Ltd* [1981] IRLR 398, CA.
56 [1996] IRLR 140, EAT. See also *MoD v Mutton* [1996] ICR 590, EAT.

returning to work rather than make findings of fact. There are three relevant questions:
a) 'What are the chances that, had she been given maternity leave and an opportunity to return to work, the applicant would have returned?' In *Cannock* the EAT said that account may be taken of statistics (which show that under 50 per cent of servicewomen who have been given the choice since 1990 have elected not to return). However, in *Hunt* the EAT stressed that the tribunal must base its assessment on the individual's evidence and said that 'statistics contain severe limitations'.
b) 'What are the chances that the woman would have been in a position to return to work, had she been given the opportunity?'
c) 'What is the length of service which the woman had hypothetically lost?'

In some cases the IT assessed the chances of the woman returning as being 100 per cent – ie, she would certainly return. The MoD argued that assessment of a chance at 100 per cent was perverse. The EAT held that whilst the assessment of a long-term chance at 100 per cent is exceptional, it is not perverse per se.

If the chance of the woman returning to work is 80 per cent but the chance of her completing her contract only 40 per cent, the 80 per cent must be applied to the first period and 40 per cent of the 80 per cent (ie, 32 per cent) to the subsequent period.

Mitigation. There is a duty on the applicant to mitigate her losses by seeking alternative employment. Unless active steps are taken to find alternative work, the tribunal may well ask whether the applicant would have returned to work at all. Failure to apply to rejoin the armed forces may be relevant.

The burden of proving a failure to mitigate is on the respondent, who must provide evidence. A vague submission of failure to mitigate unsupported by any evidence is unlikely to succeed.

In *Hunt* the EAT held that the triunal was entitled to find that there was a disadvantage in the labour market in being a woman with a young child or children. This acknowledges the difficulty women may have in finding employment and applies 'collective common sense to historical circumstance'.

Loss of earnings should include an amount for loss of promotion. In *Hunt* the tribunal found there was a 100 per cent chance the applicant would have continued in the army for a 16-year term and a 100 per cent chance she would have obtained significant promotions during that time. This was upheld by the EAT.

Calculation of compensation
In the final calculation of compensation the tribunal should deduct the failure to mitigate figure *before* applying the percentage chance figure. For example, a woman earns £500 per week before her dismissal. She then earns (or could earn, acting reasonably to mitigate her loss) £250 per week. The tribunal assesses her chances of remaining in the army as 40 per cent. The loss is calculated by
– subtracting £250 from £500, leaving £250;
– taking 40% of £250, ie £100.
Her loss is £100 per week.[57]

It was wrong to take 40 per cent of £500 (£200) and then to subtract actual earnings (£250) making a weekly loss of £50. The EAT in *Hunt* thought such a result (which was argued by the MoD) could lead to injustice and was not in line with the ECJ decision in *Marshall v Southampton and South-West Hampshire Area Health Authority (Teaching) (No 2)*.[58]

If the tribunal decides there is a different percentage chance at each stage (ie, that the woman would take maternity leave and return, that she would stay for x years) there must then be a cumulative calculation on the basis of a percentage of a percentage.

Deductions for childcare costs
The EAT held that childcare costs which notionally would have had to be incurred to enable an applicant to return to work should be set off in full against her damages for loss of earnings. The fact that the applicant's husband might have borne half the burden should be ignored.

Injury to feelings
Injury to feelings must be proved. In *Ministry of Defence v Cannock and Others* (n54 above) the EAT said that, although an award was not automatic, no tribunal will take much persuasion that the anger, distress and affront caused by the act of

---

57 In coming to this conclusion, the EAT in *Hunt* did not follow *MoD v Bristow* (1995) 24 July, EAT, unreported, saying that it had received far fuller submissions than the EAT in *Bristow* where relevant cases had not been mentioned.
58 [1993] IRLR 445, ECJ at 449.

discrimination has injured the applicant's feelings. In *Murray v Powertech (Scotland) Ltd*[59] the EAT said that a claim for hurt feelings is so fundamental to a sex discrimination case that it is almost inevitable.

The award should be the going rate for compensation, even if it is more in real terms than it would have been at the date of the injury complained of. The compensation will include an amount for stress, anger, embarrassment, interference with family life, frustration at having a chosen career brought to an end and for loss of congenial employment.[60]

The amounts awarded have varied enormously.[61] It is very important to provide evidence of any injury to feelings. This may be brought out through the applicant's evidence and witnesses, including, if possible, a doctor's or psychotherapist's report.

Aggravated damages

Compensation may include aggravated damages where the respondent has behaved in a high-handed, malicious, insulting or oppressive manner in committing the act of discrimination.[62] A tribunal can take account of all matters up to and including the hearing.

In *Ministry of Defence v Meredith*[63] the EAT held that there must be a causal connection between the exceptional or contumelious conduct or motive in committing the wrong and the intangible loss, such as injury to feelings. The applicant must have had some knowledge or suspicion of the conduct or motive which caused that increase. As the applicant in this case was not aware that the employer's conduct was unlawful when she was dismissed, any injury to feelings she suffered as a result of her dismissal could not have been aggravated by any improper conduct or motive on the part of the employer of which she was wholly unaware.

In a race discrimination case, *Patel and Harewood v T & K Home Improvements Ltd and Johnson*,[64] the tribunal awarded aggravated damages of £1,750 because the respondents made matters worse by the attitude which they displayed throughout the proceedings.

---

59 [1992] IRLR 257, EAT.
60 Loss of congenial employment is not a separate head from injury to feelings.
61 The EOC has collated details of recent awards.
62 *Alexander v Home Office* [1988] IRLR 190, CA.
63 [1995] IRLR 539, EAT.
64 (1994) 24 March, Case Nos 57783/92 and 57778/92.

In *McClenaghan and Rice v British Shoe Corporation Ltd*[65] a tribunal awarded £8,000 for injury to feelings to a woman who suffered severe depression following her dismissal when illness prevented her from returning to work after maternity absence.

Exemplary damages

There is no right to exemplary damages for sex discrimination under either UK or EU law.[66]

Pension loss

In *Ministry of Defence v Cannock* (n54 above) the EAT recommended that tribunals should calculate pension losses in accordance with the guidance contained in the booklet prepared for this purpose by the Committee of Chairmen of Industrial Tribunals. This is based on the amount of the employers' contributions which are treated as a weekly loss, in the same manner as a weekly loss of earnings.

However, it is notable that there was some doubt as to the validity of this approach since the removal of the limits on compensation. The EAT said there was an argument that 'it would be more appropriate to measure pension loss by reference to the prospective loss of benefit, rather than by the contribution method, which is a rough-and-ready method suitable and appropriate for the bulk of cases'. In *Ministry of Defence v Mutton*[66A] the EAT upheld the assessment of pension loss based on specific expert evidence rather than the usual guidance set out in the booklet. The applicant was awarded £60,635, which was the value of the benefits lost. The EAT in *Cannock* rejected the MoD's argument that loss could not be recovered for a period before 1990 (the date of the ECJ's decision in *Barber v Guardian Royal Exchange Assurance Group Ltd*).[67]

Interest

In discrimination cases the tribunal has a discretion to award interest from the date of the act of discrimination.[68] For injury to feelings interest is for the period beginning on the date of the discrimination and ending on the day of calculation.

65 (1994) 3 March, Case No 2688/91.
66 *Deane v London Borough of Ealing and Another* [1993] IRLR 209, EAT and *MoD v Meredith* [1995] IRLR 539, EAT.
66A [1996] ICR 590, EAT.
67 [1990] IRLR 240, ECJ.
68 Sex Discrimination and Equal Pay (Remedies) Regulations 1993 SI No 2798 reg 3.

Procedures and remedies

In relation to all other sums of damages or compensation interest is awarded from the mid-point date between the act of discrimination and the date of the tribunal hearing. However, the tribunal may award interest over a different period in exceptional circumstances. In *Cannock* the EAT said payment over a longer period may be appropriate where the whole of the loss was incurred many years previously – as in the MoD cases.

Interest is payable on the loss of earnings, and injury to feelings but not in respect of pension losses.[69] The current rate of interest is 8 per cent.[70]

Assessment of totality of award

In *MoD v Cannock* (n54 above) the EAT said, *obiter*[71] that some of the large awards were wholly unjustified, manifestly excessive, wrong in principle and out of proportion to the wrong done. The EAT suggested that tribunals should not simply make calculations on various heads, and then add them up and award the total sum; the total award must seem a sensible and just reflection of the chances which have been assessed. However, in *Hunt* the EAT said that if an applicant was entitled to £X for injury to feelings, £Y for loss of earnings and £Z for loss of pension entitlement, the total should be £X + Y + Z and appropriate interest. To reduce an award would be to introduce a judicial cap in an area where there is no statutory cap and would be contrary to *Marshall (No 2)* (n58 above).

Other losses

In a sexual harassment case[72] the tribunal awarded an amount for psychotherapist's fees incurred. Costs incurred in looking for other work (such as travel and phone calls) and possibly removal costs can be claimed, though evidence must be available.

Indirect discrimination

The SDA used to provide that no compensation can be awarded for unintentional indirect discrimination.[73] An award may now be

---

69 Remedies Regulations reg 6 precludes interest in respect of a sum awarded for a loss or matter which will occur after the day of calculation.
70 Judgment Debts (Rate of Interest) Order 1993 SI No 564; White Book para 6/2/12.
71 Ie, in words not binding on tribunals.
72 *Longmore v Lee* (1989) 10 November, DCLD 4, Case No 21745/88.
73 SDA s66(3).

made for unintentional indirect discrimination where it would not be just and equitable to grant other remedies alone. This applies where the hearing takes place after 25 March 1996.[74]

Overlap with unfair dismissal compensation

There can be no double recovery of compensation under the SDA and ERA for the same loss.[75] It is more advantageous to get the compensatory award under the SDA (rather than the ERA), as there is no upper limit, interest is awarded and the recoupment provisions do not apply (see p223).

Recommendation

A recommendation must have a time limit and must be practicable for the purpose of removing or reducing the adverse effect on the complainant of any act of discrimination.

Possible recommendations could include:
- that the employer pay the applicant's psychotherapist's fees for a period (see above);
- that details of the case be posted in the workplace;[76]
- that the applicant be appointed to the post in which she would have been confirmed had she not been discriminated against.[77]

However, in *Scottish Agricultural College v O'Mara*[78] the EAT held there was no power to make a recommendation that the applicant be appointed to the first suitable post as this was positive discrimination.

It is not clear if a recommendation can be made if the complainant has left the job.

Increase in compensation for non-compliance with recommendation

If an employer fails to comply with a recommendation, the tribunal may order that compensation be paid or increased.

---

74 Sex Discrimination and Equal Pay (Miscellaneous Amendments) Regulations 1996 SI No 438.
75 ERA s126.
76 In *McClenaghan and Rice* (see n65 above) the tribunal made a recommendation that the employer post details of the cases at its head office and at the applicants' previous workplaces.
77 *Williams v British Gas plc South Western* DCLD 12; 21.4.92; Case No 26089/91.
78 (1991) 5 November, DCLD 12, Case No AT/449/91.

Remedies under Equal Pay Act

Once there is a finding of equal pay, an equality clause is automatically inserted into the woman's contract giving her the same pay and other contractual terms as her male comparator. A maximum of two years' back pay can be awarded under the EqPA but this limit may be a breach of article 119.

PROCEDURE AND REMEDIES: KEY POINTS

- Most claims are brought in the industrial tribunal; there is an appeal on a point of law to the Employment Appeal Tribunal; a tribunal or court can refer a question about the interpretation of EU law to the ECJ.
- Legal aid is not available in an IT (only the EAT and above), but advice may be sought from the Maternity Alliance, the Equal Opportunities Commission, law centres, citizens advice bureaux and trade unions.
- In sex discrimination cases a questionnaire can be served within three months of the act of discrimination or within 21 days of the commencement of proceedings.
- There is a three-month time limit for bringing a claim of unfair dismissal or discrimination; there is provision for a late claim in some circumstances. An equal pay claim must be brought within six months of the employee leaving.
- The claim is usually on form IT1 and should set out the main incidents on which the applicant will rely; in most maternity cases a claim should be made under the ERA, SDA, and possibly European provisions; the EqPA may also be relevant.
- The employer must respond to the IT1 within 21 days from receipt of the IT1, though the time limit can be extended.
- The tribunal has power to order:
  - discovery (as in the county court),
  - further and better particulars,
  - written answers to questions,
  - witness orders,
  - directions hearings.
- Costs are not normally awarded but may be if a party has acted frivolously, vexatiously, etc.

- Remedies for unfair dismissal include:
  - compensation (subject to a limit),
  - reinstatement,
  - re-engagement,
  - additional award for failure to comply with reinstatement or re-engagement order.
- Remedies under the SDA include:
  - unlimited compensation, including an amount for injury to feelings,
  - a declaration,
  - a recommendation.
- Compensation can be now be awarded for indirect discrimination.
- The EAT has laid down detailed guidelines for assessing compensation in pregnancy dismissal cases.
- Under the EqPA an equality clause is inserted into the woman's contract. Back pay up to two years can be awarded.
- The EOC has power to assist individuals to make complaints, to issue codes of practice, and to conduct formal investigations.

Appendices

APPENDIX 1
Tabular summary of maternity rights

	Length of service (with same employer)	Employment Status	Earnings	Notice requirements Written notice is often essential and usually advisable	Medical evidence	Other conditions and points to note
A. 14 weeks general maternity leave can start from 11th week before EWC	None. All women irrespective of length of service are entitled to general maternity leave	Employee including employees on fixed-term contracts	Not relevant	– Written notice at least 21 days before start of leave of pregnancy and EWC and – at least 21 days notice of start of maternity leave. If not reasonably practicable to give 21 days notice, it must be given as soon as possible	If requested by employer, doctor or midwife's certificate giving EWC	If you cannot give 21 days notice because, eg, the baby is born early, you must give notice of the birth as soon as possible. Notice of pregnancy-related absence in 6 weeks before EWC must be given
B. Extended maternity absence – of up to 29 weeks after beginning of week baby was born	2 years' continuous service at the beginning of the 11th week before the EWC	Employee as above	Not relevant	As above and in addition – inform employer in writing, 21 days before leave begins, of intention to return – written notice at least 21 days before date of return, of proposal to return on that day	As above	Where not earlier than 21 days before end of MLP, the employer makes a written request for written confirmation that she intends to return the woman must provide such written confirmation within 14 days
C. Right to return to same job after 14 weeks general maternity leave	None	Employee as above	Not relevant	– Notice is required before taking leave – No notice is required for return at end of 14 weeks – 7 days notice must be given if return is before end of 14 weeks	N/A	If you cannot return at the end of the 14 weeks because you are sick you are protected from unfair dismissal for 4 weeks if you give your employer a medical certificate before the end of your leave
D. Right to return after extended maternity absence to substantially the same job	2 years service (as B above)	Employee as above	Not relevant	– 21 days written notice of date of return (as B above) – confirmation of intention to return if requested by employer (11 weeeks after start of maternity leave)	N/A	There are two exceptions to the right to return – the employer can postpone your return for 4 weeks – you can postpone your return for 4 weeks if you are sick or there is a strike

Tabular summary of maternity rights

	Length of service (with same employer)	Employment Status	Earnings	Notice requirements Written notice is often essential and usually advisable	Medical evidence	Other conditions and points to note
E. Statutory maternity pay 6 weeks on 90% of pay subsequent 12 weeks (max) on £54.55 payable from start of MPP	26 weeks up to and into qualifying week (ie 15th week before EWC)	Employee as above Holder of elective office	Average earnings of at least £61 p.w. for 8 weeks or 2 months before end of qualifying week (i.e. 15th week before EWC)	21 clear days' notice of date maternity leave is to start – or if not practicable **as** much notice as possible	Medical evidence (usually a MATB1 showing EWC must be given to the employer before the end of the 3rd week of the maternity pay period	– SMP is not repayable if you do not return to work – you can claim SMP from 2 or more employers (if you qualify) – SMP is payable during MPP even if there is no contract
F. Maternity allowance Higher rate of £54.55 for 18 weeks	Employed in the 15th week before the EWC	The woman must have been working (employed or self-employed) for at least 26 weeks in the 66 weeks immediately before the EWC	Paid 26 Class 1 National Insurance contributions in the 66 week period	A claim from the Benefits Agency should be made as soon as possible after the 14th week before the EWC	MAT B1 showing week baby is due	If woman is working for an employer she must send form SMP1 on which employer states why SMP is not payable
G. Maternity allowance Lower rate of £47.55 for 18 weeks	None	Self-employed or not working in 15th week	As above	As above	As above	
H. Paid time off for ante-natal care during working hours	None	Employee	Not relevant	Written proof of 2nd and subsequent appointments if requested by employer	Medical certificate showing woman is pregnant, if requested	
I. Protection from automatically unfair dismissal on grounds of pregnancy, childbirth, maternity leave	None	Employee including employees on fixed-term contracts	Not relevant	Not relevant	Not relevant	In case of pregnancy dismissal employer must be aware of pregnancy
J. Protection from ordinary unfair dismissal	2 years	Employee as above	Not relevant	Not relevant	Not relevant	

APPPENDIX 2
Common questions

The following is a list of common questions. Because of the complexity of the law it is only possible to give general guidance, which may not provide the full answer. Reference should therefore always be made to the text.

1. **Refusal to recruit a woman because she is pregnant**
Can an employer refuse to employ me because I am pregnant?
No. It is discriminatory to refuse to appoint a woman because she is pregnant (see p25). This applies even where the appointment is to a fixed-term contract unless the woman will be unavailable for the whole of the fixed term (see pp177-178).

2. **Informing employer of pregnancy and maternity leave**
When should I tell my employer that I am pregnant?
Although you do not generally *have* to tell your employer until 21 days before you go on leave (see p32), it is advisable to do so at an early stage for three main reasons:
- if you want paid time off for antenatal care you must tell your employer (see p18);
- if there are health and safety risks, you must inform your employer you are pregnant in order to get the statutory protection (see p118);
- if you are off sick, the employer may be able to dismiss you because of long or frequent sickness absences; however, it is automatically unfair to dismiss a woman if she has a pregnancy-related sickness and the employer is aware of this (see p21).

Do I need to tell my employer in writing?
Not in the early stages (though see above and p32). However, you should tell someone in authority. In one case a woman told a colleague and it was not clear if she passed the information on to the employer. The woman was dismissed because of sickness absence and the employer said he did not know she was pregnant. The dismissal was held by the tribunal to be fair.

When must I tell my employer of my pregnancy?
You *must* inform your employer *in writing* at least 21 days before you start your maternity leave and you must also give the expected date of childbirth. In addition you must tell your employer the date when you intend to start your leave (see p33) and, if you are entitled to extended maternity absence, that you intend to return to work (see p41). You must give the proper notice in order to get maternity leave (and absence) and SMP (see p142).

3. Paid time off for antenatal care

Does antenatal care cover relaxation and other classes?
Yes, almost certainly (see p17).

Is there a limit to how much time off I can have?
Yes. Time off includes the appointment or class and reasonable travelling time. If you can attend work for part of the day then you must do so unless you agree otherwise with your employer (see pp18-19).

Do I have a right to paid time off for antenatal care during working hours if I work part-time?
There is nothing which limits time off in working hours to full-time workers. A part-time worker *should not* have to attend solely on her days off, though one tribunal has suggested that she should (see p19).

If I work nights, can I get any compensatory time off for antenatal care?
No. You only get paid time off during working hours.

4. When to resign if you do not intend to return

If I have definitely decided not to return to work, when should I resign?
It is often difficult to know whether you want to return to work after maternity leave (or absence) and circumstances may change. Remember that if you resign or fail to give the right notice, you will probably not be able to change your mind later. However, if you assume you are going back (and comply with the notice provisions), you can change your mind and not return – at no loss to yourself (see p42).

Although you may not want to take advantage of maternity leave, your contractual rights continue during this period, so it is generally advisable to continue your employment contract during the 14 weeks (see pp45ff). You need to be employed at the 11th week before the expected week of childbirth in order to get the benefits of maternity leave (see p35).

If you are entitled to extended maternity absence, you *may* be entitled to continued benefits during this time if your contract subsists. The position is very unclear (see p56).

In order to get statutory maternity pay (SMP) you must be employed into the 15th week before the expected week of the birth (see p137).

5. Health and safety

My job involves standing for most of the day and I am getting backache. What can I do?
It is accepted that 'postures' can be a potential risk to pregnant women, but there are a number of factors to take into account (see chapter 8). If the work you do affects the health of you or your baby, your employer must take steps to avoid the risk, either by altering your working conditions, providing suitable alternative work or, if this is not possible, suspending you on full pay (see p123). You should not have to go off sick and lose pay if there is a health and safety risk arising out of your work.

I am always feeling tired at work; can I have rest periods?
From 1 January 1996, all employers must provide suitable facilities for a pregnant woman or nursing mother to rest (The Workplace (Health, Safety and Welfare) Regulations 1992, reg 25). The Code of Practice says that rest facilities should include the facility to lie down.

I have a long journey which is exhausting; is there anything I can do?
The rules do not cover travelling to and from work, only travelling within working hours. You could ask your employer if you can work shorter hours or flexible hours (see p81).

How long does the health and safety protection last?
From the beginning of your pregnancy until either six months after the birth or for as long as you are breastfeeding.

My employer refuses to take any notice of the health and safety provisions. What can I do?
You should contact your local Health and Safety Executive office or local authority environmental health officer. You should also contact your union and health and safety representative at work.

If your employer fails to carry out a proper risk assessment and then dismisses you for refusing to work when you have real concerns about health and safety, this is likely to be unfair. It may also be discriminatory, as it is a reason connected to your pregnancy.

If you believe the risk is serious and imminent and cannot be avoided and as a result you leave work, it will be automatically unfair for your employer to dismiss you (see p93 and chapter 8).

It will also be automatically unfair where your employer dismisses you in order to avoid health and safety requirements or recommendations (see p126).

Can I extend my maternity leave because I am breastfeeding?
No (see p124).

Can I express milk at work?
There is no reason why you should not do that, though you may have to fit it in around your work. The legal position is not clear.

6. Sickness

Can I be dismissed if I am off sick because of my pregnancy?
No. It is automatically unfair to dismiss a woman because she is pregnant or for any reason connected to her pregnancy. Even if you are sick for a long period you are almost certainly protected (see p21). It may also be discriminatory to dismiss you in these circumstances (see p23).

If I am sick during my pregnancy, will it affect my SMP?
Not usually. However, if you are sick during the eight weeks (or two months) up to and including the last payday before the end of the qualifying week, you may not have earned enough to qualify for SMP. You must have earned on average the lower earnings limit (currently £61 per week) over the period (see pp132ff).

If I am off work because of my pregnancy, will this affect my maternity leave?
If you are absent because of your pregnancy during the six weeks before the expected week of childbirth, you will have to start your maternity leave immediately unless your employer agrees otherwise. Your SMP period will start immediately (see p144).

Can I claim statutory sick pay during my pregnancy?
Yes. However, if you are off sick in the six weeks before the week the baby is due and your sickness is related to your pregnancy, you will have to claim SMP. If your absence is not connected to your pregnancy, you can claim SSP (see p145).

The occupational sick scheme excludes pregnancy-related illness. Can I do anything about this?
The exclusion of pregnancy-related sickness from sick pay schemes is probably discriminatory and you can challenge it (see p28).

Can I claim sick pay if I am ill during my 14 weeks' maternity leave?
You cannot get statutory sick pay (SSP) for 18 weeks after the beginning of your maternity leave. You are unlikely to get contractual sick pay.

What happens if I am sick at the end of my 14 weeks' maternity leave?
There is protection against dismissal for women unable to return to work because of sickness in the four weeks after the end of maternity leave. The dismissal will be automatically unfair where the dismissal was for reasons connected to the birth. The illness need not be related to your

pregnancy or childbirth. You must give your employer a doctor's certificate before the end of the leave (see p92).

If you are still sick at the end of the four weeks, you should be treated like any other sick employee who is sick at the end of a period of authorised absence (see p69). However, if the sickness is not connected to your pregnancy, childbirth or maternity leave (and so you cannot claim automatically unfair dismissal), you can only claim ordinary unfair dismissal if you have two years' qualifying service (but see p93). You may also have a sex discrimination claim if a man would not have been dismissed in comparable circumstances (see p96).

What happens if I am sick at the end of my maternity absence?
You may postpone your return for up to four weeks provided you give appropriate notice (see p70). If you are ill at the end of this period, you should be treated like any other sick employee, though it is advisable, if possible, to return to work for a short time (see p72).

What if I am ill after I return to work?
If the illness is related to your pregnancy, it may be automatically unfair to dismiss you. If it is not pregnancy-related, you should be treated like any other sick employee (ignoring the maternity absence) (see p111).

What happens if my baby is sick when I am due to return?
You have no particular protection and you will need to negotiate with your employer. You may be entitled to compassionate leave or some other leave under your contract. Arguably, it is discriminatory to dismissal a woman in these circumstances, but this has not been tested (see p102).

7. Maternity leave (14 weeks) and extended maternity absence

Who is entitled to maternity leave and what happens if I only have a fixed-term contract?
All employees, whether permanent or temporary, irrespective of the hours they work or their length of service, are entitled to 14 weeks' maternity leave (see p32).

In addition, employees who have worked for the same employer for two years at the beginning of the 11th week before the EWC are entitled to return to work up to 29 weeks after the beginning of the week the baby is born (see p40). This applies to women who have had a series of fixed-term contracts and may apply if there have been gaps between the contracts (see p40).

There are strict notice requirements for both general maternity leave and extended maternity absence.

What happens if the contract expires during my maternity leave?
Your statutory maternity leave will come to an end but you will still be

entitled to SMP (see p131). However, failure to renew a fixed-term contract will be a dismissal and if the reason is because of your pregnancy, childbirth or maternity leave it will be automatically unfair and discriminatory (see pp91 and 96).

If the fixed-term contract was for a specific purpose, which has come to an end, the dismissal may be fair. The employer should also consider if there is any suitable alternative work (see p105). No claim for unfair dismissal can be made if you are employed under a fixed-term contract of a year or more and you have agreed, in writing, to exclude your right to claim unfair dismissal; you may, however, be protected under EU law.

Do I lose my right to maternity leave if I do not comply with the notice provisions?
You lose your right to *statutory* maternity leave. But this does not mean your employer can dismiss you. Any dismissal connected to your pregnancy, childbirth or maternity leave will be automatically unfair (see p91).

8. Rights during 14 weeks' maternity leave

What rights am I entitled to during my maternity leave?
You are entitled to all your contractual rights except for full remuneration – ie, wages, salary (see pp47ff). Thus you should continue to receive continued use of a company car (provided it is not exclusively for business use), health insurance, professional subscriptions etc.

What about my pension?
Your employer must continue paying contributions as though you were earning your full salary. Your proportion is based on your maternity pay (see p53).

Am I entitled to a bonus payable when I am on maternity leave?
The position is not clear. A contractual bonus may count as remuneration in which case it is not payable (see p50). If it relates to a period outside the maternity leave, it should be paid on a proportionate basis.

It may be possible to bring an equal pay claim if a man on comparable leave would receive a bonus (see p50).

Do I accrue holiday leave while I am on maternity leave?
Yes. But if you are not able to take holiday in the holiday year, you are not necessarily entitled to be paid instead. You should either take holiday before you go on leave or negotiate with your employer to take it after you return (see p52).

What happens if I am made redundant during my maternity leave?
If the reason is related to your pregnancy, childbirth or maternity leave,

it will automatically be unfair. You are entitled to be offered suitable available work (see p107).

9. Extended maternity absence

What happens if I am dismissed during my maternity absence?
You can claim unfair dismissal if your contract continues during this period. The law is very unclear and it will depend on your individual circumstances (see p98).

What happens if I am made redundant during my maternity absence?
You must be consulted about any redundancy. You are entitled to be given suitable alternative work that is available during the maternity absence. This applies even if there are other employees (not on maternity leave or absence) who are made redundant at the same time (see p108).

10. Rights during maternity absence

What rights am I entitled to during my absence?
This will depend on whether your contract continues and what it says. The law is very unclear. If the contract does not make it clear, you can argue that you are entitled to contractual benefits during your absence.

You may have an equal pay claim if a man (doing like work, equivalent work or work of equal value), on comparable leave, does receive the benefit of his terms and conditions. This will depend on how the decision in *Gillespie* is interpreted (see pp58-59).

If there is no continuing contract during leave, for the purposes of your seniority and similar contractual rights, the period of employment after maternity leave is treated as continuous with the period of employment before the leave (see p60).

For the purpose of statutory rights (such as protection from unfair dismissal) your maternity absence will count towards your continuous service (see p60).

11. Returning to work

What if I am not allowed to return to work?
This is treated as a dismissal (provided you have complied with the notice provisions). It will be automatically unfair and discriminatory if the dismissal is related to your pregnancy, childbirth or maternity leave (see p91). It may also be an ordinary unfair dismissal (see p93).

What happens if my employer has changed while I was away?
If the business has been transferred, your rights are preserved and the new employer will take over the obligations of the old employer. Your service will be treated as continuous and all existing contractual terms and conditions will be transferred (see p80).

Common questions 243

My employer has told me that my job is to be done by my replacement and I will be given another job; what can I do?
If you have lost your original job because of being on maternity leave or absence, this will be automatically unfair (see p91) and discriminatory (see p96).

What happens if there has been a reorganisation while I was away and I am to be given a lower-status job?
Unless there is a genuine redundancy situation (when you are entitled to suitable alternative work), you are entitled to your job back. If you are given a job on lower pay or lower status or in a different location, you can claim you have been denied the right to return and this will be a dismissal, which may be unfair or discriminatory, depending on the reason for the dismissal (see pp75ff).

If I don't want to resign, but I want my original job back, is there anything I can do?
You can continue working under protest and bring a claim for dismissal with a request for reinstatement. You must make it clear that you do not accept the new job.

Do I have a right to return to work part-time?
If your employer does not allow you to return to work part-time or work flexible hours to fit in with your childcare, you may be able to argue this is indirectly discriminatory (see pp81ff).

If I have agreed with my employer that I will not return for a year, can I then change my mind and return earlier?
Probably, provided you have complied with the statutory notice provisions.

Can I change my notified date of return once I have given it?
Only if you are unable to return because you are sick (see p70). Otherwise you cannot change it unless the employer agrees.

12. Dismissal and redundancy

What happens if I am dismissed before the beginning of my maternity leave?
You will not be entitled to maternity leave (or absence) if you have been dismissed before being able to give the appropriate notice. However, if the dismissal was connected with your pregnancy or maternity leave, it will be automatically unfair and discriminatory (see pp20ff).

What happens if I am dismissed while on maternity leave?
The maternity leave and contract will come to an end. The dismissal will be automatically unfair and discriminatory if connected to your

pregnancy, childbirth or maternity leave (see p91). If you are entitled to extended maternity absence, you can still exercise your right to return, provided you comply with the notice provisions (see p101).

Can my employer make me redundant while I am on maternity leave?
In theory yes, but if you are made redundant *because* you are on leave or have had a baby, this will be automatically unfair (see p107). You are entitled to any suitable alternative work which is available (see p107).

Does this apply even if I am on a fixed-term contract?
Yes. Failure to renew a fixed-term contract is a dismissal (see p90).

Can my employer take my leave or absence into account when deciding who to make redundant?
No. This will almost certainly lead to a finding of unfair dismissal. Nor should the employer take account of pregnancy-related sickness absences, though where these occur after you have returned to work the position is less clear (see p111).

13. **What happens to four weeks of my SMP if I am only entitled to 14 weeks maternity leave?**
If you are only entitled to 14 weeks' leave, you will lose 4 weeks SMP – unless you are unable to return because of sickness or decide not to return at all.

14. **SMP and contractual maternity pay**
What is the earliest I can leave work in order to qualify for SMP?
You must be employed for at least one day of the qualifying week (ie, the 15th week before the expected week of childbirth). You will still be entitled to SMP if you resign or are dismissed after then. You do not have to work until the 11th week, but your SMP will not start before the 11th week.

If I do not return from maternity leave, do I have to pay back the SMP I receive?
No.

I have been told that if I do not return I will have to pay back my contractual maternity pay. Is this right?
It is not clear. If an employee who does not return from sick leave would not have to repay any contractual sick pay received, it is arguably discriminatory to require a woman to repay her maternity pay in these circumstances.

What happens if I have several jobs? Do I get SMP for each?
Yes, if you are earning above the lower earnings level in each job. You

get the 90% from each job and the £54.55 twice over. If you are self-employed as well, you do not get maternity allowance as you cannot get SMP and maternity allowance.

I have been told I cannot get 18 weeks' SMP; why not?
If you are only entitled to 14 weeks maternity leave (and it is not extended because, for example, of sickness) and you return at the end of the 14 weeks, you lose 4 weeks SMP. You cannot get SMP while you are working.

I am on maternity leave and my employer has asked me to come back to work to help out. Can I?
You will lose one week's SMP for each week, or part of week, you work. You will lose SMP at the lower rate first (£54.55). You can receive SMP, if you then stop working, for the following week.

Do part-timers qualify for maternity allowance after two years service?
It is irrelevant how many hours per week you work, as long as you have paid 26 class 1 NI contributions in the 66-week period (see p154).

Remember that a claim for unfair dismissal or sex discrimination must be made within three months of the date of the dismissal, unless you have a very good reason for a late claim (see p214).

APPENDIX 3
Precedents

IT1: Redundancy: claim for unfair dismissal and discrimination

1. The Applicant commenced employment with the Respondents as a surveyor on 11 February 1995.
2. On 17 June 1996 the Applicant wrote to the Respondents to inform them that she was pregnant, that her expected week of childbirth was 2 September and she would start her maternity leave on 5 August.
3. On or about 29 July the Respondents employed Mr Smith to take on the Applicant's work while she was on maternity leave.
4. The Applicant commenced her maternity leave on 5 August and her baby was born on 4 September.
5. The Applicant received a letter on 27 August informing her that her post was redundant as the work she had been doing on a contract with X Building Society had come to an end.
6. The Respondents have continued to employ Mr Smith.
7. The Applicant's maternity leave period was ended by dismissal and the reason or principal reason for the dismissal was her pregnancy, childbirth or the fact that she had taken maternity leave or the benefits of maternity leave. This constitutes an automatically unfair dismissal under the Employment Rights Act 1996.
8. In the alternative, if, as is alleged, there was a redundancy situation, the Applicant was unfairly selected for redundancy.
9. Further, the Respondents failed to consult the Applicant about the redundancy and the possibility of alternative employment. The Applicant was entitled to be offered a suitable available vacancy to take effect immediately on the ending of her employment under the previous contract.
10. The Respondents discriminated against the Applicant in breach of the Sex Discrimination Act [the Equal Treatment Directive or the Pregnant Workers Directive] by dismissing the Applicant because of her pregnancy and/or the fact that she had given birth and/or because she had taken maternity leave.

11. The Applicant claims:
    a. unfair dismissal
    b. a declaration that the Respondents unlawfully discriminated against the Applicant;
    c. compensation;
    d. interest.

Note:
(a) A claim could also be made for ordinary unfair dismissal if the two-year qualifying period is held to be unlawful indirect discrimination as in *R v Secretary of State for Employment ex p Seymour Smith and Perez*.
(b) A claim based directly on European directives can only be made against a public-sector body.

Questionnaire: Redundancy

Section 6

1. What is the Respondent's normal redundancy procedure and/or what redundancy procedure was being followed at the time of the redundancy situation?
2. When was the decision taken to make the Applicant redundant and by whom? Please specify the reasons why the Applicant was made redundant.
3. When was the Respondent first aware that the work which the Applicant had been doing was to come to an end?
4. What experience and qualifications does Mr Smith have? Please provide his application form or curriculum vitae or other document taken into account when deciding to employ him.
5. What work has Mr Smith done since he started employment with the Respondent? Please specify when the work was done.
6. Please provide details of work undertaken or taken on by the surveyors working for the Respondent between June and December 1966, specifying:
   - the type of work done
   - the extent of the work, including the estimated cost
   - the qualifications required for such work
   - dates when the work was first requested to be done and when the work was commenced
   - details of future work, when it is likely to commence and the amount involved.
7. Please provide details of all vacancies in the posts of surveyor or like jobs, whether permanent or temporary, which have become vacant since July 1995 and details of all such posts which are likely to become vacant in the next six months.

8. Of employees who have been pregnant and/or on maternity in the past three years please state:
   a. the total number
   b. how many of the total returned to their original posts
   c. how many were offered alternative posts
   d. how many accepted the alternative post
   e. how many were dismissed (including redundancy)
   f. how many were offered voluntary redudancy
   g. length of service at date of going on maternity leave.
9. Of employees who have been dismissed (including redundancy) in the past three years please state:
   a. how many were women
   b. of these how many had taken maternity leave in the previous five years
   c. how many were pregnant at the time of the dismissal
   d. how many were men
   e. how many women were offered alternative work
   f. how many men were offered alternative work?
10. Please supply a copy of your equal opportunities policy.
11. Please provide a breakdown of the Respondent's workforce by sex and grade of employee.
12. Please provide a copy of your maternity leave policy including any instructions to managers relating to maternity leave and the return to work.

IT3: Redundancy

1. The Applicant's claim is denied as alleged or at all.
2. It is admitted that the Applicant went on maternity leave on 5 August.
3. Mr Smith was employed on 29 July partly to cover for the Applicant's maternity leave and also to do work on a major new project.
4. The Applicant's post became redundant as the contract on which she was working came to an end.
5. The Respondent denies that there was suitable available work for the Applicant. The Applicant was not qualified for the work which was allocated to Mr Smith.
6. The Respondent denies that the Applicant was made dismissed for a reason relating to her pregnancy, childbirth or the fact that she had taken maternity leave or the benefits of maternity leave.
7. The Respondent denies that the Applicant has been discriminated against either as alleged or at all.

IT1: Dismissal at end of maternity absence for failure to return because of sickness

1. The Applicant was employed by the Respondents as a secretary on 7 December 1992.
2. On 20 May 1996 the Applicant wrote to the Respondents to inform them that she was pregnant, that her expected week of childbirth was 22 July, that she would start her maternity leave on 17 June and that she intended to return to work.
3. The Applicant went on maternity leave on 17 June. Her baby was born on 30 July. The Applicant was entitled to return to work at any time up to 29 weeks after the beginning of the week in which childbirth occurs, the last day being 21 February 1997.
4. On .... the Applicant complied with the Respondents' request for written confirmation of her intention to return to work.
5. On 21 October the Applicant wrote to the Respondents stating that she intended to return to work on 18 November.
6. On 7 November the Applicant suffered complications arising out of childbirth and was admitted to hospital for an operation.
7. On 11 November the Applicant wrote to the Respondents explaining that she would be unable to return to work on 18 November as she would need a further four weeks to recover from her operation. The Applicant sent to the Respondents a certificate from a registered medical practitioner stating that by reason of bodily disablement she would be incapable of work on 18 November and for a further four-week period until 16 December.
8. On 13 December the Applicant was still not well enough to work and she telephoned the Respondents to inform them that she was ill and would not be able to go into work for a further two weeks. The Applicant requested sick leave in accordance with the Respondents' occupational sick pay scheme.
9. On 18 December the Respondents informed the Applicant that as she had failed to return to work at the end of her maternity absence she had lost the right to return and her contract was terminated.
10. The dismissal was automatically unfair under Employment Rights Act 1996 s99 in that the Applicant was dismissed:
    a. for a reason connected with her pregnancy; and/or
    b. because her contract of employment was terminated after the end of her maternity leave period and the reason or principal reason was that she took maternity leave.

    The Applicant claims that if she had not been pregnant and/or had not taken maternity leave and/or absence, she would not have been dismissed.
11. Further or in the alternative, the Applicant has also been unfairly dismissed in that she was prevented from returning to work in accordance with Employment Rights Act 1996 s79.

12. Further or in the alternative, the Applicant's dismissal was unfair in that, in particular, the Respondents failed to:
    a. investigate the Applicant's sickness and in particular to find out the likely date of the Applicant's return;
    b. consult with the Applicant and discuss her medical condition.
13. Further or in the alternative, the Applicant's dismissal was sex discrimination and a breach of the Sex Discrimination Act 1975, the Equal Treatment Directive and the Pregnant Workers Directive.
14. Further the failure to allow the Applicant to take sick leave was discrimination.
15. The Applicant claims:
    a. a declaration that the Respondents unlawfully discriminated against the Applicant on the ground of her sex;
    b. compensation for unfair dismissal and discrimination;
    c. interest.

Note:
(a) There may also be an equal pay claim (under the Equal Pay Act 1970 or Article 119 EEC) for failure to pay sick pay.
(b) There may also be a breach of contract claim on the basis that the woman had effectively exercised her right to return and should then have been able to claim sick pay.
(c) It is unclear at present whether a woman would have a claim for dismissal and/or discrimination if she was unable to return to work after the four-week period (see p72).

IT1: Refusal of request to work part-time on return from maternity leave

1. The Applicant was employed as an administrative supervisor by the Respondents from September 1994.
2. On 8 July 1996 the Applicant went on maternity leave.
3. On 2 September the Applicant wrote to the Respondents asking if she could return to her job on a part-time basis. The Applicant told her manager, Mr X, that she did not want to leave the baby for such long periods and in addition she could only find a childminder for three days a week.
4. The Respondents replied on 16 September saying that it was not practicable for the Applicant to work part-time because the nature of the work required a full-time person.
5. The requirement to work full-time is indirectly discriminatory on the grounds of sex, as:
    a. the Respondents applied to the Applicant a condition or requirement (namely: if you want to continue in our employment,

you must work full-time) which they applied equally to men; but
  b. the proportion of women who can comply with this requirement or condition is considerably smaller than the proportion of men who can comply with it.¹
  c. the condition or requirement is to the Applicant's detriment because she could not comply with it;
  d. the condition or requirement is not justifiable.
[6. The Applicant felt she had no alternative but to resign, which she did on 30 September. By virtue of the Respondents' conduct towards the Applicant, she was entitled to terminate her contract.]

Alternatively, if the Applicant wants to return to work (working full time) but make a claim of indirect discrimination:
[6. The Applicant seeks a recommendation that the Respondents allow the Applicant to work part-time.²]
7. The Applicant claims compensation for discrimination and interest.

Note
The time limit for bringing a claim is three months (less one day) from 16 September – ie, from the date the employer *first* refused to allow the applicant to return part-time.³

Questionnaire: Request to return to work part-time

1. Please provide a copy of your equal oportunities policy.
2. Please state what criteria you use when deciding to allow an employee to work part-time or to job-share and provide any relevant documents. Please provide details of the procedure followed and who is responsible for making a decision about whether an employee can work part-time or job-share.
3. How many male employees are employed by .... [the employer] and how many female employees? How many are employed:

---

1 The evidence for the above proportion is as follows:
  (i) In winter 1995/96 88 per cent of male employees usually worked 36 or more hours per week; while only 47 per cent of female employees worked 36 or more hours per week.
  (ii) In winter 1995/96 7 per cent of male employees worked part-time; while 45 per cent of female employees worked part-time.
  (iii) These differentials are too large to be mere reflections of individual choice.
  (iv) These figures are for the whole of Britain, but there is no reason to suppose that they do not accurately reflect the position in the catchment area for employment with the Respondents. Figures are taken from Winter 1995/96 Labour Force Survey.
2 There is a danger that the employer will say that the Applicant *can* in fact work full time and she will therefore fall foul of 5(c).
3 *Cast v Croydon College* EAT/161/95. This is arguably wrong (see p212).

a. on a part-time basis;
   b. as job-sharers?
   Please state, in each case, the sex, grade and job title of each employee.
4. Please name all those who were involved in discussion about the possibility of offering me part-time work, stating in each case:
   a. when the discussions took place;
   b. what was agreed.
5. Please provide details of why it is considered that I cannot work part-time and in particular:
   a. what arrangements are made to cover for sickness and holidays;
   b. [other questions relating to the employer's reason for not allowing a job to be done part-time].

IT3: Refusal of request to work part time

1. The Applicant's claim is denied as alleged or at all.
2. It is denied that within the Respondents' workforce a considerably smaller proportion of women than men can work full-time.
3. If, which is denied, there is a requirement or condition to work full-time, such requirement or condition is justifiable irrespective of the sex of the person to whom it is applied in that:
   (i) the requirement or condition is genuinely necessary to enable supervisors to carry out their duties properly and in particular to supervise effectively the work of more junior staff; and
   (ii) the need for supervisors to work full time outweighs any possible discriminatory effect.

IT1: Claim for damages for breach of contract

1. On ..... the Respondent employed the Applicant as an assistant solicitor.
2. There were express terms of the contract set out in a letter from the Respondent to the Applicant of .... that the Applicant would be entitled to the following benefits:
   a. private health insurance to be arranged and paid for by the Respondent;
   b. a car provided by the Respondent for the Applicant's personal as well as business use;
   c. a Christmas bonus of ....
3. The Applicant became pregnant. On 2 September 1996 the Applicant gave to the Respondent written notice of her pregnancy, that the expected week of childbirth was 14 October and that her maternity leave was due to start on 23 September 1996.

4. The Applicant began her maternity leave on 23 September and gave birth on 18 October. She remained on maternity leave until 30 December 1996.
5. As a result of Employment Rights Act 1996 s71 the Applicant was entitled during her maternity leave period to the benefit of the terms and conditions of employment (apart from remuneration) which would have been applicable to her if she had not been absent (and had not been pregnant or given birth to a child).
6. In breach of the said terms and conditions the Respondent:
   a. failed to continue the Applicant's private health insurance during her maternity leave period;
   b. failed to continue to provide the Applicant with the use of a company car during her maternity leave period;
   c. failed to give the Applicant her Christmas bonus.
7. As a result of the breach of contract, the Applicant has suffered the following loss:
   a. cost of alternative health insurance at £......
   b. cost of hiring a car at £.......
   c. loss of Christmas bonus of £.....
8. The Applicant claims damages for breach of contract.
9. The Applicant claims interest.

Note

(a) A breach of contract claim can only be brought in an IT if the contract has come to an end.[4] The time limit is the same as for other IT claims. If that time limit has passed the claim must be made in the county court. In some cases a claim could be made under Part II of the Employment Rights Act for a deduction of wages (see p62).

(b) It is not clear whether a bonus is 'remuneration' and therefore not payable during maternity leave (see p50).

(c) An equal pay claim could also be brought using as a comparator a man (doing like work, equivalent work or work of equal value) who is on sick leave. The legal position is not clear (see p51).

---

4. Industrial Tribunals (Extensions of Jurisdiction) (England and Wales) Order 1994 SI No 623.

APPENDIX 4

Test period table 1996/7 (maternity allowance)

Help if you are expecting a baby and have been working but cannot get statutory maternity pay

You may be able to get Maternity Allowance if, among other things, you have paid National Insurance (NI) contributions as an employee or as a self-employed person in the 66 weeks before you expect to have your baby.

We have to look at the contributions you have paid in the 66 weeks up to the Saturday at the end of the week before the week when you expect to have your baby. These 66 weeks are called the *Test Period*.

Find the week in *column 1* of the table that includes the date you expect to have your baby. Then find the first and last days of your Test Period by reading across the table. Enter these 2 dates on *page 3* of the claim form *MA 1*.

There is an example of how to work out your Test Period at the end of these notes.

Maternity Allowance is paid at a fixed rate depending on your employment status in the qualifying week in column 4 of the table. This is the 15th week before your Expected Week of Confinement (EWC).

If you are employed, you will be paid the higher rate of Maternity Allowance. This will be equivalent to the standard rate of Statutory Maternity Pay (SMP).

If you are self-employed or non-employed, you will get the lower rate of Maternity Allowance, as shown in leaflet *NI 196 Social Security Benefit Rates*. You can get this leaflet from any social security office.

You may also get extra money added on to your Maternity Allowance for your husband, if you have one, or for someone else who looks after children for you. The current rates are shown in leaflet *NI 196*.

If the week you expect to have your baby is not shown in column 1 of this table, please get in touch with your social security office. Ask them for a new Maternity Allowance Test Period Table.

Example of how to work out your Test Period and your Qualifying Week

See the week underlined in the table (p257).

Date you expect to have your baby 30 November 1996

The week that includes the date you expect to have your baby (column 1)	24–30 November 1996
Your Test Period is (columns 2 and 3)	20 August 1995 – 23 November 1996
Your Qualifying Week is (column 4)	11 August 1996

Maternity rights/Appendix 4

1 The week that includes the date you expect to have your baby	2 The first day of your Test Period	3 The last day of your Test Period	4 Your Qualifying Week
April 1996			
7–13	1 Jan 1995	6 Apr 1996	24 Dec 1995
14–20	8 Jan 1995	13 Apr 1996	31 Dec 1995
21–27	15 Jan 1995	20 Apr 1996	7 Jan 1996
28– 4 May	22 Jan 1995	27 Apr 1996	14 Jan 1996
May			
5–11	29 Jan 1995	4 May 1996	21 Jan 1996
12–18	5 Feb 1995	11 May 1996	28 Jan 1996
19–25	12 Feb 1995	18 May 1996	4 Feb 1996
26– 1 June	19 Feb 1995	25 May 1996	11 Feb 1996
June			
2– 8	26 Feb 1995	1 Jun 1996	18 Feb 1996
9–15	5 Mar 1995	8 Jun 1996	25 Feb 1996
16–22	12 Mar 1995	15 Jun 1996	3 Mar 1996
23–29	19 Mar 1995	22 Jun 1996	10 Mar 1996
30– 6 July	26 Mar 1995	29 Jun 1996	17 Mar 1996
July			
7–13	2 Apr 1995	6 Jul 1996	24 Mar 1996
14–20	9 Apr 1995	13 Jul 1996	31 Mar 1996
21–27	16 Apr 1995	20 Jul 1996	7 Apr 1996
28– 3 Aug	23 Apr 1995	27 Jul 1996	14 Apr 1996
August			
4–10	30 Apr 1995	3 Aug 1996	21 Apr 1996
11–17	7 May 1995	10 Aug 1996	28 Apr 1996
18–24	14 May 1995	17 Aug 1996	5 May 1996
25–31	21 May 1995	24 Aug 1996	12 May 1996
September			
1– 7	28 May 1995	31 Aug 1996	19 May 1996
8–14	4 Jun 1995	7 Sep 1996	26 May 1996
15–21	11 Jun 1995	14 Sep 1996	2 Jun 1996
22–28	18 Jun 1995	21 Sep 1996	9 Jun 1996
29– 5 Oct	25 Jun 1995	28 Sep 1996	16 Jun 1996

Maternity allowance test period table

1 The week that includes the date you expect to have your baby	2 The first day of your Test Period	3 The last day of your Test Period	4 Your Qualifying Week
October 1996			
6–12	2 Jul 1995	5 Oct 1996	23 Jun 1996
13–19	9 Jul 1995	12 Oct 1996	30 Jun 1996
20–26	16 Jul 1995	19 Oct 1996	7 Jul 1996
27– 2 Nov	23 Jul 1995	26 Oct 1996	14 Jul 1996
November			
3– 9	30 Jul 1995	2 Nov 1996	21 Jul 1996
10–16	6 Aug 1995	9 Nov 1996	28 Jul 1996
17–23	13 Aug 1995	16 Nov 1996	4 Aug 1996
<u>24–30</u>	<u>20 Aug 1995</u>	<u>23 Nov 1996</u>	<u>11 Aug 1996</u>
December			
1– 7	27 Aug 1995	30 Nov 1996	18 Aug 1996
8–14	3 Sep 1995	7 Dec 1996	25 Aug 1996
15–21	10 Sep 1995	14 Dec 1996	1 Sep 1996
22–28	17 Sep 1995	21 Dec 1996	8 Sep 1996
29– 4 Jan	24 Sep 1995	28 Dec 1996	15 Sep 1996
January 1997			
5–11	1 Oct 1995	4 Jan 1997	22 Sep 1996
12–18	8 Oct 1995	11 Jan 1997	29 Sep 1996
19–25	15 Oct 1995	18 Jan 1997	6 Oct 1996
26– 1 Feb	22 Oct 1995	25 Jan 1997	13 Oct 1996
February			
2– 8	29 Oct 1995	1 Feb 1997	20 Oct 1996
9–15	5 Nov 1995	8 Feb 1997	27 Oct 1996
16–22	12 Nov 1995	15 Feb 1997	3 Nov 1996
23– 1 Mar	19 Nov 1995	22 Feb 1997	10 Nov 1996
March			
2– 8	26 Nov 1995	1 Mar 1997	17 Nov 1996
9–15	3 Dec 1995	8 Mar 1997	24 Nov 1996
16–22	10 Dec 1995	15 Mar 1997	1 Dec 1996
23–29	17 Dec 1995	22 Mar 1997	8 Dec 1996
30– 5 Apr	24 Dec 1995	29 Mar 1997	15 Dec 1996

(©Crown copyright is reproduced with the permission of the Controller of HMSO. Issued with maternity allowance claim form MA1, by the Benefits Agency, an executive agency of the Department of Social Security.)

APPENDIX 5

Pregnant Workers Directive

Council Directive 92/85/EEC of 19 October 1992

SECTION I
PURPOSE AND DEFINITIONS

Article 1: Purpose
1. (1) The purpose of this Directive, which is the tenth individual Directive within the meaning of Article 16 (1) of Directive 89/391/EEC, is to implement measures to encourage improvements in the safety and health at work of pregnant workers and workers who have recently given birth or who are breastfeeding.

(2) The provisions of Directive 89/391/EEC, except for Article 2 (2) thereof, shall apply in full to the whole area covered by paragraph 1, without prejudice to any more stringent and/or specific provisions contained in this Directive.

(3) This Directive may not have the effect of reducing the level of protection afforded to pregnant workers, workers who have recently given birth or who are breastfeeding as compared with the situation which exists in each Member State on the date on which this Directive is adopted.

Article 2: Definitions
2. For the purposes of this Directive:
   (a) *pregnant worker* shall mean a pregnant worker who informs her employer of her condition, in accordance with national legislation and/or national practice;
   (b) *worker who has recently given birth* shall mean a worker who has recently given birth within the meaning of national legislation and/or national practice and who informs her employer of her condition, in accordance with that legislation and/or practice;
   (c) *worker who is breastfeeding* shall mean a worker who is breastfeeding within the meaning of national legislation and/or national practice and who informs her employer of her condition, in accordance with that legislation and/or practice.

SECTION II
GENERAL PROVISIONS

Article 3: Guidelines

3. (1) In consultation with the Member States and assisted by the Advisory Committee on Safety, Hygiene and Health Protection at Work, the Commission shall draw up guidelines on the assessment of the chemical, physical and biological agents and industrial processes considered hazardous for the safety or health of workers within the meaning of Article 2.

The guidelines referred to in the first subparagraph shall also cover movements and postures, mental and physical fatigue and other types of physical and mental stress connected with the work done by workers within the meaning of Article 2.

(2) The purpose of the guidelines referred to in paragraph 1 is to serve as a basis for the assessment referred to in Article 4 (1).

To this end, Member States shall bring these guidelines to the attention of all employers and all female workers and/or their representatives in the respective Member State.

Article 4: Assessment and information

4. (1) For all activities liable to involve a specific risk of exposure to the agents, processes or working conditions of which a non-exhaustive list is given in Annex I, the employer shall assess the nature, degree and duration of exposure, in the undertaking and/or establishment concerned, of workers within the meaning of Article 2, either directly or by way of the protective and preventive services referred to in Article 7 of Directive 89/391/EEC, in order to:
   – assess any risks to the safety or health and any possible effect on the pregnancies or breastfeeding of workers within the meaning of Article 2,
   – decide what measures should be taken.

(2) Without prejudice to Article 10 of Directive 89/391/EEC, workers within the meaning of Article 2 and workers likely to be in one of the situations referred to in Article 2 in the undertaking and/or establishment concerned and/or their representatives shall be informed of the results of the assessment referred to in paragraph 1 and of all measures to be taken concerning health and safety at work.

Article 5: Action further to the results of the assessment

5. (1) Without prejudice to Article 6 of Directive 89/391/EEC, if the results of the assessment referred to in Article 4 (1) reveal a risk to the safety or health or an effect on the pregnancy or breastfeeding of a worker within the meaning of Article 2, the employer shall take the necessary measures to ensure that, by temporarily adjusting the

working conditions and/or the working hours of the worker concerned, the exposure of that worker to such risks is avoided.

(2) If the adjustment of her working conditions and/or working hours is not technically and/or objectively feasible, or cannot reasonably be required on duly substantiated grounds, the employer shall take the necessary measures to move the worker concerned to another job.

(3) If moving her to another job is not technically and/or objectively feasible or cannot reasonably be required on duly substantiated grounds, the worker concerned shall be granted leave in accordance with national legislation and/or national practice for the whole of the period necessary to protect her safety or health.

(4) The provisions of this Article shall apply *mutatis mutandis* to the case where a worker pursuing an activity which is forbidden pursuant to Article 6 becomes pregnant or starts breastfeeding and informs her employer thereof.

Article 6: Cases in which exposure is prohibited

6. In addition to the general provisions concerning the protection of workers, in particular those relating to the limit values for occupational exposure:
(1) pregnant workers within the meaning of Article 2 (a) may under no circumstances be obliged to perform duties for which the assessment has revealed a risk of exposure, which would jeopardize safety or health, to the agents and working conditions listed in Annex II, Section A;
(2) workers who are breastfeeding, within the meaning of Article 2 (c), may under no circumstances be obliged to perform duties for which the assessment has revealed a risk of exposure, which would jeopardize safety or health, to the agents and working conditions listed in Annex II, Section B.

Article 7: Night work

7. (1) Member States shall take the necessary measures to ensure that workers referred to in Article 2 are not obliged to perform night work during their pregnancy and for a period following childbirth which shall be determined by the national authority competent for safety and health, subject to submission, in accordance with the procedures laid down by the Member States, of a medical certificate stating that this is necessary for the safety or health of the worker concerned.

(2) The measures referred to in paragraph 1 must entail the possibility, in accordance with national legislation and/or national practice, of:
(a) transfer to daytime work; or
(b) leave from work or extension of maternity leave where such a transfer is not technically and/or objectively feasible or cannot reasonably be required on duly substantiated grounds.

Article 8: Maternity leave
8. (1) Member States shall take the necessary measures to ensure that workers within the meaning of Article 2 are entitled to a continuous period of maternity leave of at least 14 weeks allocated before and/or after confinement in accordance with national legislation and/or practice.
(2) The maternity leave stipulated in paragraph 1 must include compulsory maternity leave of at least two weeks allocated before and/or after confinement in accordance with national legislation and/or practice.

Article 9: Time off for ante-natal examinations
9. Member States shall take the necessary measures to ensure that pregnant workers within the meaning of Article 2 (a) are entitled to, in accordance with national legislation and/or practice, time off, without loss of pay, in order to attend ante-natal examinations, if such examinations have to take place during working hours.

Article 10: Prohibition of dismissal
10. In order to guarantee workers, within the meaning of Article 2, the exercise of their health and safety protection rights as recognized under this Article, it shall be provided that:
(1) Member States shall take the necessary measures to prohibit the dismissal of workers, within the meaning of Article 2, during the period from the beginning of their pregnancy to the end of the maternity leave referred to in Article 8 (1), save in exceptional cases not connected with their condition which are permitted under national legislation and/or practice and, where applicable, provided that the competent authority has given its consent;
(2) if a worker, within the meaning of Article 2, is dismissed during the period referred to in point 1, the employer must cite duly substantiated grounds for her dismissal in writing;
(3) Member States shall take the necessary measures to protect workers, within the meaning of Article 2, from consequences of dismissal which is unlawful by virtue of point 1.

Article 11: Employment rights
11. In order to guarantee workers within the meaning of Article 2 the exercise of their health and safety protection rights as recognized in this Article, it shall be provided that:
(1) in the case referred to in Articles 5, 6 and 7, the employment rights relating to the employment contract, including the maintenance of a payment to, and/or entitlement to an adequate allowance for, workers within the meaning of Article 2, must be ensured in accordance with national legislation and/or national practice;

(2) in the case referred to in Article 8, the following must be ensured:
   (a) the rights connected with the employment contract of workers within the meaning of Article 2, other than those referred to in point (b) below;
   (b) maintenance of a payment to, and/or entitlement to an adequate allowance for, workers within the meaning of Article 2;
(3) the allowance referred to in point 2 (b) shall be deemed adequate if it guarantees income at least equivalent to that which the worker concerned would receive in the event of a break in her activities on grounds connected with her state of health, subject to any ceiling laid down under national legislation;
(4) Member States may make entitlement to pay or the allowance referred to in points 1 and 2 (b) conditional upon the worker concerned fulfilling the conditions of eligibility for such benefits laid down under national legislation.

These conditions may under no circumstances provide for periods of previous employment in excess of 12 months immediately prior to the presumed date of confinement.

Article 12: Defence of rights
12. Member States shall introduce into their national legal systems such measures as are necessary to enable all workers who find themselves wronged by failure to comply with the obligations arising from this Directive to pursue their claims by judicial process (and/or, in accordance with national laws and/or practices) by recourse to other competent authorities.

Article 13: Amendments to the Annexes
13. (1) Strictly technical adjustments to Annex I as a result of technical progress, changes in international regulations or specifications and new findings in the area covered by this Directive shall be adopted in accordance with the procedure laid down in Article 17 of Directive 89/391/EEC.

(2) Annex II may be amended only in accordance with the procedure laid down in Article 118a of the Treaty.

Article 14: Final provisions
14. (1) Member States shall bring into force the laws, regulations and administrative provisions necessary to comply with this Directive not later than two years after the adoption thereof or ensure, at the latest two years after adoption of this Directive, that the two sides of industry introduce the requisite provisions by means of collective agreements, with Member States being required to make all the necessary provisions to enable them at all times to guarantee the results laid down by this Directive. They shall forthwith inform the Commission thereof.

(2) When Member States adopt the measures referred to in paragraph 1, they shall contain a reference of this Directive or shall be accompanied by such reference on the occasion of their official publication. The methods of making such a reference shall be laid down by the Member States.

(3) Member States shall communicate to the Commission the texts of the essential provisions of national law which they have already adopted or adopt in the field governed by this Directive.

(4) Member States shall report to the Commission every five years on the practical implementation of the provisions of this Directive, indicating the points of view of the two sides of industry.

However, Member States shall report for the first time to the Commission on the practical implementation of the provisions of this Directive, indicating the points of view of the two sides of industry, four years after its adoption.

The Commission shall inform the European Parliament, the Council, the Economic and Social Committee and the Advisory Committee on Safety, Hygiene and Health Protection at Work.

(5) The Commission shall periodically submit to the European Parliament, the Council and the Economic and Social Committee a report on the implementation of this Directive, taking into account paragraphs 1, 2 and 3.

(6) The Council will re-examine this Directive, on the basis of an assessment carried out on the basis of the reports referred to in the second subparagraph of paragraph 4 and, should the need arise, of a proposal, to be submitted by the Commission at the latest five years after adoption of the Directive.

15. This Directive is addressed to the Member States.

Done at Luxembourg, 19 October 1992.

ANNEX I

NON-EXHAUSTIVE LIST OF AGENTS, PROCESSES AND WORKING CONDITIONS

rererred to in Article 4 (1)

A. **Agents**

1. *Physical agents* where these are regarded as agents causing foetal lesions and/or likely to disrupt placental attachment, and in particular:
   (a) shocks, vibration or movement;
   (b) handling of loads entailing risks, particularly of a dorsolumbar nature;
   (c) noise;
   (d) ionizing radiation;
   (e) non-ionizing radiation;
   (f) extremes of cold or heat;
   (g) movements and postures, travelling – either inside or outside the establishment – mental and physical fatigue and other physical burdens connected with the activity of the worker within the meaning of Article 2 of the Directive.

   2 *Biological agents*
   Biological agents of risk groups 2, 3 and 4 within the meaning of Article 2 (d) numbers 2, 3 and 4 of Directive 90/679/EEC, in so far as it is known that these agents or the therapeutic measures necessitated by such agents endanger the health of pregnant women and the unborn child and in so far as they do not yet appear in Annex II.

   3. *Chemical agents*
   The following chemical agents in so far as is known that they endanger the health of pregnant women and the unborn child and in so far as they do not yet appear in Annex II:
   (a) substances labelled R40, R45, R46 and R47 under Directive 67/548/EEC in so far as they do not yet appear in Annex II;
   (b) chemical agents in Annex I to Directive 90/394/EEC;
   (c) mercury and mercury derivatives;
   (d) antimitotic drugs;
   (e) carbon monoxide;
   (f) chemical agents of known and dangerous percutaneous absorption.

B. **Processes**
   Industrial processes listed in Annex I to Directive 90/394/EEC.

C. **Working conditions**
   Underground mining work.

ANNEX II
NON-EXHAUSTIVE LIST OF AGENTS AND WORKING CONDITIONS
referred to in Article 6

A. Pregnant workers within the meaning of Article 2 (a)
  1. *Agents*
     (a) *Physical agents* Work in hyperbaric atmosphere e.g. pressurized enclosures and underwater diving.
     (b) *Biological agents* The following biological agents:
        – toxiplasma,
        – rubella virus
        unless the pregnant workers are proved to be adequately protected against such agents by immunization.
     (c) *Chemical agents* Lead and lead derivatives in so far as these agents are capable of being absorbed by the human organism.
  2. *Working conditions*
     Underground mining work.
B. Workers who are breastfeeding within the meaning of Article 2 (c)
  1. *Agents*
     (a) *Chemical agents*
        Lead and lead derivatives in so far as these agents are capable of being absorbed by the human organism.
  2. *Working conditions*
     Underground mining work.

Statement of the Council and the Commission concerning Article 11 (3) of Directive 92/85/EEC, entered in the minutes of the 1608th meeting of the Council (Luxembourg, 19 October 1992)

THE COUNCIL AND THE COMMISSION stated that:
'In determining the level of the allowances referred to in Article 11 (2)(b) and (3) reference shall be made, for purely technical reasons, to the allowance which a worker would receive in the event of a break in her activities on grounds connected with her state of health. Such a reference is not intended in any way to imply that pregnancy and childbirth be equated with sickness. The national social seurity legislation of all Member States provide for an allowance to be paid during an absence from work due to sickness. The link with such allowance in the chosen formulation is simply intended to serve as a concrete, fixed reference amount in all Member States for the determination of the minimum amount of maternity allowance payable. In so far as allowances are paid in individual Member States which exeeed those provided for in the Directive, such allowances are of course retained. This is clear from Article 1 (3) of the Directive.'

APPENDIX 6
Hazards for new and expectant mothers at work

(Extracts from the Health and Safety Executive pamphlet, *New and expectant mothers at work: a guide for employers* (December 1994). © Crown copyright is reproduced with the permission of the Controller of HMSO.)

Maternity rights/Appendix 6

HAZARDS, RISKS, AND WAYS OF AVOIDING THEM *(Including physical, chemical and biological agents and working conditions*	
List of agents/ working conditions	What is the risk?
PHYSICAL AGENTS – where these are regarded as agents causing foetal	
Shocks, vibration or movement	Regular exposure to shocks, low frequency vibration, for example driving or riding in off-road vehicles, or excessive movement, may increase the risk of a miscarriage. Long-term exposure to vibration does not cause foetal abnormalities but often occurs with heavy physical work, so there may be an increased risk of prematurity or low birth weight.
Manual handling of loads where there is a risk of injury	Pregnant workers are especially at risk from manual handling injury – for example hormonal changes can affect the ligaments, increasing susceptibility to injury; and postural problems may increase as the pregnancy progresses.
	There can also be risks for those who have recently given birth, for example after a caesarean section there is likely to be a temporary limitation on lifting and handling capability. There is no evidence to suggest that breastfeeding mothers are at greater risk from manual handling injury than any other workers.
Noise	There appears to be no specific risk to new or expectant mothers or to the foetus, but prolonged exposure to loud noise may lead to increased blood pressure and tiredness.
	No particular problems for women who have recently given birth or who are breastfeeding.

Hazards for new and expectant mothers at work 269

listed in Annexes 1 and 2 to the EC Directive on Pregnant Workers (92/85/EEC))

How to avoid the risk	Other legislation
lesions and/or likely to disrupt placental attachment, and in particular:	
Pregnant workers and those who have recently given birth are advised to avoid work likely to involve uncomfortable whole body vibration, especially at low frequencies, or where the abdomen is exposed to shocks or jolts. Breastfeeding workers are at no greater risk than other workers.	None specific
The changes an employer should make will depend on the risks identified in the assessment and the circumstances of the business. For example it may be possible to alter the nature of the task so that risks from manual handling are reduced for all workers including new or expectant mothers. Or it may be necessary to address the specific needs of the worker and reduce the amount of physical work, or provide aids for her in future to reduce the risks she faces.	Manual Handling Operations Regulations 1992 require employers to: • avoid the need for hazardous manual handling, so far as is reasonably practicable; • assess the risks from those operations that cannot be avoided; and • take steps to reduce these risks to the lowest level reasonably practicable.
The requirements of the Noise at Work Regulations 1989 should be sufficient to meet the needs of new or expectant mothers.	Noise at Work Regulations 1989 apply to all workers exposed to loud noise where there is a risk to hearing.

Maternity rights/Appendix 6

List of agents/ working conditions	What is the risk?
PHYSICAL AGENTS *continued*	
Ionising radiation	Significant exposure to ionising radiation can be harmful to the foetus and this is recognised by placing limits on the external radiation dose to the abdomen of the expectant mother for the declared term of her pregnancy
	If a nursing mother works with radioactive liquids or dusts, these can cause exposure of the child, particularly through contamination of the mother's skin.
	Also, there may be a risk to the foetus from significant amounts of radioactive contamination breathed in or ingested by the mother and transferred across the placenta.
Non-ionising electromagnetic radiation (NIEMR)	*Optical radiation:* Pregnant or breast-feeding mothers are at no greater risk than other workers.
	Electromagnetic fields and waves (eg radio-frequency radiation): Exposure to electric and magnetic fields within current recommendations is not known to cause harm to the foetus or the mother. However, extreme overexposure to radio-frequency radiation could cause harm by raising body temperature.

How to avoid the risk	Other legislation
Work procedures should be designed to keep exposure of the pregnant woman as low as reasonably practicable and certainly below the statutory dose limit for pregnant women. Special attention should be paid to the possibility of nursing mothers receiving radioactive contamination and they should not be employed in work where the risk of such contamination is high. The working conditions should be such as to make it unlikely that a pregnant woman might receive high accidental exposures to radioactive contamination.	Ionising Radiations Regulations 1985 and supporting Approved Codes of Practice.
Exposure to electric and magnetic fields should not exceed the restrictions on human exposure published by the National Radiological Protection Board.	None specific

List of agents/ working conditions	What is the risk?
PHYSICAL AGENTS *continued*	
Extremes of cold or heat	When pregnant, women tolerate heat less well and may more readily faint or be more liable to heat stress. The risk is likely to be reduced after birth but it is not certain how quickly an improvement comes about.

Breastfeeding may be impaired by heat dehydration.

No specific problems arise from working in extreme cold, although clearly for other health and safety reasons, warm clothing should be provided. |
| Movements and postures, travelling – either inside or outside the establishment – mental and physical fatigue and other physical burdens connected with the activity of new or expectant mothers | Fatigue from standing and other physical work has long been associated with miscarriage, premature birth and low birth weight.

Excessive physical or mental pressure may cause stress and can give rise to anxiety and raised blood pressure.

Pregnant workers may experience problems in working at heights, for example ladders, platforms and in working in tightly fitting workspaces or with workstations which do not adjust sufficiently to take account of increased abdominal size, particularly during the later stages of pregnancy. This may lead to strain or sprain injuries. Dexterity, agility co-ordination, speed of movement, reach and balance may also be impaired, and an increased risk of accidents may need to be considered. |

How to avoid the risk	Other legislation
Pregnant workers should take great care when exposed to prolonged heat at work, for example when working near furnaces Rest facilities and access to refreshments would help.	None specific
Ensure that hours of work and the volume and pacing of work are not excessive and that, where possible, the employees themselves have some control over how their work is organised. Ensure that seating is available where appropriate. Longer or more frequent rest breaks will help to avoid or reduce fatigue. Adjusting workstations or work procedures may help remove postural problems and risk of accidents.	

List of agents/ working conditions	What is the risk?
WORKING CONDITIONS	
Work with Display Screen Equipment (VDUs)	There has been considerable public concern about reports of higher levels of miscarriage and birth defects among some groups of visual display unit (VDU) workers, in particular due to electromagnetic radiation. Many scientific studies have been carried out, but taken as a whole their results do not show any link between miscarriages or birth defects and working with VDUs. Research and reviews of the scientific evidence will continue to be undertaken. In the light of the scientific evidence, pregnant women do not need to stop work with VDUs. However, to avoid problems caused by stress and anxiety, women who are pregnant or planning children and worried about working with VDUs should be given the opportunity to discuss their concerns with someone adequately informed of current authoritative scientific information and advice. See also Display Screen Equipment Regulations 1992.

Hazards for new and expectant mothers at work 275

APPENDIX 1 – Aspects of pregnancy that may affect work

Apart from the hazards listed in the table, there are other aspects of pregnancy that may affect work. The impact will vary during the course of the pregnancy and you will want to keep their effects under review, for example the posture of expectant mothers changes to cope with increasing size.

Aspects of pregnancy	Factors in work
Morning sickness	Early shift work
	Exposure to nauseating smells
Backache	Standing/manual handling/posture
Varicose veins	Standing/sitting
Haemorrhoids	Working in hot conditions
Frequent visits to toilet	Difficulty in leaving job/site of work
Increasing size	Use of protective clothing
	Work in confined areas
	Manual handling
Tiredness	Overtime
	Evening work
Balance	Problems of working on slippery, wet surfaces
Comfort	Problems of working in tightly fitting workspaces

Dexterity, agility, co-ordination, speed of movement, reach, may be impaired because of increasing size.

APPENDIX 2 – Removal from risk

(This is not reproduced. It explains the legislative provisions already summarised on pp119ff in chapter 8).

APPENDIX 3 – References and further reading

Carbon monoxide HSE Guidance Note EH43 1984 ISBN 0 11 883597 1

Control of lead at work Approved Code of Practice (rev) 1985 ISBN 0 11 883780 X

COSHH: a brief guide for employers IND(G) 1 36(L) 1993 Free leaflet

5 steps to risk assessment Free leaflet IND(G) 1 63(L)

Getting to grips with manual handling. A short guide for employers Free leaflet IND(G) 1 43(L)

Introducing the Noise at Work Regulations – a brief guide to the requirements for controlling noise at work IND(G)75(L) Free leaflet

Management of Health and Safety at Work Approved Code of Practice L21 1992 ISBN 0 7176 0412 8

Manual Handling Operations Regulations 1992. Guidance on Regulations L23 1992 ISBN 0 7176 0411 X

Mercury – health and safety precautions HSE Guidance Note EH17 1977 ISBN 0 11 883176 3

Mercury – medical surveillance HSE Guidance Note MS 12 1978 ISBN 0 11 883191 7

Occupational exposure limits HSE Guidance Note EH40/94 1994 ISBN 0 7176 0722 4

Personal Protective Equipment at Work Regulations 1992. Guidance on Regulations L25 1992 ISBN 0 7176 0415 2

Precautions for the safe handling of cytotoxic drugs HSE Guidance Note MS21 1983 ISBN 0 11 883571 8

VDUs: An easy guide to the Regulations HS(G)90 1994 ISBN 0 7176 0735 6

APPENDIX 7
Statutory maternity pay tables

© Crown copyright is reproduced with the permission of the Controller of HMSO. Extracts from leaflet CA29, issued by the Contributions Agency.

Explanation of statutory maternity pay tables

Column 1 – Expected week of confinement (EWC)
This is the calendar week in which the baby is expected. The dates in this column show a complete calendar week, Sunday to Saturday.

Column 2 – Qualifying week (QW)
This is the 15th week before the start of the expected week of confinement. The woman must either have been employed by you or treated as employed for some time during this week.

A woman may be treated as employed in the qualifying week if:
- her baby was born earlier than this week
or
- she was not employed during the qualifying week because she was absent from work for specific reasons and, depending on the type of employment, has returned to the employment since the qualifying week, see Statutory Maternity Pay Manual, CA29, page 10.

Column 3– Latest start date for 26 weeks' employment
This column shows the Saturday date for the last week in which an employee must have started working for you for there to be 26 weeks of continuous employment up to and including the qualifying week. Please note:
- if you employed the woman, or she can be treated as your employee, for some time during the qualifying week, the qualifying week counts as as full week of continuous employment.
- certain breaks in employment can be treated as part of continuous employment, for further details see Statutory Maternity Pay Manual, CA29, pages 7 to 11.

Column 4 – 11th week before the EWC
This column shows the Sunday of the earliest week that the maternity pay period can start, unless the baby was born earlier.

Colunm 5 – 6th week before the EWC
This column shows the Sunday of the 6th week before the expected week of confinement.

278 Maternity rights/Appendix 7

| COLUMN 1
Expected week of confinement (EWC) commencing Sunday
(see note 1) | COLUMN 2
Qualifying week (QW) commencing Sunday
(see note 2) | COLUMN 3
Latest start date for 26 weeks employment
(see note 3) | COLUMN 4
11th week before the EWC commencing Sunday
(see note 4) | COLUMN 5
6th week before the EWC commencing Sunday
(see note 5) |
|---|---|---|---|---|
| 01 09 96 to 07 09 96 | 19 05 96 | 02 12 95 | 16 06 96 | 21 07 96 |
| 08 09 96 to 14 09 96 | 26 05 96 | 09 12 95 | 23 06 96 | 28 07 96 |
| 15 09 96 to 21 09 96 | 02 06 96 | 16 12 95 | 30 06 96 | 04 08 96 |
| 22 09 96 to 28 09 96 | 09 06 96 | 23 12 95 | 07 07 96 | 11 08 96 |
| 29 09 96 to 05 10 96 | 16 06 96 | 30 12 95 | 14 07 96 | 18 08 96 |
| 06 10 96 to 12 10 96 | 23 06 96 | 06 01 96 | 21 07 96 | 25 08 96 |
| 13 10 96 to 19 10 96 | 30 06 96 | 13 01 96 | 28 07 96 | 01 09 96 |
| 20 10 96 to 26 10 96 | 07 07 96 | 20 01 96 | 04 08 96 | 08 09 96 |
| 27 10 96 to 02 11 96 | 14 07 96 | 27 01 96 | 11 08 96 | 15 09 96 |
| 03 11 96 to 09 11 96 | 21 07 96 | 03 02 96 | 18 08 96 | 22 09 96 |
| 10 11 96 to 16 11 96 | 28 07 96 | 10 02 96 | 25 08 96 | 29 09 96 |
| 17 11 96 to 23 11 96 | 04 08 96 | 17 02 96 | 01 09 96 | 06 10 96 |
| 24 11 96 to 30 11 96 | 11 08 96 | 24 02 96 | 08 09 96 | 13 10 96 |
| 01 12 96 to 07 12 96 | 18 08 96 | 02 03 96 | 15 09 96 | 20 10 96 |
| 08 12 96 to 14 12 96 | 25 08 96 | 09 03 96 | 22 09 96 | 27 10 96 |
| 15 12 96 to 21 12 96 | 01 09 96 | 16 03 96 | 29 09 96 | 03 11 96 |
| 22 12 96 to 28 12 96 | 08 09 96 | 23 03 96 | 06 10 96 | 10 11 96 |
| 29 12 96 to 04 01 97 | 15 09 96 | 30 03 96 | 13 10 96 | 17 11 96 |
| 05 01 97 to 11 01 97 | 22 09 96 | 06 04 96 | 20 10 96 | 24 11 96 |
| 12 01 97 to 18 01 97 | 29 09 96 | 13 04 96 | 27 10 96 | 01 12 96 |
| 19 01 97 to 25 01 97 | 06 10 96 | 20 04 96 | 03 11 96 | 08 12 96 |
| 26 01 97 to 01 02 97 | 13 10 96 | 27 04 96 | 10 11 96 | 15 12 96 |
| 02 02 97 to 08 02 97 | 20 10 96 | 04 05 96 | 17 11 96 | 22 12 96 |
| 09 02 97 to 15 02 97 | 27 10 96 | 11 05 96 | 24 11 96 | 29 12 96 |
| 16 02 97 to 22 02 97 | 03 11 96 | 18 05 96 | 01 12 96 | 05 01 97 |
| 23 02 97 to 01 03 97 | 10 11 96 | 25 05 96 | 08 12 96 | 12 01 97 |
| 02 03 97 to 08 03 97 | 17 11 96 | 01 06 96 | 15 12 96 | 19 01 97 |
| 09 03 97 to 15 03 97 | 24 11 96 | 08 06 96 | 22 12 96 | 26 01 97 |
| 16 03 97 to 22 03 97 | 01 12 96 | 15 06 96 | 29 12 96 | 02 02 97 |
| 23 03 97 to 29 03 97 | 08 12 96 | 22 06 96 | 05 01 97 | 09 02 97 |
| 30 03 97 to 05 04 97 | 15 12 96 | 29 06 96 | 12 01 97 | 16 02 97 |
| 06 04 97 to 12 04 97 | 22 12 96 | 06 07 96 | 19 01 97 | 23 02 97 |
| 13 04 97 to 19 04 97 | 29 12 96 | 13 07 96 | 26 01 97 | 02 03 97 |
| 20 04 97 to 26 04 97 | 05 01 97 | 20 07 96 | 02 02 97 | 09 03 97 |
| 27 04 97 to 03 05 97 | 12 01 97 | 27 07 96 | 09 02 97 | 16 03 97 |
| 04 05 97 to 10 05 97 | 19 01 97 | 03 08 96 | 16 02 97 | 23 03 97 |
| 11 05 97 to 17 05 97 | 26 01 97 | 10 08 96 | 23 02 97 | 30 03 97 |
| 18 05 97 to 24 05 97 | 02 02 97 | 17 08 96 | 02 03 97 | 06 04 97 |
| 25 05 97 to 31 05 97 | 09 02 97 | 24 08 96 | 09 03 97 | 13 04 97 |
| 01 06 97 to 07 06 97 | 16 02 97 | 31 08 96 | 16 03 97 | 20 04 97 |
| 08 06 97 to 14 06 97 | 23 02 97 | 07 09 96 | 23 03 97 | 27 04 97 |
| 15 06 97 to 21 06 97 | 02 03 97 | 14 09 96 | 30 03 97 | 04 05 97 |
| 22 06 97 to 28 06 97 | 09 03 97 | 21 09 96 | 06 04 97 | 11 05 97 |
| 29 06 97 to 05 07 97 | 16 03 97 | 28 09 96 | 13 04 97 | 18 05 97 |
| 06 07 97 to 12 07 97 | 23 03 97 | 05 10 96 | 20 04 97 | 25 05 97 |
| 13 07 97 to 19 07 97 | 30 03 97 | 12 10 96 | 27 04 97 | 01 06 97 |
| 20 07 97 to 26 07 97 | 06 04 97 | 19 10 96 | 04 05 97 | 08 06 97 |
| 27 07 97 to 02 08 97 | 13 04 97 | 26 10 96 | 11 05 97 | 15 06 97 |

APPENDIX 8
Useful addresses

ACAS
Brandon House
180 Borough High Street
London SE1 1LW
Tel: 0171 210 3613

Central Office of Industrial Tribunals
Southgate Street,
Bury St Edmunds,
Suffolk IP33 2AQ
Tel: 01284 762300
Fax: 01284 766334

Equal Opportunities Commission
Overseas House
Quay Street
Manchester M3 3HN
Tel: 0161 833 9244
Fax: 0161 835 1657

Free Representation Unit
Room 140, First Floor,
49–51 Bedford Row,
London WC1R 4LR
Tel: 0171 831 0692

Health and Safety Executive
HSE Books: PO Box 1999,
Sudbury, Suffolk CO10 6FS
Tel: 01787 881165
Fax: 01787 313995
HSE Information Centre:
Broad Lane,
Sheffield S3 7HQ
Tel: 0114 289 2345
Fax: 0114 289 2333

Law Centres Federation
Duchess House
18 Warren Street
London W1P 5DB
Tel: 0171 387 8570
Fax: 0171 387 8368

Maternity Alliance
45 Beech Street
London EC2P 2LX
Tel: 0171 588 8582
(information line)
Fax: 0171 588 8584

National Association of Citizens
Advice Bureaux
115 Pentonville Road
London N1 9LP
Tel: 0171 833 2181

New Ways to Work
309 Upper Street
London N1 2TU
Tel: 0171 226 4026

Rights of Women
52 Featherstone Street
London EC1Y 8RT
Tel: 0171 251 6577

Tribunal Enquiry Service
(for information about which office
to send applications to)
Tel: 0345 959775

Index

Abortion
  dismissal, to avoid, 24–25
Abroad
  women ordinarily working outside Great Britain, 14
Absence
  extended. See Extended maternity absence
  pregnancy-related,
    during six weeks before EWC, 36–37
    employer, duty to notify, 37
    meaning, 37
    woman's right to work following, 37–38
  pregnancy-related, limit to amount of, 21–22
Actual week of childbirth (AWC)
  meaning, 8
Actual week of confinement (AWC)
  meaning, 9
Addresses, useful, 279
Adjudication officer
  maternity allowance, dispute relating to, 162
Agency workers
  statutory maternity pay, eligibility for, 138–139
Allowance. See Maternity allowance
Annual shut-down
  general maternity leave, rights during, 52
Ante-natal care
  appointment for, requirement for, 18
  certificate, requirement for, 18
  employer refusing time

Ante-natal care – cont
  off for, 18–19
  meaning, 17–19
  paid time off for, right to,
    ante-natal care, meaning, 17–18
    appointment, requirement for, 18
    certificate, requirement for, 18
    dismissal of woman enforcing right to time off, 20
    employer refusing time off, 18–19
    entitlement, 19–20
    generally, 17
    remedies, 20
Appeal
  maternity allowance, dispute relating to, 162
  procedure, 209
Appearances
  less favourable treatment of pregnant woman, 27–28
Appointment for ante-natal care, 18
Armed forces
  general exclusions from ERA, 14
  return from, eligibility for SMP, 140
Automatically unfair dismissal. See Unfair dismissal
Baby
  sickness of, 102–103
Bank holidays
  missed, time off in lieu for, 55
Benefits in kind
  extended maternity absence, rights during, 60
  general maternity leave, rights during, 51
Birth. See Childbirth
Bonuses
  general maternity leave, rights during, 50–51
Breastfeeding
  compulsory leave after birth, 124–125
  worker who is, meaning, 11
Business
  dismissal on transfer of, 104
Car
  general maternity leave, rights during, 51

Certificate
  ante-natal care, requirement relating to, 18
  expected week of childbirth, giving,
    extended maternity absence, 43
    minimum general maternity leave, 35
Child benefit
  maternity allowance, effect of, 161
Childbirth
  actual week of, meaning, 8
  compulsory leave after, 124–125
  expected week of,
    11th week before, meaning, 7
    meaning, 8
  meaning, 8, 39
  rights before,
    ante-natal care, right to paid time off for,
      ante-natal care, meaning, 17–19
      entitlement, 19–20
      generally, 17
      remedies, 20
    generally, 17
    key points, 30
    less favourable treatment of pregnant woman,
      appearances, 27–28
      generally, 25
      promotion, 27
      recruitment, 25–27
      transfer, 27
    pregnancy-related dismissal,
      automatically unfair dismissal, 20–22
      discriminatory dismissal, 23–25
      ordinary unfair dismissal, 22
      sickness during pregnancy, 28–29
  working within two weeks of, 67–68
Commission
  general maternity leave, rights during, 50–51
Common questions, 236–245
Company car
  general maternity leave, rights during, 51

Composite right
  meaning, 8
Confinement
  actual week of, meaning, 9
  expected week of, meaning, 9
Continuity of service
  extended maternity absence, during, break for up to 26 weeks, 61
  contractual rights, continuity for, 60
  generally, 60
  statutory rights, continuity for, 60–61
  maternity leave, preserved during, 54
Contract
  breach of, 213
  extended maternity absence, rights during, 56–57
  fixed-term,
    exception, 90
    part-time, failure to renew, 83–84
  industrial tribunal, claim in, 62
  part-time fixed-term, failure to renew, 83–84
  return to work, right to, 74–75
Contract worker
  discrimination against, 169–170
Contractual sick pay. *See* Sick pay
Costs
  hearing, of, 219–220
Council tax benefit
  maternity allowance, effect of, 160
County court
  action in, 62
Courts
  county court, action in, 62
  European Court of Justice, 205
  UK, EU law in, 200–204
Dental treatment
  free, 161, 162
Direct discrimination. *See* Discrimination
Directive. *See* Pregnant Workers' Directive (PWD)
Discrimination
  contract worker, against, 169–170
  direct,
    comparing like with like, 175–179

Discrimination – *cont*
  establishing pregnancy-related reason, 179–182
  key points, 183–184
  less favourable treatment, 175–183
  marital discrimination, 165
  relevant evidence, 182–183
  sex discrimination, 165
  whether justified, 183
  discriminatory dismissal,
    abortion to avoid dismissal, 24–25
    birth, rights before, 23–25
    fertility treatment, 24
    moral grounds, dismissal on, 24
  EU law, under, 170
  equal pay, 58–59, 63
  extended maternity absence, rights during, 57, 63
  generally, 164–165
  health and safety, relating to, 126–127
  indirect,
    generally, 185
    key points, 196–197
    marital discrimination, 165–170
    meaning, 185–186
    proof of, 186–196
    sex discrimination, 165–170
  interview, discriminatory questions at, 26–27
  job sharer, against, 81–86
  key points, 173–174
  part-timer, against, 81–86
  protection from, 15
  sex. *See* Sex discrimination
  unfair dismissal, 96
  vicarious liability, 168
  victimisation, 165–166
Dismissal
  ante-natal care, woman enforcing right to time off for, 20
  before 11th week, 35
  deemed, 95
  discriminatory,
    abortion to avoid dismissal, 24–25
    birth, rights before, 23–25
    fertility treatment, 24
    moral grounds, dismissal on, 24

Dismissal – *cont*
  extended maternity absence, rights during, 61–62
  general principles relating to, 88–90
  pregnancy-related,
    automatically unfair dismissal, 20–22
    discriminatory dismissal, 23–25
    ordinary unfair dismissal, 22
    protection from, 67, 68
  unfair. *See* Unfair dismissal
  week's pay for employment rights under ERA, 10
Disputes
  maternity allowance, relating to, 162
Employee
  meaning, 15
  postponement of return by, 70–73
Employer
  ante-natal care, refusal of time off for, 18–19
  general maternity leave, advice about rights relating to, 34
  health and safety. *See* Health and safety
  insolvency of, effect on SMP, 149
  knowledge of pregnancy, 21
  postponement of return by, 70
  pregnancy-related absence, duty to notify of, 37
  prohibited sex discrimination by, 166–168
  same, right to return to, 75
  small,
    exceptions to right to return, 79–80
    recovery of SMP, 151
  statutory maternity pay. *See* Statutory maternity pay (SMP)
Employment agency
  prohibited sex discrimination by, 169
Employment Rights Act 1996
  employees only protected, 13
  exclusions, 15–16
  general exclusions from, 14
  ordinary unfair dismissal provisions of, 14–15
  out-of-time claims, 214

284 *Index*

Employment Rights Act 1996 – *cont*
  summary of maternity rights under, 12-16
  week's pay for employment rights under, meaning, 10
Equal Opportunities Commission (EOC)
  financial help and legal advice, 210
Equal Opportunities Review
  survey of maternity arrangements, 2
Equal pay
  Act of 1970, 170-172
  Article 119, 172
  Directive, 173
  extended maternity absence, rights during, 58-59, 63
  key points, 173-174
  time limits for bringing claim, 213
Equal Treatment Directive
  discrimination, 170
  health and safety, 127-128
European Commission
  challenging UK law through, 204-206
European Community. *See* European Union (EU)
European Court of Justice
  powers of, 205
  reference to, 205
European Union (EU)
  discrimination under law of, 170
European Communities Act 1972, 198-199
  generally, 198
  indirect discrimination, meaning, 186
  key points, 207-208
  legislation, 199
  maternity leave, trigger provisions relating to, 38-39
  Pregnant Workers Directive. *See* Pregnant Workers Directive (PWD)
  summary of maternity rights under, 11-12
  time limits under law of, 206
  UK courts and tribunals, EU law in, 200-204

European Communities Act – *cont*
  usefulness of law of, 206-207
Evidence
  direct discrimination, of, 182
  hearing, at, 219
  medical, eligibility for SMP, 142
  part-time working, support for, 84-85
Expected week of childbirth (EWC)
  11th week before, meaning, 7
  meaning, 8
Expected week of confinement (EWC)
  meaning, 9
Extended maternity absence
  continuity of service during, break for up to 26 weeks, with, 61
  contractual rights, 60
  generally, 60
  statutory rights, 60-61
  contract, rights relating to, 56-57
  discrimination, rights relating to, 57, 63
  dismissal during, 98-103
  dismissal, rights relating to, 61-62
  duration of, 43
  equal pay, rights relating to, 58-59, 63
  full pay during, no right to, 47
  general maternity leave compared with, 31-32
  generally, 40
  meaning, 7, 31
  pensions, rights relating to, 60
  Pregnant Workers Directive, rights relating to, 59
  qualifying conditions,
    certificate giving EWC, provision of, 43
    continuous employment, 40-41
    duration of absence, 43
    notice provisions, 41-43
  remedies relating to,
    county court, action in, 62
    discrimination, 63
    equal pay, 63
    industrial tribunal, contract claim in, 62
    wages, deduction of, 62-63

Extended maternity absence – *cont*
  return after, right to,
    composite rights, 74–75
    contractual rights, 74–75
    different hours, 78
    different location, 77–78
    exceptions, 79–80
    industrial action preventing
      return to work, 73–74
    key points, 86–87
    notice provisions, 70
    options if job not same or
      suitable, 79
    postponement of return, 70–73
    redundancy, 79
    same employer, right to return
      to, 75
    same job, right to return to,
      75–77
    small employer, 79–80
    suitable alternative work, offer
      of, 80
  rights during, 55–63, 65
Factory
  prohibition on employment in, 124
  woman working in, return to
    work of, 68
Family credit
  maternity allowance, effect of, 160
Fertility treatment
  discriminatory dismissal relating
    to, 24
General maternity leave. *See*
  Maternity leave
Health and safety
  compulsory leave after birth, 124–125
  discrimination, 126–127
  dismissal for reasons of, 22
  employer,
    child, duty and liability
      towards, 117
    employee, general duty of care
      to, 115–116
    HSWA 1974, duties under,
      116–117
    risk assessment, duty to carry
      out, 119–120
  Equal Treatment Directive,
    127–128
  general duties, 115–117

Health and safety – *cont*
  general maternity leave, returning
    after, 68–69
  generally, 115
  hazards for new and expectant
    mothers, 266–275
  implementation of review,
    120–121
  key points, 128–129
  nightwork, special provisions
    relating to, 124
  Pregnant Workers Directive, 117
  private health insurance, 52
  protection under ERA, 118
  remedies, 125–126
  risk assessment, 119–120,
    121–124
  unfair dismissal, 93
Hearing
  procedure, 219–220
  stages before, 216–218
Holidays
  annual shut-down, 52
  general maternity leave, rights
    during, 52–53
  missed bank holidays, time off in
    lieu for, 55
  school, 53
Hospital
  help with fares to, 162
Hours of work
  different, right to return to work
    and, 78
  flexible, 83
  long hours, requirement to work,
    84
House of Commons Employment
  Committee
  mothers in employment, report on,
    1
  recommendations, 4–5
Housing benefit
  maternity allowance, effect of, 160
Incapacity benefit
  maternity allowance, effect of,
    159–160
Income support
  maternity allowance, effect of, 160
Indirect discrimination. *See*
  Discrimination

Industrial action
  return to work, prevention of, 73–74
  statutory maternity pay, eligibility for, 139–140
Industrial tribunal
  contract claim in, 62
  procedure, 209
  UK, EU law in, 200–204
Insolvency
  employer, of, effect on SMP, 149
Interview
  discriminatory questions at, 26–27
Job
  meaning, 76
  options if job not same or suitable, 79
  same, right to return to,
    generally, 75–76
    job security, loss of, 77
    same job, meaning, 76–77
    status, loss of, 77
Job-sharing
  blanket policy against, 81–82
  discrimination against job-sharers, 81–86
  long hours, requirement to work, 84
  supervisory level, at, 82
Jobseekers' allowance
  maternity allowance, effect of, 159, 160
  means-tested, 160
Labour market
  mothers in, 1
  pregnant women, hostility to, 1–2
Leave. *See* Maternity leave
Legal aid
  availability of, 210
Location
  different, right to return to work and, 77–78
Lockout
  statutory maternity pay, eligibility for, 140
Luncheon vouchers
  general maternity leave, rights during, 52
Main statutory provisions, 6–7

Maternity allowance
  adjudication officer, reference of dispute to, 162
  appeals, 162
  disputes, 162
  effect on other benefits, 159–162
  generally, 153
  how to claim, 157–158
  key points, 162–163
  meaning, 9
  payment of, 16
  payment period, 155–157
  period, meaning, 9
  qualifying conditions, 153–155
  rates of, 155
  test period, meaning, 9
  table 1996/7, 254–257
Maternity certificate (MAT B1)
  meaning, 8
Maternity expenses payments
  maternity allowance, effect of, 161
Maternity leave
  development of law, 3–5
  extended absence. *See* Extended maternity absence
  fourteen weeks, entitlement to, 3, 4
  general,
    annual shut-down, right to, 52
    bonuses, right to, 50–51
    certificate giving EWC, provision of, 35
    commencement of leave, 35–39
    commission, right to, 50–51
    company car, right to, 51
    continuity of service preserved during, 54
    contractual sick pay, entitlement to, 55
    dismissal before 11th week, 35
    extended maternity absence compared with, 31–32
    extending, 67
    full pay during, no right to, 47
    holidays, right to, 52–53
    luncheon vouchers, right to, 52
    meaning, 31
    minimum for all employees, certificate giving EWC, 35

Maternity leave – *cont*
  commencement of leave, 35–39
    dismissal before 11th week, 35
    notice provisions, 32–34
    resignation before 11th week, 35
  mobile phone, right to, 51
  notice provisions, 32–34
  occupational pensions, right to, 53–54
  overtime pay, no right to, 49
  pay reviews or increase, right to, 49
  perks, right to, 51
  premature birth, 39
  private health insurance, right to, 52
  remuneration, right to, 48–53
  resignation before 11th week, 35
  return to work, right to, 66–69, 86
  salary, right to, 49
  school holidays, right to, 53
  statutory sick pay, entitlement to, 54
  stillbirth, 39
  time off in lieu for missed bank holidays, 55
  trigger provisions, whether in breach of EU law, 38–39
  wages, right to, 49
  general, meaning, 7
  key points, 43–45
  notified leave date, meaning, 7
  period,
    agreement, extension by, 102
    dismissal at end of, 98
    dismissal during, 97
    failure to return after end of, 102
    meaning, 7
    sickness after end of, 101–102
    sickness, protection from dismissal for four weeks due to, 98
  rights during,
    extended maternity absence, during, 55–63
    full pay, no right to, 47

Maternity leave – *cont*
  general maternity leave, 47–55
  key points, 64–65
  meaning, 46
Maternity pay
  allowance. *See* Maternity allowance
  full pay, no right to, 47
  period, meaning, 9
  statutory. *See* Statutory maternity pay (SMP)
Maternity rights
  development of law on, 3–5
Medical evidence
  statutory maternity pay, eligibility for, 142
Milk
  free, 161–162
Moral grounds
  dismissal on, 24
National insurance costs
  part-time work, 82
Nightwork
  special provisions relating to, 124
Normal weekly earnings
  meaning, 10
Notice
  extended maternity absence, provisions for, 41–43, 70
  failure to comply with provisions, dismissal, protection from, 67
  extending general maternity leave, 67
  return before expiry of 14 weeks, 67
  return to work, right to, 66–67
  minimum general maternity leave, 21 clear days' notice, 34
  contractual rights to return, 33–34
  employer's obligation to advise about rights, 34
  not reasonably practicable, 34
  requirements relating to, 32–33
  pay, 90
  proper notice to return, failure to give, 104
  statutory maternity pay, eligibility for, 142–143
Notified day of return (NDR)
  meaning, 8

Notified leave date
  meaning, 7
Occupational pensions
  general maternity leave, rights during, 53–54
One-parent benefit
  maternity allowance, effect of, 161
Ordinary unfair dismissal. *See* Unfair dismissal
Overtime pay
  general maternity leave, rights during, 49
Part-time work
  accommodation, 82
  alternative job on part-time basis, 83
  blanket policy against, 81–82
  discrimination against part-timers, 81–86
  evidence to support, 84–85
  failure to promote, 83
  fixed-term contract, failure to renew, 83–84
  flexible working hours, 83
  national insurance costs, 82
  options for women not allowed to work part-time, 85–86
  women's labour, growth in, 1
  working every day on part-time basis, 82
Partner
  prohibited sex discrimination by, 168
Pay
  full, no right to, 47
  notice, 90
  See also Maternity pay; Statutory maternity pay (SMP);
Pensions
  extended maternity absence, rights during, 60
  occupational, 53–54
Police officers
  general exclusions from ERA, 14
Precedents, 246–253
Pregnancy
  duty to notify employer of, 118
Pregnant women
  development of law, 3–5
Pregnant Workers Directive (PWD)
  definitions under, 10–11
  extended maternity absence, rights during, 59
  government opposition to, 3
  health and safety, 117
  implementation of, 3 5
  pregnant worker, meaning, 10
  statutory maternity pay, 130–131
  summary of maternity rights under, 11–12
  text, 258–265
  unfair dismissal, 96–97
  worker who has recently given birth, meaning, 10–11
  worker who is breastfeeding, meaning, 11
Premature birth
  maternity leave period, commencement of, 39
Prescription charges
  maternity allowance, effect of, 161
Private health insurance
  general maternity leave, rights during, 52
Procedure
  financial help and legal advice, 210
  framework, 209–210
  generally, 209
  hearing, 219–220
  how to apply, 215
  initial steps in bringing claim, 210–215
  key points, 231–232
  stages before hearing, 216–218
  See also Remedies
Promotion
  failure to promote, 83
  less favourable treatment of pregnant woman, 27
Qualifying week (QW)
  meaning, 9
Reasonableness test
  unfair dismissal, relating to, 95
Recruitment
  cost of training new recruit, 2
  interview, discriminatory questions at, 26–27
  refusal to recruit, 25–26

Redundancy
  duty to consult, 106
  entitlement to payment, 111
  exercising right to return, 110–111
  general maternity leave, during, 69, 107
  generally, 105
  maternity absence, during, 79 107–109
  meaning, 105–106
  pregnancy, during, 107
  selection due to pregnancy, 22
  suitable alternative work,
    increased travelling time, 110
    lack of, 110
    meaning, 109
    obligation to provide, 107
    refusal of, 110
    status of job, 109
    terms and conditions, 109
  time limits for bringing claim, 213
Remedies
  ante-natal care, right to paid time off for, 20
  county court, action in, 62
  discrimination, relating to, 63
  equal pay, relating to, 63, 230–231
  extended maternity absence, rights during, 62–63
  health and safety, relating to, 125–126
  industrial tribunal, contract claim in, 62
  job-sharing, relating to, 86
  key points, 231–232
  part-time work, relating to, 86
  settlements, 220–221
  Sex Discrimination Act, under, 223–230
  unfair dismissal, for, 221–223
  wages, deduction of, 62–63
Remuneration
  benefits in kind, 51
  bonuses, 50–51
  commission, 50–51
  company cars, 51
  full pay, no right to, 47
  general maternity leave, rights during, 48–53
  holidays,

Remuneration – *cont*
  annual shut-down, 52
  right to, 52–53
  school, 53
  luncheon vouchers, 52
  mobile phones, 51
  overtime pay, 49
  pay reviews or increase, 49
  perks, 51
  private health insurance, 52
  salary, 49
  wages, 49
Replacement
  dismissal of, 112
Resignation
  before 11th week, 35
Return to work, right to
  dismissal after return to work, 111–112
  dismissal while exercising right to return, 103–104
  extended maternity absence, after,
    composite rights, 74–75
    contractual rights, 74–75
    different hours, 78
    different location, 77–78
    exceptions, 79–80
    industrial action preventing return to work, 73–74
    job security, loss of, 77
    key points, 86–87
    notice provisions, 70
    options if job not same or suitable, 79
    postponement of return, 70–73
    redundancy, 79
    same employer, to, 75
    same job, to, 75–77
    small employer, 79–80
    status, loss of, 77
    suitable alternative work, offer of, 80
  failure to give proper notice to return, 104
  general maternity leave, after,
    generally, 69
    health and safety reasons, 68–69
    key points, 86
    notice provisions, failure to comply with, 66–67

Return to work – *cont*
- redundancy, 69
- statutory prohibitions, 67–68
- generally, 66
- industrial action, 73–74
- job sharer, discrimination against, 81–86
- key points, 86–87
- meaning, 8
- part-timer, discrimination against, 81–86
- postponement of return,
  - employee, by, 70–73
  - employer, by, 70
  - sickness, 70–73
- statutory prohibitions,
  - childbirth, working within two weeks of, 67–68
  - factory, woman working in, 68
  - general maternity leave, relating to, 67–68
  - illness, protection from dismissal for further four weeks in case of, 68
  - workshop, woman working in, 68
- transfer of undertaking, 80–81

Right to return. *See* Return to work, right to

Rights before birth. *See* Childbirth

Salary
- general maternity leave, rights during, 49

School holidays
- general maternity leave, rights during, 53

Seasonal worker
- statutory maternity pay, eligibility for, 139

Sex discrimination
- direct, 165
- employer, by, 166–168
- employment agency, by, 169
- indirect, 165–170
- out-of-time claims, 214–215
- partner, by, 168
- remedies for, 223–230
- time limits for bringing claim, 212–213
- unfair dismissal, 96
- vocational training body, by, 169

Share fisherwomen
- general exclusions from ERA, 14

Sick pay
- contractual,
  - general maternity leave, rights during, 54–55
  - pregnancy-related sickness, exclusion of, 28
- statutory,
  - general maternity leave, rights during, 54
  - maternity allowance, effect of, 159

Sickness
- baby, of, 102–103
- during pregnancy,
  - contractual sick pay, exclusion from, 28
  - statutory maternity pay, effect on entitlement to, 28–29
  - triggering provisions, 29
- maternity absence, during and at end of, 103
- maternity leave period, after end of, 101–102
- maternity pay period, during, 145–146
- ordinary, followed by pregnancy sickness, 22
- postponement of return by employee due to,
  - exercising right to return while sick, 72–73
  - generally, 70–71
  - only allowed once, 71–72
- pregnancy-related, meaning, 21
- protection from dismissal for four weeks due to, 98

Social fund payments
- maternity allowance, effect of, 161

Statutory framework
- main statutory provisions, 6–7
- Pregnant Workers' Directive, definitions under, 10–11
- summary of main provisions, 11–16
- UK law, definitions under, 7–10

Statutory maternity pay (SMP)
- administration by employers, 150–151
- calculation of, 146–148

Index 291

Statutory maternity pay – *cont*
  eligibility for,
    26 weeks' continuous
      service, 137–142
    exemptions, 136
    generally, 131–132
    lower earnings limit, 132–136
    medical evidence, 142
    notice requirements, 142–143
    pregnancy at 11th week, 142
    stillbirth, 132
    woman must be employee, 132
    woman must have stopped
      working, 143
  employee, meaning, 15
  entitlement to, effect of sickness
    during pregnancy on, 28–29
  exclusions, 15–16
  explanation of tables, 276–277
  generally, 130–131
  key points, 151–152
  legislation, 131–148
  meaning, 9
  method of payment, 148–150
  normal weekly earnings, meaning,
    10
  payment of, 15
  period,
    commencement of, 38, 144–145
    end of, 145
    sickness during, 145–146
    working for another employer,
      146
    working in, 146
  Pregnant Workers Directive,
    130–131
  recovery by employers, 151
Statutory sick pay. *See* Sick pay
Stillbirth
  maternity leave period,
    commencement of, 39
  statutory maternity pay, eligibility
    for, 132
Stoppage of work
  statutory maternity pay, eligibility
    for, 139–140
Suitable alternative work
  increased travelling time, 110
  lack of, 110
  meaning, 109

Suitable alternative work – *cont*
  obligation to provide, 107
  offer of, 80
  refusal of, 110
  status of job, 109
  terms and conditions, 109
Tabular summary of maternity rights,
  234–235
Test period table 1996/7, 254–257
Time limits
  bringing claim, 212–213
  EU law, under, 206
Time off
  ante-natal care, for,
    appointment for ante-natal care,
      requirement for, 18
    certificate, requirement for, 18
    dismissal of woman enforcing
      right to time off, 20
    employer refusing time off for
      ante-natal care, 18–19
    entitlement, 19–20
    paid time off, right to, 17–20
    remedies, 20
  missed bank holidays, for, 55
Transfer
  less favourable treatment of
    pregnant woman, 27
Transfer of undertaking
  return to work, right to, 80–81
  unfair dismissal, 104
Tribunal. *See* Industrial tribunal
Unemployment benefit. *See*
  Jobseekers' allowance
Unfair dismissal
  automatically unfair dismissal,
    burden of proof, 93
    employer's knowledge of
      pregnancy, 21
    health and safety reasons,
      dismissal for, 22
    meaning, 10
    ordinary sickness followed by
      pregnancy sickness, 22
    pregnancy-related absence, limit
      to amount of, 21–22
    pregnancy-related dismissal, 20–
      22
    pregnancy-related sickness,
      nature of, 21

Unfair dismissal – *cont*
  protection from, 91– 93
  redundancy, selection for, 22
  statutory framework, 91– 93
  written reasons for dismissal, 92
deemed dismissal, 95
dismissal, meaning, 89– 90
extended maternity absence,
  dismissal during, 98– 103
  right to return after, 70
fixed-term contract exception, 90
general law, 93– 95
general principles relating to
  dismissal, 88– 90
generally, 88
health and safety case, 93
key points, 113– 114
maternity leave period,
  dismissal at end of, 98
  dismissal during, 97
  sickness, protection for four
    weeks due to, 98
maternity replacement, dismissal
  of, 112
notice pay, 90
ordinary unfair dismissal,
  meaning, 10
pregnancy-related dismissal, 22
provisions of ERA, 14– 15
Pregnant Workers Directive, 96–97
protection from dismissal,
  statutory framework, 91– 97
reasonableness test, 95
redundancy,
  duty to consult, 106
  entitlement to payment, 111
  exercising right to return, 110
  general maternity leave, during, 107
  generally, 105
  maternity absence, during, 107–109
  meaning, 105– 106
  pregnancy, during, 107
  suitable alternative work, 109–110
remedies for, 221– 223

Unfair dismissal – *cont*
  return to work, dismissal after, 111– 112
  right not to be unfairly dismissed, 87
  right to return,
    dismissal while exercising, 103–104
    extended maternity absence, after, 70
    failure to give proper notice to return, 104
  redundancy, after, 110
  sex discrimination claim, 96
  statutory right, dismissal for assertion of, 93
  time limits for bringing claim, 212
  transfer of business, dismissal on, 104
Useful addresses, 278
Vitamins
  free, 161– 162
Vocational training body
  prohibited sex discrimination by, 169
Wages
  claim for wrongful deduction of, 213
  deduction of, 62–63
  general maternity leave, rights during, 49
  meaning, 63
Week's pay
  meaning, 10
Worker
  meaning, 62
  Pregnant Workers Directive. *See*
    Pregnant Workers Directive (PWD)
  who has recently given birth, meaning, 11
  who is breastfeeding, meaning, 11
Workshop
  prohibition on employment in, 124
  woman working in, return to work of, 68